# THE LITERARY CAREER OF
## WILLIAM FAULKNER

# The Literary Career of
# William Faulkner

## A BIBLIOGRAPHICAL STUDY

### BY JAMES B. MERIWETHER

UNIVERSITY OF SOUTH CAROLINA PRESS

COLUMBIA, SOUTH CAROLINA

# PREFACE TO THE UNIVERSITY
# OF SOUTH CAROLINA PRESS REISSUE

Only 750 copies of *The Literary Career of William Faulkner* were printed when the book was first published, in 1961. It soon went out of print, and in the antiquarian book market began fetching relatively high prices which often placed it beyond reach of the students and scholars for whom it was compiled. At some point in the fall of 1968 it became available again in a fraudulent reissue by a book pirate in or near Philadelphia who marketed it at prices ranging from twenty to thirty-five dollars for the next two years. The copies I have seen are all apparently from the same shoddy photo-offset impression, differing from the original in the binding, which is crudely done in sturdy buckram; in the title-page, which is in one color instead of two; and in the reproduction of the text and plates, which is sloppy and occasionally illegible. This illegal reissue was marketed by several firms, or one firm under several names, chiefly to libraries.

Although eventually the book should be brought up to date in a revised edition, for the present a good offset reissue, properly priced, seems the simplest and most appropriate answer to the problem produced by the original publisher's reluctance to reprint the book and by the pirate's lack of such reluctance. This, then, so far as I am aware, is the third issue and third impression of the original edition, differing textually only in the addition of this preface and a list of errata at the end to correct such errors of fact as have come to my attention, and one change in the table of contents.

In addition to the acknowledgments made in the foreword of the first issue, I wish to record my continuing obligation to Mrs. Paul D. Summers, Jr., William Faulkner's daughter and literary executrix; and to the following scholars and collectors who have helped me to catch errors in the original text: Matthew Bruccoli, Stephen Dennis, Michel Gresset, and Carl Petersen.

Columbia, South Carolina                    James B. Meriwether
January 1971

*In Memory*

*of*

SAXE COMMINS

HAROLD OBER

# CONTENTS

# FOREWORD

THIS catalogue and the several bibliographical listings which here supplement it have been compiled to serve as a published record of the exhibition, "The Literary Career of William Faulkner," held in the Princeton University Library from May 10 through August 30, 1957. The exhibition was first planned during the early fall of 1956, at which time I was writing a dissertation on Faulkner for the Princeton English Department, and compiling a check list of Faulkner's writings for publication in the *Princeton University Library Chronicle*. Through the cooperation of William S. Dix, University Librarian, and Saxe Commins, Faulkner's editor and long a devoted friend of the Library, arrangements were made which enabled me to begin gathering materials and information for an exhibition.

After the opening of the exhibition the following spring, the check list of Faulkner's published writings appeared in an issue of the *Chronicle* (Vol. XVIII, No. 3) devoted to Faulkner. At the same time, in the belief that the annotations for the exhibition would prove useful to have available in more permanent form, it was planned to publish them, along with accompanying bibliographical material that would further illustrate the scope of the exhibition and supplement the basic information in the Faulkner check list, which in the meantime had been made available separately, under the imprint of the Princeton University Library.

The five parts of this book, then, are designed to bring up to date and make available the information contained in, or collected for, that exhibition, and are to be considered in connection with the previously published check list as a basic bibliographical reference for the study of Faulkner's literary career. Mr. Faulkner's kindness in depositing his own collection of his manuscripts in the Princeton University Library made it possible, both in the text of the annotations and in the handlist of the manuscripts, to make available for the first time much significant material about this aspect of his work. The listing of English editions and translations has its basis in the emphasis placed in the exhibition upon Faulkner's reputation abroad. Their compilation delayed the publication of this book but it has thereby gained, I trust, in inclusiveness. Motion picture and television productions of Faulkner's writings, and his own work for those media, form another category which has benefited from the delay by expansion of the information made available in the exhibition itself. Finally, the presentation in tabular form in an appendix of the information in one of the Faulkner manuscripts, a sending schedule which he at one time kept for his short stories, provides valuable information about a neglected aspect of Faulkner's career at one of its most interesting periods.

In accordance with the Library's policy of bringing out in the *Chronicle*, if practicable, the annotations for its major exhibitions, Part I of this book was published in the Spring, 1960 issue (Vol. XXI, No. 3). Also included were the first twenty-one of the illustrations used here. In preparing the annotations for republication in book form, a few changes and additions were made, but their format remains, as it was, largely determined by the needs and policies of publication in the *Chronicle*.

Individual aid rendered in the preparation of all but Part I of this book has been acknowledged in the introduction to each. But thanks are due here for assistance given in preparing the exhibition itself, and in making possible this published record of it. Because publication was several times delayed, it is with apologies for their tardiness that the following acknowledgments are made to the individuals and institutions whose cooperation made possible the original exhibition, and the publication of this material from and related to it:

First, very grateful acknowledgment is made to William Faulkner, who consented to the transfer to Princeton of his own collection of his manuscripts, which had been stored for several years at Random House, his publishers. None of this material had been previously shown or made available for study, and any distinction which the exhibition may have had was due to his kindness.

To acknowledge the debt of this exhibition to Saxe Commins is to recall with sadness the loss suffered at his death in July, 1958, by his friends, by the Library, and by Princeton University. As Faulkner's editor, he arranged for the transfer of the Faulkner manuscripts to Princeton, he made available his own files and collection of Faulkner material for the exhibition, and he gave the necessary permissions for the publication of Faulkner manuscript material in the Faulkner issue of the *Chronicle* and in this catalogue.

It is also saddening to recall here the death of Harold Ober, in October, 1959. Likewise a friend for many years of the Library, and Faulkner's literary agent, Mr. Ober was responsible not only for assistance in making arrangements for the exhibition, but also for permission to reproduce or quote from unpublished Faulkner writings.

In all the processes of assembling and organizing the materials for the exhibition, and subsequently in preparing this catalogue, I have been grateful for the invaluable assistance of Alexander D. Wainwright, of the Library's Department of Rare Books and Special Collections, and Editor of the *Chronicle*. I am also grateful to him for help in the preparation of the annotations in Section XXX of the catalogue. For his help with the annotations of Sections II and XII I am indebted to George P. Garrett, Jr., though final responsibility for the form and accuracy of all the annotations is mine. To Mr. Garrett, too, I am greatly indebted for his assistance with the task of identifying, sorting, and arranging the two packing boxes of Faulkner manuscripts when they arrived at the Princeton Library.

Of the individual collectors who lent materials to the exhibition, the greatest debt is to Linton R. Massey, of Keswick, Virginia. Only the most significant of the many items which he made available from his notable Faulkner collection are individually acknowledged in this catalogue, but special thanks are given him here for his willingness to supply, on the shortest notice, whatever the exhibition needed to fill a gap in a showcase or to illustrate a manuscript page by a printed one.

Other lenders to whom thanks are due are C. Waller Barrett, Hodding Carter, Maurice E. Coindreau, Carvel Collins, George P. Garrett, Jr., Miss Mary Killgore, Leon Picon, Edward Shenton, James Silver, Phil Stone, and Ben Wasson. Items were also kindly lent by the New York Public Library, the Mary Buie Museum of Oxford, Mississippi, Random House, the Newberry Library, CBS Television, Lever Brothers Company, and Paramount Pictures Corporation. John Sykes Hartin, Director of Libraries of the University of Mississippi, was kind enough to make available photostats of Faulkner material from local newspapers.

In June, 1959, the Faulkner manuscripts were transferred to the Alderman Library of the University of Virginia, where they are now on deposit. For making them available to me there in order to complete work on the catalogue, I am indebted to Faulkner's daughter, Mrs. Paul D. Summers, Jr., and I am grateful to Miss Anne Freudenberg, Assistant in Manuscripts at the Alderman Library, for frequent and generous assistance.

The drawing of the Oxford courthouse and Confederate monument on the title-page is reproduced from the cover of the original exhibition leaflet, for which it was made by Gillett G. Griffin. Also taken from the leaflet is the Introduction to the exhibition annotations.

The list of items shown, freed from the case-by-case limitations of the exhibition itself, has been partially rearranged, and the annotations have been expanded, where necessary, by descriptions of or quotations from the items they originally accompanied. Where the original note is now out of date or misleading, a footnote has been used to correct it, though no change has been made in the present tense originally used in the leaflet and annotations. Throughout, the catalogue follows the final arrangement of the exhibition, though during its progress several additions and changes were made, both in the items shown and the accompanying annotations.

With the entry for each item in the catalogue is given the name of the lender, or, in the case of material owned by the Princeton University Library, the call number or name of the collection in which the item may be found. Many of the periodicals actually exhibited were single copies borrowed for the purpose, but, in order to make the catalogue as useful a reference as possible, these are listed with the call numbers (the majority of which represent bound files) of the copies in the Princeton University Library. In most cases where more than one copy of an item was exhibited only the designation of the Library's copy is given.

The John E. Annan Memorial Fund generously subsidized the costs of this book, and for their efforts in behalf of its publication I am particularly indebted to William S. Dix and to two members of the Princeton English Department, Willard Thorp and Lawrance Thompson, who have befriended the project at every stage.

JAMES B. MERIWETHER
*University of North Carolina*

# PART ONE

## *THE EXHIBITION*

# CATALOGUE OF THE EXHIBITION

# INTRODUCTION

A SPAN of nearly forty years, from the appearance of the poem "L'Apres-Midi d'un Faune" in *The New Republic* on August 6, 1919, to the publication of the novel *The Town* by Random House on May 1, 1957, is covered by this exhibition tracing the literary career of William Faulkner. Included among the works displayed are all of his twenty-five books, from two presentation copies of *The Marble Faun*, a volume of poems published in 1924, to the limited, signed issue of *The Town*, as well as many of his short stories, poems, articles, and other publications. Thanks to the deposit in the Library of Mr. Faulkner's own collection of his manuscripts, and through the co-operation of his editor, Saxe Commins, and of his publishers, Random House, it is possible to show manuscript material for all of his books, and for much of the other published work included in the exhibition.

William Faulkner was born on September 25, 1897, in New Albany, Mississippi, but has lived most of his life in the nearby college town of Oxford, where his family moved when he was a boy, and where his father was later to hold several administrative posts at the university. There his literary career began, upon his return to college after service in World War I, with the appearance of "L'Apres-Midi d'un Faune" and the pieces, mostly poems, which he contributed to the college weekly, *The Mississippian*. Shortly after the publication of *The Marble Faun*, his first book, he left Oxford for New Orleans. There, during the first half of 1925, he wrote fiction for the Sunday magazine section of the *Times-Picayune*, became a friend of Sherwood Anderson, and wrote his first novel, *Soldiers' Pay*, which was published the following year by Liveright, Anderson's publisher. A trip abroad was followed, in 1927, by a second novel, *Mosquitoes*.

The publication of his third novel, *Sartoris*, in 1929, marked a turning point in Faulkner's career. It was the first volume in what has become the Yoknapatawpha series. "With *Soldiers' Pay* I found out writing was fun," he has said in an interview. "But I found out after that not only each book had to have a design but the whole output or sum of an artist's work had to have a design." *Sartoris* marked not only the inception of the design that was eventually, after years of neglect, to bring Faulkner in 1950 the Nobel Prize for literature, but it was the first of his works whose setting was the author's own north Mississippi countryside, a land of small farms and rolling hills: "Beginning with *Sartoris*," he said, "I discovered that my own little postage stamp of native soil was worth writing about and that I would never live long enough to exhaust it."

The more than a dozen books and three dozen short stories of the Yoknapatawpha series which have followed *Sartoris* have indeed shown no signs of exhausting the materials of Faulkner's county. No two Faulkner novels, within or outside the Yoknapatawpha series, are alike, and such works as *The Sound and the Fury* (1929), *As I Lay Dying* (1930), *Light in August* (1932), *Absalom, Absalom!* (1936), *The Hamlet* (1940), *Go Down, Moses* (1942), and *The Town* (1957), show, in their rich variety, the constant, restless urge of their author to experiment with new forms and methods. Neither critical nor (in the case of *Sanctuary*) popular acclaim has ever led him to repeat an experiment or imitate a success, and this refusal to remain within a literary pigeonhole, to be classified, has made the proper recognition of his achievement far more difficult.

In Faulkner a literary pioneer's interest in technical innovation has been combined with a craftsman's care to perfect his work. A glance at the manuscripts in the exhibition shows how painstaking has been the process of revising and rewriting, and displayed are many works which not only went through several manuscript versions but have undergone subsequent revision in their various published appearances.

The history of the Snopes family of Yoknapatawpha, which is a minor theme in several of Faulkner's novels and the main subject of a number of short stories, of *The Hamlet*, and of *The Town*, is given special emphasis in the exhibition. By the inclusion of numerous translations, the exhibition also suggests the widespread influence and reputation of Faulkner's writings throughout the world.

# 1. FAULKNER AT THE UNIVERSITY OF MISSISSIPPI

In World War I William Faulkner served briefly in the Royal Air Force, although he was still a cadet, in training in Canada, at the end of the war. After his return to Mississippi, he enrolled as a special student in the fall term of 1919 at the University of Mississippi, where his father, Murry C. Falkner, was Assistant Secretary. (William Faulkner apparently first added the "u" to his surname while in the RAF, and afterward retained it as his "literary" signature.) He soon became a well-known campus figure in his British uniform.

During the academic year 1919-1920 thirteen of his poems appeared in *The Mississippian*, the weekly student newspaper, where they were attacked, defended, and parodied energetically. Drawings by Faulkner had appeared in *Ole Miss*, the yearbook of the University of Mississippi, before his departure for service in the RAF, and other drawings and poems appeared in the volumes for 1919-1920 and 1920-1921.

1. Photograph of Faulkner in RAF uniform. Glossy photostat, enlarged, from *Ole Miss . . . 1919-1920* [University, Miss., 1920], p. 107. [Original lent by Carvel Collins]

2. "L'Apres-Midi d'un Faune."
   Faulkner's literary career may be said to have begun with the publication of the poem "L'Apres-Midi d'un Faune" in *The New Republic* on August 6, 1919. With the exception of a few drawings, this is his first known published work. His first contribution to *The Mississippian* was a reprinting, with minor alterations, of this poem a few months later.

a. *The New Republic*, August 6, 1919, p. 24. [Lent by Linton R. Massey; Library copy, 0901.N562q]

b. Photostat of "L'Apres-Midi D'un Faune" from *The Mississippian*, October 29, 1919, p. 4. [Original in the University of Mississippi Library]

3. "Cathay" and "Clair de Lune."

Faulkner's first poem originally published in *The Mississippian* was "Cathay." "Clair de Lune" was one of several poems 'From Paul Verlaine' which appeared during the spring semester.

a. Photostat of "Cathay" from *The Mississippian*, November 12, 1919, p. 8. [Original in the University of Mississippi Library]

b. Typescript of "Cathay." 1 p. It differs slightly from the published version. [Lent by Mr. Faulkner]. See Fig. 3

c. Photostat of "Clair de Lune" from *The Mississippian*, March 3, 1920, p. 6. [Original in the University of Mississippi Library]

4. "Landing in Luck." Photostat from *The Mississippian*, November 26, 1919, pp. 2, 7. [Original in the University of Mississippi Library]

The short story "Landing in Luck" won Faulkner a prize for the best story published in *The Mississippian* during the academic year 1919-1920. Apparently Faulkner's first piece of published fiction, it describes a near-crash by a cadet at what is obviously an RAF flight training field.

5. Critical pieces in *The Mississippian*.

Most of Faulkner's contributions to *The Mississippian* were poems, but he also published book reviews, essays, and dramatic criticism.

a. Photostat of essay on Conrad Aiken's *Turns and Movies* from *The Mississippian*, February 16, 1921, p. 5. [Original in the University of Mississippi Library]

b. Photostat of article on Eugene O'Neill from *The Mississippian*, February 3, 1922, p. 5. [Original in the University of Mississippi Library]

6. "The Marionettes."

The list of members of the student dramatic group in the 1920-1921 *Ole Miss* is accompanied by a drawing that is almost certainly by Faulkner, who appears in the list as property-man. The drawing and the caption, with its characteristic reversed s's, are similar to those of the poem "Nocturne," in the same volume.

The manuscript play, "The Marionettes," which has never been published, dates from this period in Faulkner's career and his association with the dramatic group. According to Faulkner's letter of authentication, he made six copies of the play. On the verso of the title-page of the copy exhibited Faulkner printed "FIRST EDITION 1920" and the flyleaf is signed by Ben Wasson, the president of the dramatic group, who later became Faulkner's literary agent.

a. Photostat of drawing and list of members of the Marionettes from *The Ole Miss, 1920-1921* [University, Miss., 1921], p. 135. [Original lent by Carvel Collins]

b. "The Marionettes: A Play in One Act," by W. Faulkner. 55-page manuscript, with nine pen-and-ink drawings by the author. [Lent by Miss Mary Killgore]. Opened to the first page of the text, a description of the setting of the opening scene, with its accompanying drawing of Pierrot at a garden table beneath the full moon. See Fig. 1

c. Letter from Raymond Green to William Faulkner, February 9, 1932, requesting confirmation of his authorship of the play, with Faulkner's reply written at the bottom: "I wrote a play by that name once. It was never printed. I made and bound 6 copies by hand. I signed none of them. There may also be a mss. It was long ago and I dont remember." [Lent by Miss Mary Killgore]

7. "To a Co-ed." *Ole Miss . . . 1919-1920* [University, Miss., 1920], p. 174. [Lent by Carvel Collins]

The sonnet "To a Co-ed" was reprinted in an article on Faulkner by his college friend Louis Cochran in the Memphis *Commercial Appeal* Sunday magazine section, November 6, 1932, p. 4, and became the first of his writings in student publications to be more widely known after Faulkner became a novelist.

> The dawn herself could not more beauty wear
> Than you 'mid other women crowned in grace,
> Nor have the sages known a fairer face
> Than yours, gold-shadowed by your bright sweet hair
> Than you does Venus seem less heavenly fair;
> The twilit hidden stillness of your eyes,
> And throat, a singing bridge of still replies,
> A slender bridge, yet all dreams hover there.
>
> I could have turned unmoved from Helen's brow,
> Who found no beauty in their Beatrice;
> Their Thais seemed less lovely then as now,
> Though some had bartered Athens for her kiss.
> For down Time's arras, faint and fair and far,
> Your face still beckons like a lonely star.

8. "Nocturne." *The Ole Miss, 1920-1921* [University, Miss., 1921], pp. 214-215. [Lent by Carvel Collins]. See Fig. 2

The unsigned poem "Nocturne" is almost certainly by Faulkner, and is characteristic of the poetry he was writing at the time of its appearance. The lettering and the accompanying drawing are similar to those of the manuscript play "The Marionettes." The text on p. 215 was obviously reversed with that on p. 214 in printing.

9. Drawing. *Ole Miss . . . 1917-1918* [University, Miss., 1918], p. 111. [Lent by Carvel Collins]

Faulkner contributed drawings, both signed and unsigned, to the *Ole Miss* annuals of 1917, 1918, and 1922.

## 2. *THE MARBLE FAUN*, 1924

*The Marble Faun,* a pastoral cycle of nineteen poems, is William Faulkner's first book. It appeared in December, 1924, just before he left Oxford for New Orleans. Faulkner's friend Phil Stone, a lawyer in Oxford, wrote the introduction to the book, noting the talent of the author and his potential. It has never been reprinted.

10. *The Marble Faun.* Boston, The Four Seas Company [1924]. Two copies. [Lent by Linton R. Massey; Ex 3734.92.361]

The Massey copy contains on the front flyleaf two inscriptions: "To Miss Sallie McGuire from W Faulkner"; and "Autographed for Mr. Raymond Green. Oxford, Mississippi, April 15, 1932. Phil Stone". It is signed on the title-page: "William Faulkner Oxford, Miss. 24 December 1924".

The Princeton copy also has two inscriptions on the front flyleaf: "To Polly Clark, from her friend, Bill Faulkner 19 December 1924"; and "With love to Cousin Polly. Phil Stone." It is signed on the title-page: "William Faulkner 19 December 1924".

11. Typescript of *The Marble Faun.* [Lent by Ben Wasson]. See Fig. 26

This 27-page carbon typescript is nearly a third shorter than the published book of poems. The manuscript corrections are not in Faulkner's hand. Shown is the beginning of the second group of poems, entitled "Summer." In the published version the titles of the seasons were omitted.

12. Review by John McClure of *The Marble Faun.* Photostat from the New Orleans *Times-Picayune* Sunday magazine section, January 25, 1925, p. 6. [Original in the Louisiana State University Library]

John McClure, who was book editor of the New Orleans *Times-Picayune* and one of the editors of *The Double Dealer*, was one of the first of the reviewers of William Faulkner to recognize his achievement and promise. His perceptive and favorable review of *The Marble Faun* appeared not long after Faulkner reached New Orleans, early in 1925.

13. "Study." Photostat from *The Mississippian*, April 21, 1920, p. 4. [Original in the University of Mississippi Library]

The poem "Study" is indicative of the pastoral mode which Faulkner developed for *The Marble Faun*. It was published in April, 1920, and Faulkner gave the date *"April, May, June, 1919"* at the end of *The Marble Faun*, though it is likely that the poems of the book, if they were originally conceived at that date, were considerably changed in the five years that elapsed before their publication.

14. "Portrait." *The Double Dealer*, III (June, 1922), 337. [0901 .D727]

Faulkner's first appearance in *The Double Dealer*, the little magazine published in New Orleans in the 1920's, was "Portrait," a poem characteristic of the verse (both published and unpublished) Faulkner was writing in the years preceding *The Marble Faun*.

## 3. FAULKNER IN NEW ORLEANS

Early in January, 1925, Faulkner left Oxford for New Orleans, where he spent nearly six months before leaving for Europe. In New Orleans he became a friend of Sherwood Anderson, contributed poems and articles to *The Double Dealer* and fiction to the *Times-Picayune*, and wrote his first novel, *Soldiers' Pay*.

15. *Sherwood Anderson & Other Famous Creoles*, 1926.

This book of drawings by the artist William Spratling was published in New Orleans in December, 1926, in a limited edition, a few of the copies bound in fancy boards and with some of the drawings tinted.

As John McClure said in his review in the *Times-Picayune* (January 2, 1927), the drawings are "Amusing caricatures of familiar figures in the artistic and literary circles of New Orleans, with not a line drawn in malice," and the book as a whole is "frankly a take-off" on Miguel Covarrubias' *The Prince of Wales and Other Famous Americans*. "William Faulkner," McClure noted, "has written the introduction and arranged the subtitles for the two-score sketches in the volume. The introduction is a whimsical interpretation of Sherwood Anderson's attitude to the Vieux Carre." Years later, in an article about Anderson, Faulkner himself described the introduction as a parody of Anderson's "primer-like style" which had led to a coolness between the two men (*Atlantic*, June, 1953).

a. *Sherwood Anderson & Other Famous Creoles*. New Orleans, Pelican Bookshop Press, 1926. One of about forty copies in fancy boards, signed by the artist. [Ex 3734.92.3867, copy 2]. Opened to the title-page and tinted frontispiece (a view of the cathedral and Cabildo Alley roofs in the French Quarter).

b. Photostat, enlarged, of the final caricature of the volume. Drawn from the mirror, it shows Faulkner and Spratling at a table, writing and drawing. [From Ex 3734.92.3867, copy 2]. See illustration on p. 11.

16. Drawing of Faulkner by William Spratling. Photostat, slightly enlarged, from the New Orleans *Times-Picayune* Sunday magazine section, April 26, 1925, p. 6. [Original in the Louisiana State University Library]
This drawing by Spratling of the twenty-seven-year-old author of *The Marble Faun* originally appeared in the *Times-Picayune* and was reproduced on the dust jacket of *Mosquitoes* two years later.

17. Undated typewritten letter from Faulkner to Sherwood Anderson. 3 pp. [Lent by the Newberry Library]. See Figs. 27-29
In his 1953 *Atlantic* article on Sherwood Anderson, Faulkner referred to the tall tales which he and Anderson concocted about the mythical Jackson family when the two men were in New Orleans together. The legends were recorded in an exchange of letters, of which this undated typescript account by Faulkner of the adventures of Al, Elenor, and Herman Jackson is part. Parts of the Jackson legend also appear in *Mosquitoes* (pp. 277-281).

18. *Soldiers' Pay*. New York, Boni & Liveright, 1926. First edition, in dust jacket. [Ex 3734.92.384]
Faulkner's first novel, *Soldiers' Pay*, was written during his stay in New Orleans. On Anderson's recommendation, it was accepted by Boni and Liveright, Anderson's publishers at that time.

19. Bound typescript of *Soldiers' Pay*. 476 pp. [Lent by Mr. Faulkner]. See Fig. 5
Opened to p. 151, showing manuscript addition to the text.

20. *Mosquitoes*. New York, Boni and Liveright, 1927. First edition, in dust jacket with drawing of mosquitoes. [Ex 3734.92 .3655]
Faulkner's second novel, *Mosquitoes*, was written after his return from the trip abroad, and has its setting in New Orleans. The verse read aloud by one of the characters on p. 252 (p. 336 of the bound typescript) appeared, revised, in Faulkner's 1933 book of poems, *A Green Bough*.
The first impression of the novel was issued in two different dust jackets.

21. *Mosquitoes*. First edition, in dust jacket with drawing of bridge players. [Lent by Miss Mary Killgore]

22. Bound typescript of *Mosquitoes*. 464 pp. [Lent by Mr. Faulkner]. See Fig. 6
Opened to p. 336, showing manuscript corrections.

23. Sketches in the *Times-Picayune*.
Faulkner contributed sixteen short pieces of fiction in 1925 to the New Orleans *Times-Picayune*, the first of which was "Mirrors of Chartres Street" and the last was "Yo Ho and

Two Bottles of Rum." Several of the characters in these sketches resemble those in "New Orleans," which appeared in *The Double Dealer* at about the same time. Although thirteen of these sketches have been known, in recent years, and have been reprinted in two different collections, three of the last four have been previously unrecorded.

a. Photostat of "Mirrors of Chartres Street" from the *Times-Picayune* Sunday magazine section, February 8, 1925, pp. 1, 6. [Original in the Louisiana State University Library]

b. Photostat of "Out of Nazareth" from the *Times-Picayune* Sunday magazine section, April 12, 1925, p. 4. [Original in the Louisiana State University Library]. This was the only one of the series to be illustrated by William Spratling.

c. The section subtitled 'The Cobbler' from "New Orleans," *The Double Dealer*, VII (January-February, 1925), 104. [0901.D727]

d. Photostat of "The Cobbler" from the *Times-Picayune* Sunday magazine section, May 10, 1925, p. 7. [Original in the Louisiana State University Library]

e. Photostat of "Yo Ho and Two Bottles of Rum" from the *Times-Picayune* Sunday magazine section, September 27, 1925, pp. 1, 2. [Original in the Louisiana State University Library]. One of three previously unrecorded sketches; the others are "The Liar" (July 26) and "Country Mice" (September 20). All three appeared after Faulkner's departure for Europe, July 7, 1925, aboard the freighter "West Ivis."

24. "Elmer." 130-page typescript, several versions, incomplete. [Lent by Mr. Faulkner]. See Fig. 7

After finishing *Soldiers' Pay* and leaving New Orleans, Faulkner began a second novel, which he variously entitled "Elmer," "Portrait of Elmer Hodge," "Elmer and Myrtle," and "Growing Pains." Never completed, it contains some of the elements of humor and satire that he was to use in *Mosquitoes*. In one version, the central character lived in Jefferson, Mississippi, as a small boy.

## 4. FAULKNER'S COUNTY

25. The maps of Yoknapatawpha County.

From the publication of *Sartoris* in 1929 to *The Town* in 1957, more than a dozen books and three dozen short stories by Faulkner have had their setting in his mythical north Mississippi county of Yoknapatawpha. He has twice drawn maps of this county—"WILLIAM FAULKNER, *Sole Owner & Proprietor*"—once for *Absalom, Absalom!* in 1936, and ten years later for the Viking *Portable Faulkner*. (The 1936 map was redrawn but not brought up to date for the Modern Library issue of *Absalom, Absalom!* in 1951.)

a. Map from the first edition of *Absalom, Absalom!* [Lent by James B. Meriwether]

b. Photostat, enlarged, of map from the Modern Library issue of *Absalom, Absalom!* [Original: L 3734.92.311]

c. Photostat, enlarged, of map from the Viking *Portable Faulkner*. [Original: 3734.92.1946]

26. Lafayette County.

William Faulkner's home county of Lafayette (accented on

the second syllable: La-fay′-ette) is similar in many ways to Yoknapatawpha. The Tallahatchie River is on the northern boundary of both, and in the southern part of Lafayette County is the Yocona River, which on old maps appears in longer form and in various spellings, one of which is Yoknapatawpha, the same spelling that Faulkner gives to his imaginary county and to the river that is its southern boundary.

a. Photostat, enlarged, of Lafayette County and northern Mississippi from the United States Department of Commerce, Bureau of Public Roads, "Mississippi Transportation Map," 1949. Sheet 1 of 8 sheets. [Original in Maps Division]

b. Photostat, enlarged, of detail from "Railroad Commissioners' Map of Mississippi," 1906 (copyright by Brandon Printing Co., Nashville), showing spelling "Yoknapatawpha." [Original in Maps Division]

27. The courthouse and the Confederate monument.

Descriptions in Faulkner's works of the courthouse in Jefferson, the county seat of Yoknapatawpha, correspond with the appearance of the actual courthouse in his home town of Oxford. However, the monument of the Confederate soldier in front of the Jefferson courthouse seems modeled after the monument on the University of Mississippi campus, rather than the one by the Oxford courthouse.

a. Reproduction of picture of the courthouse and Confederate monument in Oxford, Mississippi, from David E. Scherman and Rosemarie Redlich, *Literary America*, New York, 1952, p. 148. [3570.815]

b. Photograph of Confederate monument on the University of Mississippi campus. [Lent by Carvel Collins]

c. Description of the courthouse and Confederate monument in Jefferson from *Sartoris*, p. 166:

> The courthouse was of brick too, with stone arches rising amid elms, and among the trees the monument of the Confederate soldier stood, his musket at order arms, shading his carven eyes with his stone hand. Beneath the porticoes of the courthouse and on benches about the green, the city fathers sat and talked and drowsed. . . .

## 5. *SARTORIS*, 1929

In New Orleans, Sherwood Anderson had advised Faulkner to write about his native north Mississippi. This Faulkner did for the first time in *Sartoris*, his third novel, although the small-town Georgia setting of *Soldiers' Pay* and the unidentified rural setting of one of the *Times-Picayune* sketches, "The Liar," seem to some extent to draw upon Oxford and Lafayette County.

Faulkner dedicated *Sartoris* "TO SHERWOOD ANDERSON *through whose kindness I was first published*," and he recalled the importance of Anderson's advice and the significance of *Sartoris* in the "design" of his literary career in his 1953 *Atlantic* tribute to Anderson and in an interview in *The Paris Review* in 1956.

28. *Sartoris*. New York, Harcourt, Brace and Company [1929]. First edition, in dust jacket. [Ex 3734.92.383]

29. Three pages from the manuscript of *Sartoris*: 01, 42-C, and 76. [Lent by Mr. Faulkner]. See Fig. 9

This manuscript of an earlier version of *Sartoris* is entitled "Flags in the Dust." The Evelyn Sartoris who appears on p. 01 is the John Sartoris, twin brother of young Bayard, of the published book. The flyer whose marginal remark "I am Comyn of the Irish nation" occurs on p. 01 was omitted from the typescript and the published book, but appears, with his remark, in the short story "Ad Astra," published in 1931.

30. Bound typescript of *Sartoris* (entitled "Flags in the Dust" in this version). 594 pp. [Lent by Mr. Faulkner]. See Fig. 8

Opened to p. 221 for comparison with p. 76 of the manuscript.

31. *Sartoris*. London, Chatto & Windus, 1932. First English edition. [Lent by Random House]

32. *Sartoris*. [Milan], Garzanti [1955]. Translation into Italian by Maria Stella Ferrari. [Ex 3734.92.383.6]

33. *Sartoris*. Stockholm, Albert Bonniers Förlag [1955]. Translation into Swedish by Th. Warburton. [Lent by Random House]

34. Interview with Faulkner by Jean Stein, *The Paris Review*, IV (Spring, 1956), [28]-52. [0901.P237]

35. William Faulkner. "Sherwood Anderson: An Appreciation." *The Atlantic*, CXCI (June, 1953), [27]-29. [0901.A881]

36. Colonel William C. Falkner.

One of the characters of *Sartoris*, the Civil War officer and railroad builder John Sartoris, is modeled after Faulkner's great-grandfather, Colonel William C. Falkner (d. 1889). Lawyer, Confederate soldier, and railroad builder, Colonel Falkner was also author of several books. His novel *The White Rose of Memphis*, originally published in 1881, was reprinted thirty-six times in the next thirty years. His last book, which appeared in 1884, was *Rapid Ramblings in Europe*. The description in *Sartoris* of the effigy of Colonel Sartoris in the Jefferson cemetery recalls the monument over the grave of Colonel Falkner in Ripley, Mississippi.

a. *The White Rose of Memphis*. With an introduction by Robert Cantwell. New York, Coley Taylor [1953]. This modern edition omits the epigraph and dedication of the original, as well as making numerous minor changes. [3733.754.397]

b. *Rapid Ramblings in Europe*. Philadelphia, J. B. Lippincott & Co., 1884. [Ex 1401.338]. Opened to frontispiece, a picture of Colonel Falkner.

15

c. Description of the effigy of Colonel Sartoris in Jefferson, in *Sartoris*, p. 375:

He stood on a stone pedestal, in his frock coat and bareheaded, one leg slightly advanced and one hand resting lightly on the stone pylon beside him. His head was lifted a little in that gesture of haughty pride which repeated itself generation after generation with a fateful fidelity, his back to the world and his carven eyes gazing out across the valley where his railroad ran, and the blue changeless hills beyond, and beyond that, the ramparts of infinity itself. The pedestal and effigy were mottled with seasons of rain and sun and with drippings from the cedar branches, and the bold carving of the letters was bleared with mold, yet still decipherable. . . .

d. Photograph of the monument of Colonel Falkner in Ripley, Mississippi. [Lent by James B. Meriwether]

## 6. *THE SOUND AND THE FURY*, 1929

*The Sound and the Fury* was published late in 1929 by the new firm of Jonathan Cape and Harrison Smith, after it had been rejected by Harcourt, Brace and Company, the publishers of *Sartoris*. Faulkner has often referred to it as his own favorite among his works, and the one which cost him the greatest trouble in writing. At the same time, he has emphasized the point that in one sense the writing was easy, for in this book he was striving to please no audience but himself. (It was written during the period in which his previous book, *Sartoris*, had been rejected by his old publisher, and had not yet been accepted by a new one.)

In an unpublished note on *The Sound and the Fury* written during the early 1930's (lent to the Library by Mr. Faulkner), he describes it as "the only one of the seven novels which I wrote without any accompanying feeling of drive or effort, or any following feeling of exhaustion or relief or distaste. When I began it I had no plan at all. I wasn't even writing a book. I was thinking of books, publication, only in the reverse, in saying to myself, I wont have to worry about publishers liking or not liking this at all." The writing of his first three novels had cost him progressively greater efforts, he continued, and when *Sartoris* was repeatedly turned down, "One day I seemed to shut a door between me and all publishers' addresses and book lists. I said to myself, Now I can write." The complexity, the control, and the emotional power which characterize this novel all seem to owe something to these circumstances of the writing.

37. *The Sound and the Fury*. New York, Jonathan Cape and Harrison Smith [1929]. First edition, in dust jacket. [Ex 3734.92.386]

16

38. *Le Bruit et la Fureur*. Paris, Gallimard [1938]. Translation into French by Maurice E. Coindreau. [Ex 3734.92.386.7]

39. *Schall und Wahn*. Stuttgart, Scherz & Goverts Verlag [1956]. Translation into German by Helmut M. Braem and Elisabeth Kaiser. [3734.92.386.6]

40. *L'Urlo e il Furore*. [Milan], Arnoldo Mondadori, 1956. Translation into Italian by Augusto Dauphiné. [Ex 3734.92.386.6]

41. *El Sonido y la Furia*. Buenos Aires, Editorial Futuro [1947]. Translation into Spanish by Floreal Mazía. [Lent by Random House]

42. Six pages from the manuscript of *The Sound and the Fury*: 20, 34, 70, 87, 115, and 125.[1] [Lent by Mr. Faulkner]. See Figs. 10 and 11

43. Bound typescript of *The Sound and the Fury*. 409 pp. [Lent by Mr. Faulkner]
Opened to p. 86 for comparison with p. 34 of the manuscript.

44. Undated autograph letter from Faulkner to Ben Wasson on *The Sound and the Fury*. 2 pp. [Lent by Linton R. Massey]
In this letter Faulkner discusses the problem of indicating the time shifts in the stream-of-consciousness of the idiot Benjy, who is the narrator of the first section of *The Sound and the Fury*. Against his wishes, this section was first set up by the printer with breaks in the text to indicate the dislocations in time, but Faulkner, according to this letter, restored his original device of using italics for this purpose when he corrected the proofs.

The idea of using inks of different colors to accomplish this, which Faulkner mentions as a process which he wishes the publishing business were advanced enough to allow, was returned to a few years later when a new edition of the book was planned by Random House. Though announced for publication in 1933, the project was never completed, and Faulkner has stated in a recent interview that he now feels that such a device is unnecessary and the section is sufficiently clear as it stands.

## 7. *AS I LAY DYING*, 1930

*As I Lay Dying* was published in 1930, a year after the appearance of *The Sound and the Fury*. "I wrote *As I Lay Dying* in six weeks, without changing a word," Faulkner said in 1932 (in the introduction to the Modern Library *Sanctuary*), and this has often been interpreted to mean that it was not revised. However, Faulkner has said elsewhere that writing this book "was not easy. No honest work is," and both manuscript and the bound typescript show considerable revision by the author.

[1] For a reproduction of the last page of the manuscript, see *The Princeton University Library Chronicle*, XVIII (Spring, 1957), Plate III.

45. *As I Lay Dying.* New York, Jonathan Cape: Harrison Smith [1930]. First state of first edition, in dust jacket. [Ex 3734 .92.313]

46. *As I Lay Dying.* Second state of first edition, with the initial "I" on p. 11 correctly aligned. [Lent by James B. Meriwether]

47. Page 32 of the manuscript of *As I Lay Dying.*[2] [Lent by Mr. Faulkner]

48. Bound typescript of *As I Lay Dying.* 266 pp. [Lent by Mr. Faulkner]
   Opened to p. 78 for comparison with p. 32 of the manuscript.

49. *Tandis que J'Agonise.* Burins de Courtin. Paris, Editions Jean Boisseau, 1946. Translation into French by Maurice E. Coindreau. No. 5 (of 10 "hors commerce") of 210 copies. [Lent by Maurice E. Coindreau]

50. Typewritten letter from Faulkner to Maurice E. Coindreau, February 26, 1937, about the translation of *As I Lay Dying.*[3] [Manuscripts Division]

51. *Medan jag låg och dog.* Stockholm, Albert Bonniers Förlag [1948]. Translation into Swedish by Mårten Edlund. [Lent by Random House]

52. *Uitvaart in Mississippi.* Amsterdam, Uitgeverij de Bezige Bij, 1955. Translation into Dutch by Apie Prins and John Vandenbergh. [Lent by Random House]

53. *Mientras Agonizo.* Madrid, Aguilar, 1954. Translation into Spanish by Agustin Caballero Robredo and Arturo del Hoyo. [Lent by Random House]

54. *Kun tein Kuolemaa.* [Helsinki], Kustannusosakeyhtiö Tammi [1952]. Translation into Finnish by Alex. Matson. [3734.92 .313.8]

## 8. *SANCTUARY*, 1931

*Sanctuary*, published by Cape and Smith in February, 1931, was Faulkner's first popular success. For the Modern Library issue

---

[2] For a reproduction of the last page of the manuscript, see *The Princeton University Library Chronicle*, XVIII (Spring, 1957), Plate V.

[3] This letter was reproduced as an illustration in *The Princeton University Library Chronicle*, XVIII (Spring, 1957), Plate II.

in 1932 he supplied an introduction which explained how he wrote the original version—"the most horrific tale I could imagine"—deliberately to make money. It was rejected by his publisher. Later on the publisher changed his mind, and sent the galley proofs to the author. "I saw that it was so terrible," Faulkner said, describing his reaction to the galleys, "that there were but two things to do: tear it up or rewrite it." He chose rewriting; how extensive the process was can be seen by the comparison of the manuscript, typescript, and galleys of the original version with the finished book.

55. *Sanctuary*. New York, Jonathan Cape & Harrison Smith [1931]. First edition, in dust jacket. [Ex 3734.92.382, copy 1]

56. *Sanctuary*. With an introduction by William Faulkner. New York, The Modern Library [1932]. First Modern Library issue. Binding variant in green cloth, in dust jacket. [Lent by Linton R. Massey]
The introduction is printed on two pages. In later impressions of the Modern Library issue the introduction is printed on four pages.

57. Four manuscript pages of the original version of *Sanctuary*: 1, 9, 15, and 131.[4] [Lent by Mr. Faulkner]. See Fig. 12
The beginning of the original version, as shown by manuscript p. 1, is the description of the Negro murderer that appears at the beginning of Chapter XVI of the published book. Manuscript p. 131 shows a discarded beginning of the original version, the trial scene that appears near the end of the published book.

58. Bound typescript of *Sanctuary*. 359 pp. [Lent by Mr. Faulkner]
Opened to pp. 56 verso and 57 for comparison with pp. 9 and 15 of the manuscript.

59. Galley proofs of the beginning of the original version of *Sanctuary*. [Lent by Linton R. Massey]

60. *Sanctuary*. New York, Jonathan Cape & Harrison Smith [1931]. "Sixth Printing, July, 1931". [Lent by James B. Meriwether]
*Sanctuary* went through six printings between February and July, 1931, all of them under the Cape and Smith imprint.

61. *Sanctuary*. New York, Harrison Smith and Robert Haas [date uncertain]. "Sixth Printing, July, 1931". [Lent by James B. Meriwether]
This copy of the "Sixth Printing" bears the imprint of Smith and Haas, the successors to Cape and Smith who published Faulkner after 1931, though the format is similar to that of the Modern Library issue and it contains the later, four-page version of the Modern Library introduction.

4 Page 1 of the manuscript was reproduced as an illustration in *The Princeton University Library Chronicle*, XVIII (Spring, 1957), Plate IV.

62. *Sanctuary.* Paris, Crosby Continental Editions, 1932. [Lent by Miss Mary Killgore]

63. *Sanctuaire.* Préface d'André Malraux. [Paris], Gallimard [1933]. Translation into French by R. N. Raimbault and Henri Delgove. [Lent by Maurice E. Coindreau]
This copy contains a presentation inscription from the translators to Mr. Coindreau.

64. *Die Freistatt.* Zürich, Artemis-Verlag [1951]. Translation into German by Herberth E. Herlitschka. [Ex 3734.92.382.7]

65. *Santuario.* [Milan], Arnoldo Mondadori [1946]. Translation into Italian by Paola Ojetti Zamattio. [Lent by Random House]

66. *Santuário.* Sao Paulo, Instituto Progresso Editorial [1948]. Translation into Portuguese by Lígia Junqueira Smith. [Lent by Random House]

67. *Det Allra Heligaste.* Stockholm, Albert Bonniers Förlag, 1951. Translation into Swedish by Mårten Edlund. [Lent by Random House]

68. *Det Aller Helligste.* Oslo, Gyldendal Norsk Forlag, 1951. Translation into Norwegian by Leo Strøm. [Lent by Random House]

69. *Sanctuary.* [Tokyo, Getuyō Shobō Company, 1950.] Translation into Japanese by Naotarō Tatsunokuchi and Masami Nishikawa. [Lent by Carvel Collins]

## 9. *THESE 13*, 1931

Faulkner's first collection of short stories, *These 13*, followed soon after the success of *Sanctuary*. Published in September, 1931, it was the first of his books to be brought out simultaneously in trade and limited, signed issues. Seven of its thirteen stories were published for the first time.

70. *These 13.* New York, Jonathan Cape & Harrison Smith [1931]. First trade issue, in dust jacket. [Ex 3734.92.389]

71. *These 13.* Limited, signed issue. No. 286 of 299 copies. [Ex 3734.92.389.11]

72. "A Rose for Emily." *The Forum*, LXXXIII (April, 1930), 233-238. [0901.F747]

Aside from his brief pieces of fiction in *The Mississippian* and the *Times-Picayune*, Faulkner's first published short story was "A Rose for Emily," in 1930. It was slightly revised for its appearance in *These 13*.

73. First page of the manuscript of "A Rose for Emily." [Lent by Mr. Faulkner]

74. *Treize Histoires*. [Paris], Gallimard [1939]. Translation into French by R. N. Raimbault and Ch. P. Vorce with the collaboration of M. E. Coindreau. [Ex 3734.92.3915.6]
"Une Rose pour Emily," translated by Mr. Coindreau, pp. [135]-146.[5]

75. "Ad Astra." *American Caravan IV*, New York, The Macaulay Company, 1931, pp. 164-181. [3588.668]
The short story "Ad Astra" first appeared in the fourth volume of *American Caravan*, an annual anthology of American writing. It was considerably revised for *These 13*.

76. Page 1 of the manuscript of "Ad Astra." [Lent by Mr. Faulkner]

77. "Red Leaves." *The Saturday Evening Post*, October 25, 1930, pp. 6-7, 54, 56, 58, 60, 62, 64. [0901.S254q]
One of the best stories in *These 13* is "Red Leaves," the first of several stories about the Indians in north Mississippi which Faulkner published in the 1930's. Like the other previously published stories in *These 13*, it was revised from its periodical appearance, and the manuscript and typescript differ from each other and from both published versions.

78. Page 1 of the manuscript of "Red Leaves." [Lent by Mr. Faulkner]

79. Page 1 of carbon typescript of "Red Leaves." [Lent by Mr. Faulkner]

80. *Questi Tredici*. Turin, Lattes [1948]. Translation into Italian by Francesco Lo Bue. [Lent by Random House]
"Foglie Rosse," pp. 113 ff.

## 10. *IDYLL IN THE DESERT* AND *MISS ZILPHIA GANT*

81. *Idyll in the Desert*. New York, Random House, 1931. No. 40 of 400 copies, signed by the author. [Ex 3734.92.348]
The short story *Idyll in the Desert*, issued in a limited, signed edition of 400 copies in December, 1931, and never reprinted, was the first Faulkner title to be published by Random House.

[5] This translation, the first work of Faulkner to appear in France, was first published in *Commerce*, XXIX (1932). For a reproduction of a letter, April 14, 1932, from Faulkner to Mr. Coindreau, which includes a comment on the translation, see *The Princeton University Library Chronicle*, XVIII (Spring, 1957), Plate II.

82. First page of the manuscript of *Idyll in the Desert*. [Lent by Mr. Faulkner]

83. *Miss Zilphia Gant*. [Dallas], The Book Club of Texas, 1932. No. 32 of 300 copies. [Ex 3734.92.365]

   The short story *Miss Zilphia Gant* was issued in a limited edition of 300 copies by the Book Club of Texas in June, 1932, and has never been reprinted. Although in the prospectus which announced the book it was stated that "Mr. Faulkner tells us that 'Miss Zilphia Gant' is in reality the basis for a novel which he plans to write in the near future," it bears little resemblance to any of his subsequently published work.

84. First page of the manuscript of *Miss Zilphia Gant*. [Lent by Mr. Faulkner]

85. Page 1 of a typescript version, with manuscript corrections, of *Miss Zilphia Gant*. [Lent by Mr. Faulkner]

86. Certificate of copyright registration for *Miss Zilphia Gant*, from Copyright Office, Library of Congress. [Lent by Mr. Faulkner]

   It gives June 27, 1932, as the date of publication; July 2 as the date the affidavit was received; and July 5 as the date the copyright deposit copies were received.

## 11. *LIGHT IN AUGUST*, 1932

William Faulkner's eighth novel, *Light in August,* was published in October, 1932, by the new firm of Smith and Haas. On p. 340 an error occurred in the first line, where the name "Jefferson" is printed instead of "Mottstown". This mistake was picked up as a "point" by early bibliographers of Faulkner, who believed that this error distinguished between two states of the first impression, as did the misaligned "I" in *As I Lay Dying.* That it is simply an error, and an uncorrected error, not a point, is shown by the fact that it persists in three subsequent Smith and Haas printings; in the English issue and the 1947 New Directions issue (both printed photographically from the Smith and Haas text); and in the 1950 resetting of the text for the Modern Library.

87. *Light in August*. [New York], Harrison Smith & Robert Haas [1932]. First edition, in dust jacket. [Ex 3734.92.358]

88. *Light in August*. London, Chatto & Windus, 1933. First English issue [Ex 3734.92.358.11]

89. Manuscript pages of the beginning and end of *Light in August*: 2 and 187. [Lent by Mr. Faulkner]

90. *Light in August.* [Norfolk, Conn., New Directions, 1947.] [Lent by James B. Meriwether]
Opened to p. 271 for comparison with p. 110 of the manuscript.

91. Page 110 of the manuscript of *Light in August.* [Lent by Mr. Faulkner]
That Faulkner's revisions of the manuscript involved rearrangement of this episode is indicated by the different page and chapter numbers which are cancelled.

92. The first four printings of the Smith and Haas edition of *Light in August* and a remaindered copy of the fourth printing in a Random House binding. [Lent by James B. Meriwether]

93. *Lumière d'Août.* Paris, Gallimard [1935]. Translation into French by Maurice E. Coindreau. [3734.92.358.6]

94. *Luce d'Agosto.* [Milan], Arnoldo Mondadori [1954]. Translation into Italian by Elio Vittorini. [Ex 3734.92.358.9]

95. *Licht im August.* Berlin, Verlag Volk und Welt, 1957. Translation into German by Franz Fein. [Ex 3734.92.358.6]

96. *Geboorte in Augustus.* Amsterdam, Em. Querido, 1951. Translation into Dutch by I. E. Prins-Willekes-Macdonald. [3734 .92.358.8]

97. *Mørk August.* Oslo, Gyldendal Norsk Forlag, 1951. Translation into Norwegian by Sigurd Hoel. [Lent by Random House]

98. *Svetloba v Avgustu.* Ljubljana, Cankarjeva Zalozba, 1952. Translation into Slovenian by Mira Mihelic. [Lent by Random House]

## 12. *A GREEN BOUGH,* 1933

In 1933 William Faulkner, now established and well known as a novelist and short story writer, brought out his second volume of poems, *A Green Bough.* It had been announced early in 1925, when Faulkner was in New Orleans, that he was preparing another book of verse for publication, and the dated manuscripts of several of the poems of *A Green Bough* show that they were written in the 1920's, but they were revised and tightened for book publication. Since 1933 Faulkner's published work has been exclusively in prose forms.

99. *A Green Bough*. New York, Harrison Smith and Robert Haas, 1933. First trade issue, in dust jacket. [Ex 3734.92.341.11]

100. *A Green Bough*. Limited, signed issue. No. 5 of 360 copies. [Ex 3734.92.341]

101. "My Epitaph." *Contempo*, I (February 1, 1932), 2. [Ex 3734 .92.326f, copy 1]
The last poem in *A Green Bough* had been published twice before: as "My Epitaph" in an issue of *Contempo* devoted to Faulkner, and in pamphlet form, entitled *This Earth*. All three versions differ slightly.

102. Typescript of *Contempo* text of "My Epitaph." 1 p. [Lent by Mr. Faulkner]

103. *This Earth*. New York, Equinox, 1932. [Ex 3734.92.391]

104. *Le Rameau Vert*. Paris, Gallimard [1955]. Bilingual edition of *A Green Bough*, with translation into French by R. N. Raimbault. [3734.92.341.8]

105. Typescript of sonnet "Spring," dated "13 December, 1924" in Faulkner's hand. 1 p. [Lent by Mr. Faulkner]
The sonnet which appeared, untitled, as number XXXVI of the poems in *A Green Bough* had been previously published, in a slightly different version, in the Faulkner issue of *Contempo*, entitled "Spring." According to the date of this typescript of the *Contempo* version, it was originally written about the time of the publication of *The Marble Faun*.

106. Typescript version of poem XXXII of *A Green Bough*, with a humorous inscription by Faulkner for Sam Gilmore, whom he knew in New Orleans in 1925. 1 p. [Lent by Mr. Faulkner]. See Fig. 4

## 13. *DOCTOR MARTINO AND OTHER STORIES*, 1934

*Doctor Martino* is Faulkner's second collection of short stories. Two of its fourteen stories were published for the first time, and only two of the twelve which had been previously published were revised for their appearance in the collection.

107. *Doctor Martino and other stories*. New York, Harrison Smith and Robert Haas, 1934. First trade issue, in dust jacket. [Ex 3734.92.331.11]

108. *Doctor Martino and other stories*. Limited, signed issue. No. 69 of 360 copies. [Ex 3734.92.331]

109. First page of an untitled manuscript version of "There Was a Queen." [Lent by Linton R. Massey]

Although the short story "There Was a Queen" was not revised from its original periodical publication when it was included in *Doctor Martino*, the three manuscript and typescript versions exhibited all differ from the printed texts as well as from each other.

110. First page of a manuscript version of "There Was a Queen" entitled "An Empress Passed," with cancelled title "Through the Window." [Lent by Mr. Faulkner]

111. First page of a typescript version of "There Was a Queen." [Lent by Mr. Faulkner]

112. "Death-Drag." *Scribner's Magazine,* XCI (January, 1932), [34]-42. [0901.S436]
Faulkner's interest in flying continued after his RAF service, as both the novel *Pylon* and the short story "Death-Drag" attest.

113. Page 1 of the manuscript of "A Death-Drag." [Lent by Mr. Faulkner]

114. *Le Docteur Martino et Autres Histoires.* [Paris], Gallimard [1948]. Translation into French by R. N. Raimbault and Ch. P. Vorce. [Ex 3734.92.331.8]
"La Course à la Mort" ("Death Drag"), pp. [71]-92.

115. "A Mountain Victory." *The Saturday Evening Post*, December 3, 1932, pp. 6-7, 39, 42, 44, 45, 46. [0901.S254q]
One of the best of the stories in *Doctor Martino* is "Mountain Victory," which was revised from its original appearance in *The Saturday Evening Post.*

116. First page of the manuscript of "A Mountain Victory." [Lent by Mr. Faulkner]

## 14. *PYLON,* 1935

117. *Pylon.* New York, Harrison Smith and Robert Haas, Inc., 1935. First trade issue, in dust jacket. [Ex 3734.92.374]

118. *Pylon.* Limited, signed issue. No. 96 of 310 copies. [Ex 3734.92.374.13]
Opened to the title-page and the folded, tipped-in reproduction of p. 58 of the manuscript.

119. Page 78 of the typescript setting copy of *Pylon.* [Lent by Mr. Faulkner]

120. *Pylône.* [Paris], Gallimard [1946]. Translation into French by R. N. Raimbault with the collaboration of G. Louis-Rousselet. [Lent by Random House]
Opened to pp. [68]-69, for comparison with p. 78 of the setting copy.

121. Unnumbered manuscript page of *Pylon*, containing a version of parts of pp. 9, 10, and 27 of the published book. [Lent by Mr. Faulkner]. See Fig. 13

122. *Trekanten*. Copenhagen, Winthers Forlag [1952]. Translation into Danish by Peter Toubro. [Ex 3734.92.374.9]

123. *Pylon*. Barcelona, Luis de Caralt [1947]. Translation into Spanish by Julio Fernández-Yánez. [Lent by Random House]

124. *Wendemarke*. Hamburg, Rowohlt [1951]. Translation into German by Georg Goyert. [3734.92.374.6]

## 15. *ABSALOM, ABSALOM!* 1936

*Absalom, Absalom!* was Faulkner's first novel published by Random House, who have been his publishers ever since. Faulkner appended a chronology, a genealogy of the principal characters, and a map of Yoknapatawpha County to this volume, which appeared in October of 1936.

125. *Absalom, Absalom!* New York, Random House, 1936. First trade issue, in dust jacket. [Ex 3734.92.311, copy 1]

126. *Absalom, Absalom!* Limited, signed issue. No. 187 of 300 copies. [Ex 3734.92.311.11]

127. First page of the final typescript of *Absalom, Absalom!* [Lent by Mr. Faulkner]

128. Two pages from the typescript of a version of the first chapter of *Absalom, Absalom!*: 9 and 13, with manuscript annotations by Faulkner and his editor. [Lent by Mr. Faulkner]. See Fig. 14

129. "Absalom, Absalom!" *The American Mercury*, XXXVIII (August, 1936), 466-474. [0901.A491]
Opened to pp. 466-467, the beginning of a version of the first chapter of *Absalom, Absalom!*

130. First manuscript page (unnumbered) of a version of the Chronology of *Absalom, Absalom!* [Lent by Mr. Faulkner]

131. "Wash." *Harper's Magazine*, CLXVIII (February, 1934), [258]-266. [0901.H295]
Opened to pp. [258]-259, the beginning of the story, which is an early version of the episode of Sutpen's death in Chapter VII of *Absalom, Absalom!*

132. *Absalom, Absalom!* Introduction by Harvey Breit. New York, The Modern Library [1951]. First Modern Library issue, in dust jacket. [Lent by Linton R. Massey; Library copy, L 3734.92.311]

133. *Absalon! Absalon!* [Paris], Gallimard [1953]. Translation into French by R. N. Raimbault with the collaboration of Ch. P. Vorce. [Lent by Random House]

134. *Absalom, Absalom!* Stuttgart, Rowohlt [1948]. Translation into German by Hermann Stresau. [Lent by Random House]

135. *Assalonne, Assalonne!* [Milan], Arnoldo Mondadori [1954]. Translation into Italian by Glauco Cambon. [Ex 3734.92 .311.6]

136. *¡Absalón, Absalón!* Buenos Aires, Emecé Editores [1950]. Translation into Spanish by Beatriz Florencia Nelson. [Lent by Random House]

## 16. *THE UNVANQUISHED*, 1938

*The Unvanquished*, published in February, 1938, is a novel made from six previously published short stories, revised and with a seventh and concluding chapter, "An Odor of Verbena," added. The illustrations were made by Edward Shenton, who had previously illustrated the magazine appearance of the sixth chapter.

137. *The Unvanquished.* New York, Random House [1938]. First trade issue, in dust jacket. [Ex 3734.92.393.11]

138. *The Unvanquished.* Limited, signed issue. No. 90 of 250 copies. [Ex 3734.92.393]
Opened to p. 243, the beginning of "An Odor of Verbena."

139. Page 1 of the manuscript of "An Odor of Verbena." [Lent by Mr. Faulkner]

140. Page 1 of the typescript of "An Odor of Verbena." [Lent by Mr. Faulkner]

141. "Skirmish at Sartoris." *Scribner's Magazine*, XCVII (April, 1935), [193]-200. [0901.S436]
Opened to p. [193], the beginning of the story which was revised to become the sixth chapter of *The Unvanquished*.

142. *L'Invaincu.* [Paris], Gallimard [1949]. Translation into French by R. N. Raimbault and Ch. P. Vorce. [Ex 3734 .92.393.8]

143. *Die Unbesiegten.* Zürich, Fretz & Wasmuth Verlag [1954]. Translation into German by Erich Franzen. [3734.92.393.6]

144. *Gli Invitti.* [Milan], Arnoldo Mondadori, 1948. Translation into Italian by Alberto Marmont. [Ex 3734.92.393.7]

145. *Los Invictos.* Barcelona, Luis de Caralt [1951]. Translation into Spanish by Alberto Vilá de Avilés. [3734.92.393.9]

146. *De Obesegrade.* Stockholm, Folket i Bilds Förlag [1948]. Translation into Swedish by Håkan Norlén. [Lent by Random House]

## 17. *THE WILD PALMS*, 1939

In form, *The Wild Palms* is one of Faulkner's most experimental novels. The action of the two sections of its double plot, "Wild Palms" and "Old Man," never combines. Printed in alternate chapters, their only unity is thematic.

147. *The Wild Palms.* New York, Random House [1939]. First trade issue, in dust jacket. [Ex 3734.92.397, copy 1]
Opened to pp. 22-23, the end of the first chapter of "Wild Palms" and the beginning of the first chapter of "Old Man."

148. *The Wild Palms.* Limited, signed issue. No. 164 of 250 copies. [Lent by Maurice E. Coindreau]
Opened to p. 143, the beginning of the third chapter of "Old Man."

149. Manuscript page (unnumbered) of the end of the first chapter of "Wild Palms." [Lent by Mr. Faulkner]

150. Manuscript (p. 92) of the beginning of the third chapter of "Old Man." [Lent by Mr. Faulkner]

151. Title-page of the typescript which was used as the setting copy of *The Wild Palms*, showing cancelled title, "If I Forget Thee, Jerusalem" (a reference to Psalms 137:5). [Lent by Mr. Faulkner]

152. Pages 4 and 36 of the typescript setting copy of *The Wild Palms*, the first page of each section of the novel. [Lent by Mr. Faulkner]

153. *The Old Man.* New York, New American Library [1948]. First Signet edition of this erroneously entitled paperback. [Lent by James B. Meriwether]

154. *Les Palmiers Sauvages.* [Paris], Gallimard [1952]. Translation into French by M. E. Coindreau. [3734.92.397.6]

155. *Yasei no jo Netsu.* [Tokyo], Mikasa Shobō [1951]. Translation into Japanese by Yasuo Ōkubo. [Ex 3734.92.397.83]

## 18. *THE HAMLET*, 1940

Volume One of the Snopes trilogy, *The Hamlet*, was published in April, 1940. Faulkner had planned a novel about the Snopes family from the inception of the Yoknapatawpha series in the 1920's, and *The Hamlet* incorporates four previously published short stories which had appeared in the 1930's: "Fool About a Horse," "The Hound," "Spotted Horses," and "Lizards in Jamshyd's Courtyard." All were extensively revised for the book, which also makes use of material from the short stories "Barn Burning" and "Afternoon of a Cow."

156. *The Hamlet.* New York, Random House, 1940. First trade issue, in dust jacket. [Ex 3734.92.342]

157. *The Hamlet.* Limited, signed issue. No. 220 of 250 copies. [Lent by Maurice E. Coindreau]

158. Bound carbon typescript of *The Hamlet.* 2 vols. [Lent by Phil Stone]
Opened to p. 1 of the first volume, with manuscript dedication: "To My Godson, Philip Alston Stone | May he be faithful | fortunate, and brave | William Faulkner | Xmas 1945 | Oxford, Miss".
*The Hamlet* is dedicated to Phil Stone, who wrote the preface to *The Marble Faun*, and with whom Faulkner had worked up many of the events of the Snopes stories in tall tales the two men told each other in the late 1920's. To Stone's son Philip, Faulkner presented this first carbon of the typescript setting copy of *The Hamlet.* Bound in two volumes, it is inscribed on the first page and signed on the last page of each.

159. "Barn Burning." *Harper's Magazine,* CLXXIX (June, 1939), [86]-96. [0901.H295]
Opened to p. [86], the beginning of the story. The short story "Barn Burning," first published in *Harper's,* was written to be the first chapter of *The Hamlet,* as the manuscript and typescript show.

160. Page 1 of the manuscript of "Barn Burning." [Lent by Mr. Faulkner]. See Fig. 15

161. Page 1 of the typescript of "Barn Burning." [Lent by Mr. Faulkner]

162. Page 58 of a manuscript version of the first part of the "Eula" section of *The Hamlet,* indicating that at one time Faulkner

planned to begin the section with what is the end of its first chapter in the published version.[6] [Lent by Mr. Faulkner]

163. Page 317 of a typescript version of *The Hamlet*, in which the name Mordred (nicknamed "Maud") Snopes appears for the character Launcelot (nicknamed "Lump") Snopes of the published book. [Lent by Mr. Faulkner]

164. *El Villorrio*. Buenos Aires, Editorial Futuro [1947]. Translation into Spanish by Raquel W. de Ortiz. [Lent by Random House]

165. *El Villorrio*. Barcelona, Luis de Caralt [1953]. Translation into Spanish by J. Napoletano Torre and P. Carbó Amiguet. [Ex 3734.92.342.8]

## 19. *GO DOWN, MOSES*, 1942

*Go Down, Moses and Other Stories* was published in May, 1942. Eight previously published short stories are incorporated into its seven sections, or chapters, but the volume has a basic unity which was emphasized in later printings by the omission of *"and Other Stories"* from the title.

166. *Go Down, Moses and Other Stories*. New York, Random House [1942]. Presumable first state of the binding, first trade issue, in black cloth, with top edges stained red; in dust jacket. [Lent by Linton R. Massey]

167. *Go Down, Moses and Other Stories*. Variant state of the binding, first trade issue, in red cloth, with top edges unstained; in dust jacket. [Ex 3734.92.339]
Several other binding variants of the first impression have been noted.

168. *Go Down, Moses and Other Stories*. Limited, signed issue. No. 12 of 100 copies. [Lent by Linton R. Massey]
This is the smallest of the limited issues of Faulkner's books, and the most difficult to obtain at the present time.

169. *Go Down, Moses*. New York, The Modern Library [1955]. First Modern Library edition, in dust jacket. [Lent by Alexander D. Wainwright]

170. Page 1 of a typescript version of "Was," the first section of *Go Down, Moses*. [Lent by Mr. Faulkner]. See Fig. 16

6 For a reproduction of the first page of the manuscript of *The Hamlet*, see *The Princeton University Library Chronicle*, XVIII (Spring, 1957), Plate VI.

The "Bayard" who narrates this story is a nine-year-old boy, the Bayard Sartoris of *The Unvanquished*. This is the only section of the book from which no part had been previously published.

171. Page 1 of a typescript, with alternate titles "An Absolution" and "Apotheosis," of a story, unpublished in this form, which was incorporated into the second section of *Go Down, Moses*, "The Fire and the Hearth." [Lent by Mr. Faulkner]. See Fig. 17

172. "Lion." *Harper's Magazine*, CLXXII (December, 1935), [67]-77. [0901.H295]
The longest chapter of *Go Down, Moses* is the fifth, entitled "The Bear." An early version of this section had been published in 1935, entitled "Lion," and a version of part of the section appeared, entitled "The Bear," in *The Saturday Evening Post*, May 9, 1942, just two days before the publication date of the book.

173. Page 186 of the typescript setting copy of *Go Down, Moses*, the first page of "The Bear," showing cancelled original title of the section, "Lion." [Lent by Mr. Faulkner]
"The Bear" contains some of Faulkner's most complex writing, and his note on p. 253 of the typescript setting copy indicates that it might have presented difficulties for editor and printer as well as the reader: "This is the section referred to in Red Underlining in note 9 Nov 41. Set it as written, without caps or stops at beginning and end of paragraphs. Unless put there by me. . . ."

174. "The Bear." *The Saturday Evening Post*, May 9, 1942, [30]-31, 74, 76, 77. [0901.S254q]
Opened to pp. [30]-31, showing the beginning of the story and the illustrations by Edward Shenton.

175. Page 3 of a typescript version of "Delta Autumn," the sixth section of *Go Down, Moses*. [Lent by Mr. Faulkner]

176. Page 6 of a typescript version of the title story and concluding section of *Go Down, Moses*. [Lent by Mr. Faulkner]

177. Manuscript page of genealogy of McCaslin family in *Go Down, Moses*. [Lent by Mr. Faulkner]
The genealogy differs in several particulars from the family as it appears in the published book, although Faulkner included no such genealogical chart in it.

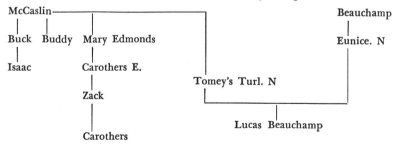

178. *¡Desciende, Moisés!* Barcelona, Luis de Caralt [1955]. Translation into Spanish by Ana-María de Foronda. [Lent by Random House]

179. *Descends, Moïse.* Paris, Gallimard [1955]. Translation into French by R. N. Raimbault. [Lent by Random House]

180. *Scendi, Mosè.* [Milan], Arnoldo Mondadori, 1947. Translation into Italian by Edoardo Bizzarri. [Ex 3734.92.339.58]

181. *Das Verworfene Erbe.* Stuttgart, Scherz & Goverts Verlag [1953]. Translation into German by Hermann Stresau. [3734.92.339.9]

## 20. *INTRUDER IN THE DUST*, 1948

Faulkner's first book in more than six years, *Intruder in the Dust* was published in September, 1948. It was his first book since 1932 to appear without a limited, signed issue.

182. *Intruder in the Dust.* New York, Random House [1948]. First edition, in dust jacket. [Ex 3734.92.349]

183. *Intruder in the Dust.* A copy of the second printing, signed by the author; in dust jacket. [Ex 3734.92.349.11]
Opened to the first page of the text.

184. Manuscript page of the beginning of *Intruder in the Dust.* [Lent by Mr. Faulkner]

185. Manuscript p. 65 of dialogue between the sheriff, Miss Habersham, and Stevens, from a version of *Intruder in the Dust.* [Lent by Mr. Faulkner]

186. Page 29 of typescript setting copy of *Intruder in the Dust,* with manuscript corrections.[7] [Lent by Mr. Faulkner]

187. *Inkräktare i Stoftet.* Stockholm, Albert Bonniers Förlag [1950]. Translation into Swedish by Th. Warburton. [Lent by Random House]

188. *Intruso en el Polvo.* Buenos Aires, Editorial Losada [1951]. Translation into Spanish by Aída Aisenson. [Lent by Random House]

189. *Griff in den Staub.* Zürich, Fretz & Wasmuth Verlag [1951]. Translation into German by Harry Kahn. [3734.92.349.7]

[7] For a reproduction of p. 65 of the corrected typescript, see *The Princeton University Library Chronicle*, XVIII (Spring, 1957), Plate VII.

190. *L'Intrus.* [Paris], Gallimard [1952]. Translation into French by R. N. Raimbault. [Lent by Random House]

191. *Non si Fruga nella Polvere.* [Milan], Arnoldo Mondadori, 1956. Translation into Italian by Fernanda Pivano. [Ex 3734.92.349.8]

192. *Intruder in the Dust.* [Tokyo], Hayakawa Shobō [1951]. Translation into Japanese by Shōzo Katō. [Lent by Random House]

193. *Ongenode Gast.* Amsterdam, Wereld-Bibliotheek, 1951. Translation into Dutch by Apie Prins. [Lent by Random House]

194. *Ubuden Gaest i Støvet.* Copenhagen, Aschehoug Dansk Forlag, 1950. Translation into Danish by Mogens Boisen. [Lent by Random House]

## 21. *KNIGHT'S GAMBIT*, 1949

*Knight's Gambit,* published in November, 1949, collects five previously published short stories, and prints for the first time the title story, a 33,000-word novella rewritten for this volume from an unpublished short story. All six pieces are detective stories in which Gavin Stevens is the main character.

195. *Knight's Gambit.* New York, Random House [1949]. First edition, in dust jacket. [Ex 3734.92.352]

196. Page 1 of the manuscript of "Smoke." [Lent by Mr. Faulkner]
The first story in *Knight's Gambit* is "Smoke," which was originally published in *Harper's* in April, 1932, and reprinted in *Doctor Martino* in 1934. The first page of the setting copy of this story, for *Knight's Gambit*, was typescript; tear sheets from *Doctor Martino* were used for the remainder of the setting copy, and tear sheets from their magazine appearances were used for the setting copy of the other four previously published stories of the book.

197. Typescript setting copy of the beginning of "Smoke." [Lent by Mr. Faulkner]

198. Tear sheet, p. 121, of the second page of "Smoke," from *Doctor Martino,* used as setting copy. [Lent by Mr. Faulkner]

199. "An Error in Chemistry." *Ellery Queen's Mystery Magazine,* VII (June, 1946), 5-19. [Ex 3734.92.3315]
"An Error in Chemistry," the fifth story of *Knight's Gambit,* was first published in *Ellery Queen's Mystery Magazine* in 1946. It had been one of 838 manuscripts

submitted for the First Annual Detective Short-Story Contest sponsored by the magazine, in which it won second prize of $500.00 and high praise from the judges, while missing first prize of $2,000.00 by a single vote.

In their introduction to the story's magazine publication, the editors called it a "strange story of almost pure detection . . . stylized, morbid, mystical, and sharply and brilliantly narrated."

200. *The Queen's Awards, 1946.* Edited by Ellery Queen [pseud.]. Boston, Little, Brown and Company, 1946. First edition, in dust jacket. [Ex 3734.92.375]
First book appearance of "An Error in Chemistry," pp. [23]-42.

201. First page of the typescript setting copy of "Knight's Gambit." [Lent by Mr. Faulkner]

202. Page 22 of a carbon typescript version of the original short story "Knight's Gambit." [Lent by Mr. Faulkner]
This final page of the story is very similar to the ending of the published novella, although here the narrator and nephew of Gavin Stevens is Charles Weddel, not Charles Mallison.

203. *Knight's Gambit.* Tokyo, Yukei-sha, 1951. Translation into Japanese by Yasuo Ōkubo. [Lent by Random House]

204. *Gambito de Caballo.* Buenos Aires, Emecé Editores [1951]. Translation into Spanish by Lucrecia Moreno de Sáenz. [Lent by Random House]

205. *Le Gambit du Cavalier.* [Paris], Gallimard [1951]. Translation into French by André du Bouchet. [Lent by Random House]

## 22. COLLECTED STORIES, 1950

*Collected Stories of William Faulkner,* published in August, 1950, was Faulkner's third miscellaneous collection of short stories and his first since 1934. During those sixteen years many of his stories had been brought together in volumes like *The Unvanquished, The Hamlet, Go Down, Moses,* and *Knight's Gambit,* and these were omitted from *Collected Stories,* which reprinted forty-two of the forty-six stories published since 1930 which had not been incorporated into less miscellaneous collections.

206. *Collected Stories of William Faulkner.* New York, Random House [1950]. First edition, in dust jacket. [Ex 3734.92.1950]

207. Page 1 of the typescript, with manuscript corrections, of an early version of "Shall Not Perish." [Lent by Mr. Faulkner]
One of several Faulkner short stories about World War II, "Shall Not Perish" was published in 1943 and reprinted in *Collected Stories.*

208. Page 1 of carbon typescript of "Shall Not Perish." [Lent by Mr. Faulkner]

On the verso of this page is part of a version of the story "A Courtship," which was apparently written about the same time as "Shall Not Perish" but remained unpublished until 1948.

209. " 'Once Aboard the Lugger.' " *Contempo*, I (February 1, 1932), [1], 4. Entire number printed on green stock. [Ex 3734.92.326f, copy 2]

One of four uncollected Faulkner short stories.

210. Page 1 of the manuscript of "Thrift." [Lent by Mr. Faulkner]

Another uncollected story, "Thrift" was published in *The Saturday Evening Post*, September 6, 1930.

211. Page 1 of a typescript of "The Wishing-Tree." [Lent by Mr. Faulkner]

Faulkner originally wrote this unpublished children's story in the 1920's for Margaret Brown, the daughter of one of his teachers at the University of Mississippi. More than twenty years later he made a copy for his godchild, Philip Stone.

212. Page 1 of a later typescript of "The Wishing-Tree," inscribed by the author: "For Philip Stone II. | from his God-father | William Faulkner | Oxford. | Xmas 1948". [Lent by Phil Stone]

213. First page of a typescript version of "With Caution and Dispatch," on verso of p. 530 of the setting copy of *The Hamlet*. [Lent by Mr. Faulkner]

This unpublished story deals with Bayard Sartoris and his adventures in the RFC in World War I. Several pages of one version of the story appear on the back of the typescript setting copy of *The Hamlet*, which might indicate that this version was written about 1939, although the other stories ("All the Dead Pilots" and "Ad Astra"), and the novel *Sartoris*, in which Bayard Sartoris appears, apparently date from at least ten years earlier.

214. First page of another typescript version of "With Caution and Dispatch." [Lent by Mr. Faulkner]. See Fig. 25

215. Page 1 of the typescript of "The Big Shot." [Lent by Mr. Faulkner]

According to the sending schedule of his stories which Faulkner kept for a time, *The Saturday Evening Post* turned down this story in April, 1930. Although it remained unpublished, Faulkner used one part of it, the episode of a poor boy's rejection by the upper class, in the novel *Absalom, Absalom!* six years later, where it provides a spur to the ambition of an earlier kind of "big shot," Thomas Sutpen.

216. Sending schedule of short stories. [Lent by Mr. Faulkner]

For the first two years of the 1930's Faulkner kept on this sheet of cardboard a record of the stories he sent to various magazines and agents. He drew a circle around each title when it was accepted.

*Requiem for a Nun*, published in September, 1951, is a novel in the form of a three-act play with a narrative prologue to each act. Adaptations for the stage have been produced in Switzerland, Germany, France, Spain, Greece, Holland, and Sweden.[8]

217. *Requiem for a Nun.* New York, Random House [1951]. First trade issue, in dust jacket. [Ex 3734.92.376]

218. *Requiem for a Nun.* Limited, signed issue. No. 606 of 750 copies. [Ex 3734.92.376.11]

219. Page 100 of the typescript of a version of *Requiem for a Nun*, showing the beginning of the narrative prologue of Act II. [Lent by Mr. Faulkner]

In the published book this material appears at the end of the prologue (pp. 110-111).

220. Manuscript of the first page of Act II of *Requiem for a Nun*. [Lent by Mr. Faulkner]

221. Two typescript versions of the first page of the narrative prologue to Act I of *Requiem for a Nun*. [Lent by Mr. Faulkner]

222. Four examples, from the galley proof of the book, of Faulkner's revisions in *Requiem for a Nun*. [Lent by Mr. Faulkner]

a. Galley proof of the end of Act II.
b. Galley proof of the beginning of the narrative prologue to Act III, with an author-to-editor note. Exhibited, for comparison, with a copy of the book opened to pp. 212-213.
c. Galley proof from Act II, Scene 1, with manuscript additions.
d. Galley proof of the final scene, with manuscript additions. See Fig. 22

223. An author-to-editor manuscript note about the title of the narrative prologue to Act II. [Lent by Saxe Commins]

> Re Title — Act II — The Golden Dome
> (Beginning Was — )
> What I wanted here was to paraphrase Eliot,
> 'In the beginning was the Word,
> Superfetation of $\tau \grave{o} \ \ddot{\epsilon}\nu$.'
> I dont know Greek.
> Can we use
> (Beginning Was $\tau \grave{o} \ \ddot{\epsilon}\nu$)?
> If not,
> (Beginning Was the Word)

The quotation is from T. S. Eliot, "Mr. Eliot's Sunday Morning Service." In the published book the title became "The Golden Dome (Beginning Was the Word)."

[8] The play was first produced in this country in Ruth Ford's version a year and a half after this exhibition had closed. Following is a chronological list of pro-

224. *Requiem pour une nonne* [Paris], Gallimard [1956]. First edition of the stage adaptation by Albert Camus. [Ex 3734 .92.376.7]

225. Program of the 1956 Paris production of the Camus adaptation of *Requiem pour une nonne*, given at the Théâtre des Mathurins. [Theatre Collection]

226. Poster for the 1956 Paris production of *Requiem pour une nonne* at the Théâtre des Mathurins. [Theatre Collection]

227. *Requiem für eine Nonne*. Frankfurt am Main, S. Fischer Verlag [1956]. The text of Robert Schnorr's German adaptation, reproduced from typewritten copy. [Ex 3734.92.376.9 .11]

228. Program of the German production of *Requiem für eine Nonne*, given during the 1956-1957 season at the Schlosspark Theater in Berlin. [Theatre Collection]

229. Poster for the 1956-1957 Berlin production of *Requiem für eine Nonne* at the Schlosspark Theater. [Theatre Collection]

230. Photograph of a scene from the 1956-1957 Berlin production of *Requiem für eine Nonne*. [Theatre Collection]

231. *Requiem for a Nun*. London, Chatto & Windus, 1953. First English edition, in dust jacket. [Ex 3734.92.376.12]

232. *Requiem für eine Nonne*. Zürich, Fretz & Wasmuth Verlag [1956]. Translation into German by Robert Schnorr. [Ex 3734.92.376.9]

233. *Réquiem para una Mujer*. Buenos Aires, Emecé Editores [1952]. Translation into Spanish by Jorge Zalamea. [Lent by Random House]

ductions of the play (the date given is of the opening only) through the spring of 1960: Switzerland (Zurich, October 1955); Germany (Berlin, November 1955); Spain (Barcelona, February 1956; Madrid, December 1956); Sweden (Gothenburg, February 1956); Holland (Amsterdam, February 1956); France (Paris, November 1956); Greece (Athens, March 1957); England (London, November 1957); Denmark (Copenhagen, March 1958); Argentina (Buenos Aires, September 1958); Italy (various cities, beginning with Florence, November 1958); Mexico (Mexico City, 1958); United States (New York, January 1959); Brazil (October 1959); Yugoslavia (October 1959). The American production appeared in New Haven and Boston before it reached New York, and it is likely that some of the foreign productions also had road tours, before or after appearing in the cities noted here. I am indebted to Miss Anne Louise Davis of Harold Ober Associates, Faulkner's agent, for supplying me with much of this information.

234. *Requiem per una Monaca.* [Milan], Arnoldo Mondadori, 1955. Translation into Italian by Fernanda Pivano. [Ex 3734 .92.376.8]

235. *Requiem pour une Nonne.* Préface d'Albert Camus. Paris, Gallimard [1957]. Translation into French by M. E. Coindreau. [Ex 3734.92.376.6]

## 24. *A FABLE,* 1954

*A Fable* was published in August, 1954. Begun in December, 1944, and not completed until November, 1953, it is one of Faulkner's longest and most complex novels.

236. *A Fable.* [New York], Random House [1954]. First trade issue, in dust jacket. [Ex 3734.92.332.11]

237. *A Fable.* Limited, signed issue. No. 600 of 1,000 copies. [Ex 3734.92.332]

238. *Eine Legende.* Stuttgart, Scherz & Goverts Verlag [1955]. Translation into German by Kurt Heinrich Hansen. [3734 .92.333.7]

239. *Una Fábula.* Mexico City, Editorial Cumbre [1955]. Translation into Spanish by Antonio Ribera. [Lent by Random House]

240. *Uma Fábula.* S. Paulo, Editôra Mérito [1956]. Translation into Portuguese by Olívia Krähenbühl. [Ex 3734.92.332.7]

241. *Notes on a Horsethief.* Greenville, Miss., The Levee Press, 1950 [1951]. An out-of-series copy of an edition of 975 numbered copies. [Lent by Hodding Carter; Library copy (No. 247), Ex 3734.92.368]

In 1951 the Levee Press of Greenville, Mississippi, brought out in a limited, signed edition *Notes on a Horsethief,* an earlier version of the episode that occurs on pp. 151-189 of *A Fable.* This copy was inscribed by Faulkner for Hodding Carter, editor of the *Delta Democrat-Times* and co-owner, with Ben Wasson, of the Levee Press. According to Carter, Faulkner's original title for the work was "A Dangling Participle from Work in Progress," and at one time the excerpt was so punctuated as to form only one or two sentences.

242. Page 267 of the typescript setting copy of *A Fable,* showing part of the *Notes on a Horsethief* episode as it occurs in the novel. [Lent by Mr. Faulkner]

Exhibited, for comparison, with a copy of *Notes on a Horsethief* opened to pp. 64-65.

243. Final typescript of *A Fable*, used as setting copy. 691 pp. [Lent by Mr. Faulkner]

244. Two typescript pages with manuscript corrections from *A Fable*: 120-Z-7 and 120-Z-8. [Lent by Mr. Faulkner]

245. Two pages of manuscript additions to the typescript of *A Fable*: inserts 17 and 18. [Lent by Mr. Faulkner]

## 25. *BIG WOODS*, 1955

*Big Woods*, published in October, 1955, is a collection of four previously published hunting stories. Five brief narrative pieces are used, at the beginning and end of the book, and between each story, to set or change the mood; Faulkner has described them, in an interview in *The New York Times Book Review*, January 30, 1955, as "interrupted catalysts."

246. *Big Woods*. New York, Random House [1955]. First edition, in dust jacket. [Ex 3734.92.317]

247. Manuscript page of a draft of Faulkner's dedication to his editor, Saxe Commins. [Lent by Saxe Commins]

248. "Race at Morning." *The Saturday Evening Post*, March 5, 1955, pp. 26-27, 103, 104, 106. [Ex 3734.92]
This story was slightly revised for the book.

249. Tear sheet of "A Bear Hunt." [Lent by Mr. Faulkner]
"A Bear Hunt," the third story in *Big Woods*, was revised from its appearance in the 1950 *Collected Stories*. This tear sheet of the earlier version, with Faulkner's manuscript corrections (p. 79), is part of the setting copy for *Big Woods*.

250. Tear sheet of "The Bear." [Lent by Mr. Faulkner]
*Big Woods* includes four of the five sections of "The Bear" from *Go Down, Moses*. This page from the setting copy, a tear sheet from *Go Down, Moses* (p. 254), shows the ending of the third section and the beginning of the omitted fourth section.

251. The last two pages of the typescript setting copy of the epilogue. [Lent by Mr. Faulkner]
The conclusion of *Big Woods* is an epilogue revised from "Delta Autumn," the sixth section of *Go Down, Moses*. These two pages of the typescript setting copy show manuscript revisions by author and editor.

252. Drawings by Edward Shenton for *Big Woods*. [Lent by Edward Shenton]
The decorations for *Big Woods* were drawn by Edward Shenton, who had illustrated *The Unvanquished* and had supplied the drawings for the May 9, 1942 *Saturday Evening Post* version of "The Bear." Shown are the originals for the following decorations in the book:

a. Bear paw print, half title
b. Head of dog, p. [1]
c. Boy by tree, p. [9]
d. Snake, p. [99]
e. Deer and hunters, p. [111]
f. Bird and steamboat, p. [139]
g. Man between plow handles, p. [143]
h. Deer in flood waters, p. [165]
i. Deer pursued by dogs, p. [173]

## 26. THE SNOPESES OF YOKNAPATAWPHA, 1929-1957

The Snopes family, who supplied the major characters of *The Hamlet* and *The Town*, published in 1940 and 1957, have also appeared as minor characters in novels and in short stories since the beginning of the Yoknapatawpha series in 1929. This section of the exhibition traces chronologically the development of the family in Faulkner's fiction, both published and unpublished.

**253.** *Sartoris.* New York, Harcourt, Brace and Company [1929]. [Ex 3734.92.383]

The first book in the Yoknapatawpha series, *Sartoris*, contains the first published reference to the tribe of Snopes. Flem, Byron, and Montgomery Ward Snopes all make their first appearance in *Sartoris*, which provides this description of the progenitor of the tribe (p. 172):

> Flem, the first Snopes, had appeared unheralded one day behind the counter of a small restaurant on a side street. . . . With this foothold and like Abraham of old, he brought his blood and legal kin household by household, individual by individual, into town, and established them where they could gain money.

**254.** *The Sound and the Fury.* New York, Jonathan Cape and Harrison Smith [1929]. [Ex 3734.92.386]

The second published appearance of the Snopes family is in *The Sound and the Fury* (published in October, 1929), where I. O. Snopes appears briefly (p. 271).

**255.** *As I Lay Dying.* New York, Jonathan Cape: Harrison Smith [1930]. [Ex 3734.92.313]

The third published appearance of the Snopeses occurs in *As I Lay Dying*, where mention is made of the episode (described fully the following year in "Spotted Horses") of Flem Snopes's sale of Texas ponies (p. 124).

**256.** *Sanctuary.* New York, Jonathan Cape & Harrison Smith [1931]. [Ex 3734.92.382]

In *Sanctuary* (published February, 1931) Virgil Snopes and Mississippi state senator Clarence Snopes appear (pp. 208-209).

**257.** "Spotted Horses." *Scribner's Magazine*, LXXXIX (June, 1931), 585-597. [0901.S436]

"Spotted Horses," in the June 1931 issue of *Scribner's*, is the first Faulkner short story about the Snopeses. The unnamed first-person narrator is the same itinerant sewing machine salesman who first appeared in *Sartoris*, named V. K. Suratt. In *The Hamlet* (1940) the same character appears as V. K. Ratliff, and "Spotted Horses," much revised, appears there in Book Four, "The Peasants."

258. Unfinished autograph note, addressed to "Mr Thompson," and dating from 1931 or not long after, in which Faulkner identifies the unnamed narrator of "Spotted Horses" as Suratt. 1 p. [Lent by Mr. Faulkner]

"As you say, I am availing myself of my prerogative of using these people when and where I see fit. So far, I have not bothered much about chronology, which, if I am ever collected, I shall have to do.

" 'Spotted Horses' occurred about 1900, at Varner's Store, a village in the county of which Jefferson is market town. Suratt must have been about 25. In Sartoris, 1919, he is 45 say."

259. Page 2 of the manuscript of "Father Abraham." [Lent by the New York Public Library]. See Fig. 18

It is apparent that Faulkner planned a novel about the Snopes family at about the same time that *Sartoris* was written. The manuscript of the virtually completed first chapter of the novel, entitled "Father Abraham," presents a version of the "Spotted Horses" episode which is closer to its appearance in *The Hamlet* than in "Spotted Horses." "Father Abraham" and another title, "Abraham's Children," which is given to a later typescript version of the episode, are reminiscent of the description in *Sartoris* of Flem's arrival in Jefferson.

260. Page 18 of a typescript version of "Abraham's Children." [Lent by Mr. Faulkner]. See Fig. 19

261. *The Hamlet*. New York, Random House, 1940. [Ex 3734 .92.342]

Opened to pp. 324-325 for comparison with p. 18 of the typescript of "Abraham's Children."

262. "The Hound." *Harper's Magazine*, CLXIII (August, 1931), [266]-274. Tear sheet of p. 271. [Lent by Mr. Faulkner]

In "The Hound," a short story published two months after "Spotted Horses," a store clerk in Frenchman's Bend named Snopes appears briefly. When the story was rewritten to become part of *The Hamlet*, the name of its central character was changed from Ernest Cotton to Mink Snopes.

263. "Centaur in Brass." *The American Mercury*, XXV (February, 1932), 200-210. [Ex 3734.92.324]

The short story "Centaur in Brass," originally published in February, 1932, was revised extensively to become part of *The Town* twenty-five years later.

264. "Lizards in Jamshyd's Courtyard." *The Saturday Evening Post*, February 27, 1932, pp. 12-13, 52, 57. [0901.S254q]

The short story "Lizards in Jamshyd's Courtyard," which also first appeared in February, 1932, was extensively revised to become the concluding episode of *The Hamlet*.

265. Page 6 of a manuscript of "There Was a Queen." [Lent by Mr. Faulkner]

In the story "There Was a Queen," published in 1933, the episode in *Sartoris* of the anonymous letters sent by Byron Snopes to Narcissa Benbow is recalled.

266. Page 17 of a typescript of "There Was a Queen." [Lent by Mr. Faulkner]

267. Page 3 of a manuscript of "Mule in the Yard." [Lent by Mr. Faulkner]

"Mule in the Yard," which first appeared in 1934, was incorporated into *The Town* in 1957, with I. O. Snopes an important character in it.

268. Page 7 of a typescript of "Mule in the Yard." [Lent by Mr. Faulkner]

269. Page 1 of manuscript of "Fool About a Horse." [Lent by Mr. Faulkner]. See Fig. 21

There were no Snopeses in the original version of "Fool About a Horse," but it was rewritten as an episode in *The Hamlet*, four years later, with Ab Snopes as its principal character. The published short story version was narrated by a boy, the son of the unnamed principal character; in manuscript and typescript versions of the story, however, the narrator is identified as the V. K. Suratt who told the story of "Spotted Horses," and in one typescript version Faulkner has changed the narrator's references to the principal character from the "Pap" of the short story to the "Ab" [Snopes] of the version in *The Hamlet*.

270. "Fool About a Horse." *Scribner's Magazine*, C (August, 1936), [80]-86. [0901.S436]

271. Page 23 of typescript of "Fool About a Horse," with Suratt as narrator. [Lent by Mr. Faulkner]. See Fig. 20

272. Page 23 of carbon of above typescript with manuscript corrections of "Pap" to "Ab." [Lent by Mr. Faulkner]

273. Page 8 of typescript of "Fool About a Horse," with description of Suratt's background as the son of a tenant farmer. [Lent by Mr. Faulkner]

". . . a race existing in complete subjection not to modern exploitation but to an economic system stubbornly moribund out of the dark ages themselves, who had escaped his birthright and into independence and even pride."

274. "The Unvanquished." *The Saturday Evening Post*, November 14, 1936, pp. 12-13, 121, 122, 124, 126, 128, 130. [0901 .S254q]

Ab Snopes, the father of Flem, first appears in the short story "The Unvanquished," which was revised to form the chapter "Riposte in Tertio" of *The Unvanquished* (1938).

275. "Vendée." *The Saturday Evening Post*, December 5, 1936, pp. 16-17, 86, 87, 90, 92, 93, 94. [0901.S254q]

The next appearance of Ab Snopes is in the story "Vendée," which was also to become a chapter in *The Unvanquished*.

276. *The Unvanquished.* New York, Random House [1938].
[L 3734.92.392]
Opened to p. 135, Ab Snopes's first book appearance in the Yoknapatawpha series.

277. Typescript of "Afternoon of a Cow." 17 pp. [Manuscripts Division]
In June, 1937, Faulkner gave a typescript of his unpublished story "Afternoon of a Cow" to Professor Maurice E. Coindreau, the translator of several of his works into French, who later presented it to the Princeton University Library. An episode of the story was drawn upon in *The Hamlet,* and the original story was published in *Furioso* in 1947. (A French translation, by Mr. Coindreau, was published in *Fontaine* in 1943.)

278. Page 17 of the manuscript of "Barn Burning," the end of the story. [Lent by Mr. Faulkner]
The story of Ab Snopes was continued in "Barn Burning," published in 1939. Originally intended as the first chapter of *The Hamlet,* it was drastically cut and rewritten to form one episode (pp. 15-21) of Chapter One of the published book. The central character is Ab's son, Colonel Sartoris ("Sarty") Snopes, who escapes from his father and his background at the end of the story. He does not appear in the published book. (See also Nos. 159-161.)

279. *The Hamlet.* New York, Random House, 1940. [Ex 3734.92 .342]
Volume One of the Snopes trilogy. (See also Section XVIII.)

280. Page 31 of the manuscript of *The Hamlet,* showing a change of the name Suratt to Ratliff. [Lent by Mr. Faulkner]

281. "My Grandmother Millard and General Bedford Forrest and the Battle of Harrykin Creek." *Story,* XXII (March-April, 1943), 68-86. [0901.S888]
Ab Snopes appears in "My Grandmother Millard," a Civil War story about the Sartoris family of *The Unvanquished.*

282. Page 9 of typescript of "My Grandmother Millard." [Manuscripts Division]

283. "Mississippi." *Holiday,* XV (April, 1954), 33-47. [0901 .H732q]
The coming of the Snopeses to Mississippi is described by Faulkner in his semi-fictional account of his native state, "Mississippi."

284. Page 4 of typescript of "Mississippi." [Manuscripts Division]

285. "By the People." *Mademoiselle,* XLI (October, 1955), 86-89, 130, 131, 132, 133, 134, 135, 136, 137, 138, 139. [Ex 3734.92 .323]
How V. K. Ratliff ended the political career of Clarence Snopes is told in "By the People," which brings the story of the Snopeses up to the period just after the Korean War.[9]

[9] This episode was included, with its date changed to the period just after World War II, in *The Mansion* (1959).

286. Page 5 of typescript of "By the People." [Manuscripts Division]. See Fig. 24

287. *The Town.* New York, Random House [1957]. [Ex 3734.92 .3925]
Volume Two of the Snopes trilogy. (See also Section XXVII.)

288. Last page of typescript setting copy of *The Town.* [Lent by Mr. Faulkner]
The final page of *The Town* marks, for the present (1957), the last completed chapter in the chronicle of the Snopeses of Yoknapatawpha, although his publishers announce that Faulkner is now at work upon the third volume of the trilogy, *The Mansion.*[10]

## 27. *THE TOWN*, 1957

*The Town*, published on May 1, 1957, is the middle volume of the Snopes trilogy, which chronicles the rise of Flem Snopes, the Snopes family, and the Snopes principles, in twentieth-century Yoknapatawpha County. *The Hamlet* (1940) is the first volume of the trilogy, which is to be completed by the publication in 1958 or 1959 of *The Mansion*, upon which Faulkner is now working.[10]

289. *The Town.* New York, Random House [1957]. First trade issue, in dust jacket. [Ex 3734.92.3925]

290. *The Town.* Limited, signed issue. No. 51 of 450 copies. [Ex 3734.92.3925.11]

291. Final typescript, used as setting copy, of *The Town.* 478 pp. [Lent by Mr. Faulkner]

292. "The Waifs." *The Saturday Evening Post*, May 4, 1957, pp. 27, 116, 118, 120. [Ex 3734.92]
The final episode of *The Town*, the story of Byron Snopes's four half-Indian children, was also printed in *The Saturday Evening Post* (from galley proof of the book), under the title "The Waifs." (Faulkner's suggestion for the title was "Them Indians.")

293. A manuscript worksheet for *The Town.* [Lent by Saxe Commins]

294. Corrected galley proof of *The Town*: 11-A, 36-A, and 83-A.[11] [Lent by Mr. Faulkner]

10 Published two years after the close of this exhibition: New York, Random House [1959].
11 For reproductions of two other sections of the corrected galley proof, see *The Princeton University Library Chronicle*, XVIII (Spring, 1957), Plate VIII.

295. "Centaur in Brass." *Collected Stories of William Faulkner,*
New York, Random House [1950], pp. 149-168. [Ex 3734.92
.1950]

The short story "Centaur in Brass," originally published in 1932, was incorporated, extensively revised, into Chapter One of *The Town.* The original version had been reprinted, with a few changes, in the 1950 *Collected Stories.*

296. Eight versions of the first page of "Mule in the Yard" (originally published in 1934), the second of two previously published short stories incorporated into *The Town.*

a. First page of manuscript of "Mule in the Yard." [Lent by Mr. Faulkner]. See Fig. 23

b. First page of typescript of "Mule in the Yard." [Lent by Mr. Faulkner]

c. "Mule in the Yard." *Scribner's Magazine,* XCVI (August, 1934), [65]. [0901 .S436]

d. "Mule in the Yard." *Collected Stories of William Faulkner,* New York, Random House [1950], p. 249. [Ex 3734.92.1950]

e. Page 303 of typescript setting copy of *The Town.* [Lent by Mr. Faulkner]

f. Galley 75-A of *The Town.* [Lent by Mr. Faulkner]

g. Page [231] of page proof of *The Town.* [Lent by Mr. Faulkner]

h. Page [231] of foundry proof of *The Town.* [Lent by Mr. Faulkner]

297. *The Town.* First printing, opened to p. 327. [Ex 3734.92
.3925]

In the first printing of *The Town* a line on p. 327 was omitted and the space filled by a repetition of another line from the same page, apparently as the result of an accident at the press, as the passage is correct in galley, page, and foundry proof.[12]

298. Page 327 of page proof of *The Town.* [Lent by Mr. Faulkner]

## 28. ANTHOLOGIES

An indication of the recent rapid growth in popularity of Faulkner's work has been the proliferation of anthologies of previously published material.

299. *Salmagundi.* Milwaukee, The Casanova Press, 1932. No. 395
of an edition of 525 copies. [Ex 3734.92.381, copy 2]

A significant early appreciation of Faulkner's importance by Paul Romaine is the introduction to the collection *Salmagundi,* which he edited. The volume reprinted three essays and five poems by Faulkner from *The New Republic* and *The Double Dealer.*

300. *A Rose for Emily and Other Stories by William Faulkner.*
[New York], Editions for the Armed Services, Inc. [Foreword dated April, 1945]. [Lent by Saxe Commins]

Edited, and with a foreword, by Saxe Commins. *A Rose for Emily and Other Stories* is one of the paperback, pocket-sized Armed Services editions which were distributed to American servicemen overseas during and immediately after World War II.

12 The error was corrected in the second printing.

301. *The Portable Faulkner.* Edited by Malcolm Cowley. New York, The Viking Press, 1946. First edition, in dust jacket. [Lent by Maurice E. Coindreau; Library copy, 3734.92.1946]

A collection of short stories and excerpts from novels, with an influential introduction by Malcolm Cowley.

302. *The Indispensable Faulkner.* New York, The Book Society [1950]. A copy of what appears to be the first issue under this imprint, in glassine wrapper, boxed. [Lent by James B. Meriwether]

A reprint of *The Portable Faulkner,* save for the omission of the map on the end papers.

303. *Mirrors of Chartres Street by William Faulkner.* Introduction by William Van O'Connor. [Minneapolis, Faulkner Studies, 1953.] No. 318 of an edition of 1,000 copies, in dust jacket. [Ex 3734.92.364]

Eleven of Faulkner's 1925 sketches for the New Orleans *Times-Picayune* were reprinted in this volume, with badly mangled text.

304. Review by Carvel Collins of *Mirrors of Chartres Street. The New York Times Book Review,* February 7, 1954, p. 4. [DR 0901.674f]

After the appearance of this review which called attention to two more Faulkner sketches in the *Times-Picayune,* the editors of *Faulkner Studies* brought them out in the periodical and, later on, in a supplementary volume. Between the publication of these two sketches in periodical and book form, an edition of all thirteen was published in Japan, under the title *New Orleans Sketches,* the text based on the Minneapolis versions.

305. "Jealousy" and "Episode." *Faulkner Studies,* III (Winter, 1954), [46]-53. [Ex 3734.92.666]

306. *Jealousy and Episode: Two Stories by William Faulkner.* Minneapolis, Faulkner Studies, 1955. No. 279 of an edition of 500 copies. [Ex 3734.92.351]

307. *New Orleans Sketches by William Faulkner.* Edited with notes by Ichiro Nishizaki. [Tokyo], Hokuseido [1955]. [3734 .92.367]

308. *Faulkner at Nagano.* Edited by Robert A. Jelliffe. Tokyo, Kenkyusha Ltd. [1956]. First edition, in dust jacket. [Ex 3734.92.333]

Faulkner's participation in the 1955 Nagano Summer Seminar in American Literature, at the invitation of the United States Department of State, is recorded in *Faulkner at Nagano,* a collection of speeches, interviews, and the text of seminar question-and-answer sessions.

309. Miscellaneous anthologies of Faulkner's work published in England, France, and Norway.

a. *Faulkner's County: Tales of Yoknapatawpha County.* London, Chatto & Windus, 1955. [Ex 3734.92.335]

b. *Jefferson, Mississippi.* Une anthologie établie et presentée par Michel Mohrt. [Paris, Le Club du meilleur livre, 1956.] [Ex 3734.92.353]

c. *Noveller.* Oslo, Gyldendal Norsk Forlag, 1951. Translation of fourteen short stories into Norwegian by Leo Strøm. [Lent by Random House]

## 29. MOVIES AND TELEVISION

For a period of twenty-five years Faulkner has made occasional appearances in Hollywood as a film writer, usually in association with producer-director Howard Hawks. "When I need money," Faulkner has said, "I write to Howard. When he needs writing he writes to me." He deprecates his movie-writing and says that "it bears about the same relation to my books as letter-writing" *(Saturday Review,* June 25, 1955, p. [24]).

"The moving picture work of my own which seemed best to me," he declared in an interview *(The Paris Review,* Spring, 1956, p. 35), "was done by the actors and the writer throwing the script away and inventing the scene in actual rehearsal just before the camera turned. If I didn't take, or felt I was capable of taking, motion picture work seriously, out of simple honesty to motion pictures and myself too, I would not have tried. But I know now that I will never be a good motion picture writer; so that work will never have the urgency for me which my own medium has."

Faulkner first went to Hollywood after *Sanctuary* had gained him wide public recognition in 1931, and he has had a hand in many scripts since then. A partial list includes: *Today We Live* (1933), an adaptation of his own story "Turn About," with Joan Crawford and Gary Cooper; *The Road to Glory* (1936), with Fredric March and Lionel Barrymore; *The Slave Ship* (1937), with Wallace Beery; *To Have and Have Not* (1945), an adaptation of the Hemingway novel, with Humphrey Bogart and Lauren Bacall; *The Big Sleep* (1946), also with Bogart and Bacall; and *Land of the Pharaohs* (1955). Faulkner has said that he has done screen writing for which he has not received screen credit, and one such script is that of *The Southerner* (1945), with Zachary Scott, according to Scott himself (Memphis *Commercial Appeal,* May 8, 1955, Section 6, p. 15).

310. Photograph of Joan Crawford and Robert Young in *Today We Live.* [Lent by the New York Public Library]

311. Review of *Today We Live* by John S. Cohen, Jr. Clipping from the New York *Sun,* April 17, 1933. [Lent by the New York Public Library]

312. Photograph of Joseph Schildkraut in *The Slave Ship*. [Theatre Collection]

313. Script of *The Big Sleep*, by William Faulkner and Leigh Brackett, produced by Howard Hawks. [Lent by the New York Public Library]

314. Movie adaptations of Faulkner works.

*Sanctuary* was transformed by Paramount into the film *The Story of Temple Drake* (1933), which starred Miriam Hopkins and Jack La Rue. Faulkner himself had a hand in the adaptation of his short story "Turn About" into *Today We Live* (1933), and in 1949 Metro-Goldwyn-Mayer produced *Intruder in the Dust*, which was filmed in Oxford, Mississippi, with many of the townspeople cast in minor roles.

a. Script of *The Story of Temple Drake*, by Oliver H. P. Garrett and Maurice Watkins. [Lent by Paramount Pictures Corporation]

b. Three stills from *The Story of Temple Drake*. [Theatre Collection]

c. Photostat of the review of the *première* of *Intruder in the Dust* by Elizabeth Spencer, the Greenville, Miss., *Delta Democrat-Times*, October 16, 1949, p. 18. [Lent by James B. Meriwether]

d. List of cast and credits for *Intruder in the Dust*, Metro-Goldwyn-Mayer publicity release sheet, dated August 22, 1949. [Theatre Collection]

e. Four stills from *Intruder in the Dust*. [Theatre Collection]

315. Television adaptations of Faulkner works.

The adaptation (by Faulkner himself) of the short story "The Brooch," televised on the Lux Video Theatre, April 2, 1953, was the first appearance of a Faulkner work on television. Two Faulkner stories, "Smoke" and "Barn Burning," were adapted by Gore Vidal and televised by the Columbia Broadcasting System in 1954. The scripts were later published in a collection of Vidal's television plays.

a. Script of "The Brooch." [Lent by Lever Brothers Company]

b. Three photographs of the filming and production of "The Brooch." [Lent by Lever Brothers Company]

c. Scripts of adaptations of "Smoke" and "Barn Burning," by Gore Vidal. [Lent by CBS Television]

d. Gore Vidal. *Visit to a Small Planet and Other Television Plays*. Boston, Little, Brown and Company [1956]. [3973.125.393]. "Smoke," pp. [217]-233; "Barn Burning," pp. [235]-252.

e. Script of adaptation of *The Sound and the Fury*, by Frank W. Durkee, Jr., televised by the National Broadcasting Company on December 6, 1955. [Manuscripts Division]

## 30. AWARDS AND PUBLIC CAREER

Since the award of the Nobel Prize for Literature in December, 1950, William Faulkner has received many additional awards and prizes, and has increasingly accepted the responsibilities of being a widely known public figure, as well as man of letters. He has made speeches, has written articles and letters on current affairs, and has made official trips abroad for the United States Department of State.

316. The Nobel Prize, 1950.

On December 10, 1950, Faulkner was awarded the 1949 Nobel Prize for Literature in Stockholm, Sweden. The text of his speech of acceptance, as printed in the official record of the 1950 Nobel Prize ceremonies the following year, differs slightly from the text of the typescript Faulkner supplied his publishers, from which were derived most of the versions which have appeared in this country.

a. *Les Prix Nobel en 1950.* Stockholm, Imprimerie Royale, P. A. Norstedt & Söner, 1951. [Ex 3734.92.837]. Faulkner's speech of acceptance, pp. 71-72.

b. " 'I Decline to Accept the End of Man.' " *New York Herald Tribune Book Review,* January 14, 1951, p. 5. [DR 0901.198f]

c. *The Nobel Prize Speech.* [New York, The Spiral Press, 1951.] A copy of the first impression inscribed by Faulkner for his editor, Saxe Commins. [Lent by Saxe Commins; Library copy, Ex 3734.92.3863]. There were three impressions of this pamphlet: the first, of 1,500 copies, was ready about March 15; the second, of 2,500 copies, about March 25; and the third, of 1,150 copies, about April 10.

d. The 1949 Nobel Prize for Literature, medal and scroll. [Lent by the Mary Buie Museum, Oxford, Mississippi]. The text of the scroll, which is in Swedish, may be translated as follows: "The Swedish Academy have, at a meeting on 10 November 1950, in accordance with the terms of the will of Alfred Nobel, drawn up on 27 November 1895, decided to confer upon William Faulkner the 1949 Nobel Prize in Literature for his powerful and independent artistic contribution to America's new fictional literature. Stockholm 10 December 1950." See Fig. 32

317. Commencement address, University High School, 1951.

On May 28, 1951, Faulkner delivered the address to the graduating class of the University High School, Oxford, Mississippi, of which his daughter, Jill, was a member.

a. Photostat of the address in *The Oxford Eagle,* May 31, 1951, p. 1. [Original in the University of Mississippi Library]

b. First page of the manuscript of the address. [Lent by Mr. Faulkner]

318. The Legion of Honor, 1951.

On October 26, 1951, in New Orleans, Faulkner was made an Officer of the Legion of Honor.

a. Photostat of manuscript copy of his speech of acceptance inscribed by Faulkner for Saxe Commins.[13] [Lent by Saxe Commins]

[13] Reproduced as an illustration in *The Princeton University Library Chronicle,* XVIII (Spring, 1957), Plate I.

b. The Legion of Honor, medal and scroll. [Lent by the Mary Buie Museum, Oxford, Mississippi]

319. Address to the Delta Council, 1952.

On May 15, 1952, Faulkner spoke in Cleveland, Mississippi, at the annual meeting of the Delta Council. The complete text of his address appeared three days later in Hodding Carter's *Delta Democrat-Times* and, later in the same month, in pamphlet form.

a. Photograph of the address in the Greenville, Miss., *Delta Democrat-Times*, May 18, 1952, p. 9. [Lent by James B. Meriwether; from the microfilm on file in the office of *The Delta Democrat-Times*]

b. *An Address Delivered By William Faulkner. . . .* [Greenville, Miss., Delta Council, 1952.] [Ex 3734.92.3115]

320. Commencement address, Pine Manor Junior College, 1953.

On June 8, 1953, Faulkner delivered the address to the graduating class of Pine Manor Junior College, Wellesley, Massachusetts. The text of his address as printed in *The Atlantic* differs slightly from that of the mimeographed copies distributed by the Pine Manor Alumnae Office after August 31 and from the shortened version published in the *Pine Manor Bulletin*.

a. "Faith or Fear." *The Atlantic*, CXCII (August, 1953), [53]-55. [0901.A881]

b. "William Faulkner Addresses Pine Manor Seniors." *Pine Manor Bulletin*, I (July, 1953), 8-9. [Ex 3734.92]

c. Mimeographed copy of address. 11 pp. [Lent by Linton R. Massey]

d. Photograph of Faulkner, with President Alfred T. Hill of Pine Manor congratulating Miss Jill Faulkner, who was graduated with the highest academic record in her class. [Manuscripts Division]

321. The National Book Award, 1951 and 1955.

Faulkner has twice won the National Book Award, in 1951 (for the *Collected Stories*, 1950) and in 1955 (for *A Fable*, 1954).

a. ". . . William Faulkner's address on the occasion of his receiving on Jan. 25 the National Book Award for his novel, 'A Fable.'" *The New York Times Book Review*, February 6, 1955, pp. 2, 24. [DR 0901.674f]

b. Typescript of the address, with manuscript corrections. 3 pp. [Manuscripts Division]

322. Address at the University of Oregon, 1955.

In April, 1955, Faulkner spoke at the University of Oregon on "Freedom American Style." Revised for publication, the speech was entitled "On Privacy: The American Dream: What Happened to It."

a. Typescript of the original speech, with manuscript corrections. 17 pp. [Manuscripts Division]. See Fig. 31

b. "On Privacy." *Harper's Magazine*, CCXI (July, 1955), [33]-38. [0901.H295]

c. Typescript of the revised version of speech, as published, with a change of title on the first page in Faulkner's hand. 16 pp. [Manuscripts Division]

323. Address to the Southern Historical Association, 1955.

On November 10, 1955, in Memphis, Tennessee, Faulkner was one of three speakers on the topic "The Segregation Decisions" at the twenty-first annual meeting of the Southern Historical Association. His address, printed in the Memphis *Commercial Appeal* the following morning, was expanded by three additional paragraphs for inclusion in the later pamphlet publication of all three papers read at the meeting.

a. Typescript of the original address. [Lent by James Silver]
b. Typescript of the three added paragraphs. [Lent by James Silver]
c. *Three Views of the Segregation Decisions* [cover title], Atlanta, Southern Regional Council, 1956. [Ex 3734.92.3835]. William Faulkner, "American Segregation and the World Crisis," pp. 9-12.

324. The Silver Medal of the Athens Academy, 1957.

On March 28, 1957, Faulkner received, while in Greece on an official visit for the United States Department of State, the Silver Medal of the Athens Academy. (The Academy annually awards two medals, one of gold and one of silver. The Gold Medal was awarded in 1957 to the people of Cyprus.) While in Athens, Faulkner attended a gala performance, on March 30, of the Greek production of his play, *Requiem for a Nun.*

a. The Silver Medal and scroll of the Athens Academy. [Lent by Mr. Faulkner]
b. Photograph of Faulkner receiving the medal and scroll from the President of the Academy, Panagiotis Poulitsas. [Manuscripts Division]
c. Press releases, by the United States Information Service in Athens, of the Greek and English texts of Faulkner's speech of acceptance, March 28, 1957. [Manuscripts Division]. The English text is as follows:

> Mr. President, Gentlemen of the Academy, Ladies and Gentlemen:
> I accept this medal not alone as an American nor as a writer but as one chosen by the Greek Academy to represent the principle that man shall be free.
> The human spirit does not obey physical laws. When the sun of Pericles cast the shadow of civilized man around the earth, that shadow curved until it touched America. So when someone like me comes to Greece he is walking the shadow back to the source of the light which cast the shadow. When the American comes to this country he 'has come back to something that was familiar. He has come home. He has come back to the cradle of civilized man. I am proud that the Greek people have considered me worthy to receive this medal. It will be my duty to return to my country and tell my people that the qualities in the Greek race—toughness, bravery, independence and pride—are too valuable to lose. It is the duty of all men to see that they do not vanish from the earth.

d. Photograph of Faulkner speaking to the Swedish ambassador, Count Stackelberg, during the intermission of *Requiem for a Nun.* [Manuscripts Division]

e. Photograph of Faulkner with the actor-producer Dimitri Myrat and the actress Voula Zoumboulaki backstage at the performance of *Requiem for a Nun*. [Manuscripts Division]

### 325. The Howells Medal of the American Academy, 1950.

In 1950 Faulkner was awarded the Howells Medal by the American Academy of Arts and Letters. This medal is awarded by the Academy "from time to time for work in the art of prose fiction over the five years last preceding."

a. The Howells Medal. [Lent by the Mary Buie Museum, Oxford, Mississippi]

b. "Letter of Acknowledgment from William Faulkner." *Proceedings of the American Academy of Arts and Letters and the National Institute of Arts and Letters*, Second Series, No. 1 (1951), 19. [0911.122]

### 326. Other awards. [Lent by the Mary Buie Museum, Oxford, Mississippi]

a. Medal from the city of Verdun, 1951.

b. Page One Award of the Newspaper Guild of New York, 1951. Awarded for *Collected Stories*, 1950.

### 327. Faulkner at Nagano, 1955.

In August, 1955, Faulkner visited Japan as a participant in the Summer Seminar in American Literature at Nagano conducted under the auspices of the United States Department of State.

a. Mimeographed State Department report on the seminar, September 27, 1955. [Manuscripts Division]

b. Scrapbook concerning Faulkner's visit to Japan, compiled by Leon Picon, of the United States Information Service. [Lent by Leon Picon]. Through the courtesy of Mr. Picon, a microfilm of this scrapbook is available in the Princeton University Library. [Film 3734.92.856]

c. *To the Youth of Japan*. [Tokyo, United States Information Service, August, 1955.] [Ex 3734.92.392]. A bilingual edition of a message Faulkner wrote August 22, 1955, for the United States Information Service to use in connection with his visit. It was reprinted in several newspapers and in *Faulkner at Nagano*. (See No. 308.)

### 328. Public letters.

On several occasions Faulkner has addressed letters to the editors of newspapers and magazines on current affairs and literary issues.

a. Photostat of letter to the editor of *The Oxford Eagle*, March 13, 1947, p. 5. [Original in the University of Mississippi Library]

b. Photostat of letter to the editor of *The New York Times*, December 26, 1954, Section IV, p. 6. [0921.6784e]

c. Letter to Richard Walser, in *The Enigma of Thomas Wolfe*, ed. Richard Walser, Cambridge, Harvard University Press, 1953, p. [vii]. [3995.23.974]. Faulkner has on several occasions been quoted as calling Wolfe the greatest contemporary American writer. In this letter he corrects the misquotations. "I rated Wolfe first," he wrote Walser, "because he had tried the hardest to say the most."

d. Part of a letter to the Batesville, Mississippi, Chamber of Commerce, quoted in the Memphis *Commercial Appeal*, August 11, 1956, p. 15. [Lent by James B. Meriwether]

e. Photostat of letter to the editor of the Memphis *Commercial Appeal*, April 17, 1955, Section V, p. 3. [Original in the Memphis State College Library]. This is the last of a series upon the integration question which Faulkner wrote to the *Commercial Appeal* in the spring of 1955.

### 329. The "Beer Broadside."

In connection with an election on the legalization of the sale of beer in Oxford, Faulkner had printed and distributed 1,500 copies of a broadside which, as he explained in a subsequent letter to *The Oxford Eagle*, "was only secondarily concerned with beer." His primary purpose, he said, was to protest against the action of three Oxford ministers who campaigned against the legalization of beer sales—"I object to ministers of God violating the canons and ethics of their sacred and holy avocation by using, either openly or underhand, the weight and power of their office to try to influence a civil election" (*The Oxford Eagle*, September 14, 1950).

"To the Voters of Oxford." Broadside printed in Oxford, Mississippi, about September 1, 1950. [Lent by James Silver]

### 330. "A Letter to the North."

Faulkner's moderate stand on the segregation question has aroused the resentment of extremists on both sides. In this article, as Faulkner explained in a letter printed in *Life* three weeks later, he was cautioning the pro-integration forces to proceed slowly because of his fear that violence would erupt over the Autherine Lucy case at the University of Alabama.

a. "A Letter to the North." *Life*, March 5, 1956, pp. 51-52. [0901.L724q]

b. Typescript of article, entitled "Letter to a Northern Editor," with manuscript corrections. 11 pp. [Manuscripts Division]. See Fig. 30

### 331. *The American Dream.*

At Nagano in 1955, Faulkner read, in a seminar, the manuscript of an unpublished essay which he said would eventually be a chapter in a book which he planned to call *The American Dream*. Apparently the essay was that which appeared, entitled "On Fear: The South in Labor," the following summer, and it would seem that the article "On Privacy: The American Dream: What Happened to It" (see No. 322), published shortly before the Nagano Seminar, is also designed for a Chapter in the book of essays.

a. *Faulkner at Nagano*, Tokyo, Kenkyusha Ltd. [1956], opened to pp. 96-97, with a reference to *The American Dream*. [Ex 3734.92.333]

b. Typescript of "On Fear: The South in Labor," with manuscript corrections. 17 pp. [Manuscripts Division]

c. "On Fear: The South in Labor." *Harper's Magazine*, CCXII (June, 1956), [29]-34. [0901.H295]

## 31. PHOTOGRAPHS OF WILLIAM FAULKNER

332. As the author of *Light in August* (1932). [Lent by Carvel Collins]

333. Four photographs of Faulkner at his home in Oxford (about 1950). [Lent by Carvel Collins]

334. By Sabine Weiss (1954?). [Manuscripts Division]

335. By Carl Van Vechten (1954). [Manuscripts Division]

(For other photographs and representations of Faulkner, see Nos. 1, 15, 16, 320-d, 324-b, 324-d, and 324-e.)

The sky is a thin trans-
parent blue, a very light blue mer-
ging into white with stars in regular
order, and a full moon. At the back
center is a marble colonnade, small
in distance, against a regular black
band of trees; on either side of it
is the slim graceful silhouette of a
single poplar tree. Both wings are
closed by sections of wall covered
with roses, motionless on the left
wall is a peacock silhouetted a-
gainst the moon. In the middle

7

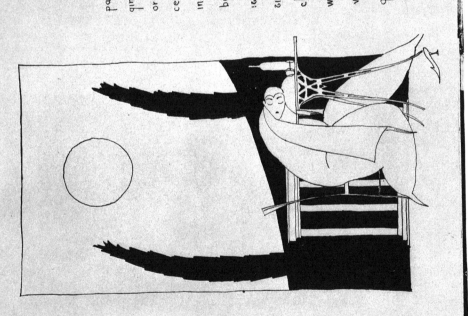

1. "The Marionettes: A Play in One Act" (Catalogue No. 6-b)

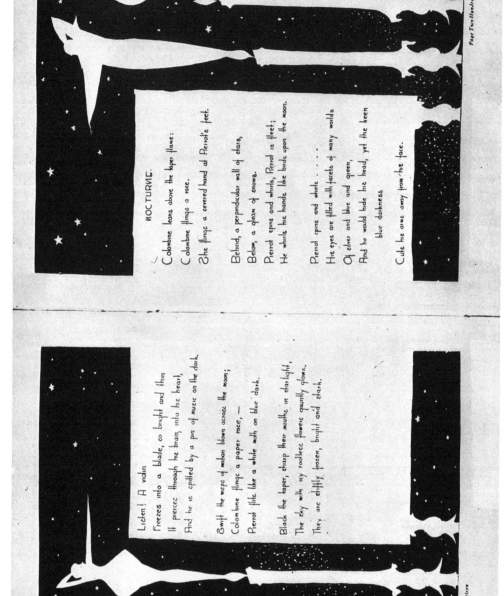

2. "Nocturne" The Ole Miss 1920-1921 (Catalogue No 8)

Cathay.

Sharp sands, those blind desert horsemen, sweep
Where yesterday tall shining caravels
Swam in her golden past. What fate fortells
That now the winds go lightly lest her sleep
Be broken? Where once her splendors rose
And shook their banners bright against the sky,
Now go the empty years infinitely
Rich with ghosts. So it is: who sows
The seed of Fame, makes grain for Death to reap.

Wanderers, with faces sharp as spears,
And flocks and herds on muffled aimless feet
Drift where glittering kings went through each street
Of her white vanished cities, and the years
Have closed like walls behind them. Still
Through spawn of lesser destinies
We stare where once her star burned, lest like these
We dose faith. They knew her not, nor will
To see her magic empire when the Hand
Thrusts back the curtain of the shifting sand
On singing stars and lifting golden hill.

3. **Typescript of "Cathay"**
(Catalogue No. 3-b)

---

La Lune ne Grade Aucune Rancune.

Look, Cynthia,
How Abelard evaporates
The brow of Time, and Paris
Tastes his bitter thumbs——

The Worm grows fat, eviscerate,
But not on love, O Cynthia.

rote for saM G8lm9re b% wУ99iam 7 mqan 3ill#a@ 7 ;ean
bY wiLMau fⓍⅡkm8R

7 ha'e toM leⅡ$on$ o$ ɧe 5Ype@rltyr "ut 7 kee!p fonfu9ing
it rrikh saw wⅣth my llute 7 meⅤn fl@rt 7 /ean FULTE

4. Typescript version of poem XXXII of *A Green Bough*
(Catalogue No. 106)

## 5. Soldiers' Pay

"You go and see what he wants. I'll
come on after a while."

The negro had turned shuffling on a-
head and the lawn mower resumed its chattering song as Gilligan mounted the steps. The rector stood on the verandah, his
face was calm but it was evident he had not slept.

"Sorry to trouble you, Mr Gilligan,
but Donald is awake and I am not familiar with his clothing
as you are. I gave away his civilian things when he——
when he——"

"Sure, sir," Gilligan answered in
sharp pity for the gray-faced man. He dont know him yet!
"I'll help him."

The divine ineffectual would have
followed but Gilligan leaped away from him, up the stairs.
So he descended to the lawn to meet Mrs Powers.

"Good morning, Doctor," she replied
to his greeting. "I have been looking at your flowers. I
hope you dont mind?"

"Not at all, not at all, my dear mad-
am. An old man is always flattered when his flowers are ad-
mired. I had thought to grow old with my books among my roses:"

*5. Soldiers' Pay*
*Page 111 of bound typescript (Catalogue No. 10)*

## 6. Mosquitoes

he brooded on a page. Here's one:

"'Tis that of thy weary all see weariest
And wearier for the curves and pallid by
Still riddle of thy secret face, and thy
Sick mossair of its own ill obsesses;

that a thing heaves thy tired mouth reconciled,
for sweating so frees thee but ill beguiled
With secret joy of thine own woman's breast.

Weary thy mouth with smiling: cause thou drive
thyself with thee, or thine own kissing shake?
Thy ... wearing down itself deride
With sleep's share absence, coming so aware;
And near thy mouth thy twinned heart's grief down me
mine

For there's no breast between: it cannot break.'

*6. Mosquitoes*
*Page 226 of bound typescript (Catalogue No. 22)*

ELMER. [Book 1.]
ELMER.
Chapter One.
1.

He thought I wish the boat were going to Liverpool, spitting over the taffrail toward Sicily asleep on the horizon like a blue floating whale, hearing his spittle smack a round spot of silence on that hissing ceaseless monotony of water creaming along the hull. Now that they were approaching land at last Elmer began to feel human again, i.e. to remember that after all he was still heir to the emotions of loneliness and impatience, to what circumstance and his fellow man could do to him. Being in the middle of the ocean never made him feel lonely at all. On the contrary it had given him a sense of firmness, of independence, as if loneliness [solitude] had herded all the floating atoms of Elmer together and had by quiet constant pressure welded him into a compact erectness.

There was really very little time to be lonely at sea. After twenty days on a freighter pushing one empty horizon before and drawing another one behind, empty too save for a green carpet of wake unrolling across that blue monotone as though before a great cathedral prepared for an elegant wedding in high life, Elmer forgot how to be anything except hungry and sleepy: his one emotional response was that [that of] a fat unenergetic pleasure like a bright lazy child's, at the sight of a lone busy ship far away or a porpoise or a spouting whale.

His days were pretty well filled. There were the officers to talk to, for instance. (To lean on the bridge rail doing nothing while the bo'sun and his watch avoided looking at him

1.

quarter hours, but saving this there was no sound from the other parts of the house. Simon's activity below stairs had long ceased, but a murmur of voices reached her at intervals from somewhere, murmurously indistinguishable. The leaves on the tree beyond the window did not stir in the hot air, and upon it a myriad noises blended in a drowsy monotone---the negroes' voices, sounds of stock from the barnyard, the rythmic groaning of the water pump; a sudden cacophony of fowls in the garden beneath the window, interspersed with Isom's meaningless cries as he drove them out.

He was asleep now, and as she realized this she realized also that she did not know just when she had stopped reading. And she sat with the page open upon her knees, a page whose words left no echoes whatever in her mind, watching his calm face. It was again like a bronze mask, purged by illness of the heat of its violence, yet with the violence still slumbering there and only refined a little, and she realized that today, for the first time since the day of his injury, that old paradox of shrinking and fascination and dread had returned; and for the moment she believed that though Horace was her cross and her derision, beyond was a curse put upon her because of her love and jealousy and selfishness toward Horace, and that there would be peace for her only in a world where there were no men.

373 --- 372

late June
One February dusk — in 1917 — one of those timeless treacherous apocryphal days neither spring nor winter — a tender drew up to an aerodrome up toward Arras and stopped before the squadron office. It contained a single occupant in a parti—

I am Comyn, of the first native, and it's bloody cold driving up from Wing," he stated.

with his cap thrust to the back of his head and the light fell on his flushed face

"Whiskey," the newcomer said. "Whiskey for everybody, everyone. My clot. Damn— Damn cold, driving down from Wing," he added, looking about. "Oh, I say, Sartoris," he said to a slight lean youth with restless blue eyes and tawny hair, "One of the new Camel squadrons came through Wing today, replacing 65. There's a Sartoris in it. Any of your people?"

"It's Bayard," Evelyn Sartoris said, springing to his feet. "Hell, I'm going up there." He too raised his voice, but at that moment the orderly returned with bottles — a tray of bottles and glasses. "Nip one and tell the Flight Sergeant of 13 to have No. gal for Sartoris' machine out," he directed.

"Don't be a pukka fool," his squadron flight-commander said from his chair, without raising his head from the Field pictorial magazine he perused. "You can't fly up there at this hour."

"Why not? It aint dark yet, is it?" Sartoris demanded of the newcomer, who was building himself a dynamic drink. "That yet, the old answered. "Let him go, Mac," he added to the oblivious flight-commander. "plenty of light of the horizon."

"And has let him work out a parfectly good machine?" the flight commander said. "Plenty more pilots of Pool, but it takes it days to replace a machine. Sit down, Sartoris."

The newcomer blundered into a chair and took a long swallow from his glass. "Damn cold, driving up from Wing," he repeated "I tell you what: there's a night-flying squadron up there somewhere; you might get on up there, and if it's too dark to set down, you might just sort of hang around until they light their flares— turn on their searchlights."

"Or you might ask the Major to 'phone up and have them put out flares for you," another suggested.

"Oh, go to hell," Sartoris snapped. "Let me have the tender, will you, Mac?"

"Sit down, Sartoris," the flight-commander so repeated, "and you all always do shut up. Oh, steward." The orderly appeared again and the flight-commander added: "Take that whiskey out. Mr Comyn's had enough." He turned to Evelyn Sartoris again "Why not telephone up there, if you could, would tomorrow?
I wouldn't go up there tonight. It'll take you all night to clean up there." He turned to his magazine again.

"Well," Evelyn Sartoris opined, "I recon that's what I'll have to do."

June Second, 1910

The shadow of the sash fell across the curtains, between 7 and 8 oclock, and then I was hearing the watch. again, ~~that I should~~ and I lay there looking at the shadow bar across the nosy and motionless curtains, listening to the watch. Hearing it, that is. I dont suppose anybody deliberately listens to a watch or a clock. You dont have to. You can be oblivious to the sound for a long while, then in a second of ticking it can create in the mind unbroken the long diminishing parade of time you did not hear. Where up the long and lonely annaring of light rays you might see Jesus walking, like. The Inne Son of Man. he had no sister. Marourne and Roman and Vinginian, they had no sister one minute she was

Beyond the wall Shreve's bedsprings complained thinly, then his carpet slippers on the floor. I got up and went to the dresser and slid Had no sister my hand along it and touched the watch and turned it face down upon the dresser and went back to bed. As soon as I knew I couldn't see it that constant speculation as to what mechanical knew it in which came to be a part of every continued man's mind, set up again. all night, I wonder what time it is. What about it? Marourne and Roman and Vinginian. ~~Come~~ Praelonium blew none of you, ye went worn away by a minute ~~to~~ clicking of little wheels

Ye were none of ye cancelled:

The curtains were like nosy gauze and then I was thinking it would be nice in them down at New London if the weather held up like this why shouldn't it the month of brides the voice that She was running when I heard it, too the minute she was running before I knew what it was but from ~~being caught-up over her arm, then out of the minute like a cloud along the annealed stones her not swimming~~ out of the minute running out of the bandied street and the voice that mouthed o'er eden Shreve stood in the door, pulling his collar on, his glasses glinty as though he had just washed them also, ~~out~~ along with his face.

"You taking a cut this morning?"

"Is it that late?"

He looked at his watch. "Bell in two minutes."

"I didn't know it was that late." He was still looking at his watch, his mouth shaping. "I'll have to hustle. I cant stand another cut. The dean told me ____" He put the watch back.

"You'd better slip on your coat and pants and run." He went out.

I got up and moved about until he closed the sitting room.

"You ready yet?"

"Not yet. Run along. I'll make it."

He went on. The door opened, closed upon his feet. I quit moving about and went to the window and drew the curtains aside. The quad was full and watched them running in chapel, the same ones rushing past at the last minute, and Spoade in the middle of them like a turtle in a street full of scuttering leaves, his coat collar about his ears, moving at his customary unhurried walk. He was from South Carolina, a union. It was his class' boast that he never

10. *The Sound and the Fury*
Page 34 of manuscript
(Catalogue No. 42)

11. *The Sound and the Fury*
Page 70 of manuscript
(Catalogue No. 42)

12. *Sanctuary*
Page 131 of manuscript (Catalogue No. 57)

Thursday

2:30 P.M. 200 cu. in. Qualifying Speed 100 m.p.h. Purse $850.00 (1) 45% (2) 30% (3) 15%
(4) 10%

3:00 A.M. Spot Parachute Jump. Purse $25.00

3:30 P.M. Scull Dash 350 cu. in. Qualifying Speed 160 m.p.h. Purse $325.00 (1,2,3,4)

4:00 P.M. Aerial Acrobatics. Solo Airplanes. France. Lieut Frank Burnham. America.

4:30 P.M. Scull Dash 550 cu. in. Qualifying Speed 200 m.p.h. Purse $500.00 (1,2,3,4)

5:00 P.M. Delayed Parachute Drop

8:00 P.M. Special Mardi Gras Event. Rocket Plane. Lieut Frank Burnham.
2000 DOLLARS 2000

13. *Pylon*
Unnumbered page of manuscript
(Catalogue No. 121)

no matter what happens out there tonight, will still be
in the family; the skeleton (if it be a skeleton) still in
the closet. Or more than that even. She may believe that
if it hadn't been for your grandfather's friendship Sutpen
could not have got a foothold here and that if he had not got
that foothold, he could not have married Ellen. So maybe she
considers you partly responsible for what happened to her
and her family through him."

Whatever the reason, whether it was that
or not, Quentin thought, the getting to it was taking a long
time. Meanwhile, as time passed and as though in inverse ratio
to the vanishing of the voice, the invoked ghost of the
brother-in-law, with whom at one time she herself had been
engaged to marry began to assume a quality almost of solid-
ity, permanence. Itself circumambient and in turn enclosed
by the effluvium of hell, its aura of unregeneration. It
mused with that quality peaceful and now harmless and not
even very attentive---the ogreshape which, as the voice went
on, began to resolve out of itself the two halfogre chil-
dreh, the three of them forming a shadowy background for
the fourth, the wraith of the mother, the dead sister Ellen:
a Niobe without tears who had conceived to the demon in a
kind of nightmare, and who even alive had moved but without life and grieved but without tears, and who now, at this
distance shadowy too, had an air of tranquil and unwitting des-
olation, not as though she had either outlived the others
or had died first, but as if she had never lived at all.

9.

any other patent of respectability) that people could look
at and read just as he would have wanted our father's—(or any
other reputable men's) faded signature on a note-of-hand:
because our father knew who his father was in Tennessee and
who his grandfather had been in Virginia and our neighbors
and the people we lived among knew that we knew and we knew
they knew we knew and we knew that they would have believed
us about who and where he came from even if we had lied, just
as anyone could have looked at him once and known that he
would be lying about who and where and why he came from by
the very fact that apparently he had to refuse to say at all.
And the very fact that he had had to chose respectability to
hide behind was proof enough (if anyone needed further proof)
that what he fled from must have been some opposite of
respectability too dark to talk about. Because he was too
young. He was just twenty-five and a man of twenty-five does
not voluntarily undertake the hardship and privation of
clearing virgin land and establishing a plantation in a new
country just for money; not a young man without any past
that he apparently cared to discuss, in Mississippi in 1833,
with a river full of steamboats loaded with drunken fools
covered with diamonds and bent on throwing away their cotton
and slaves before the boat reached New Orleans--not with all
this just one night's hard ride away and the only handicap
or obstacle being the other blackguards or the risk of being
put ashore on a sandbar, and at the remotest, a hemp rope.
And he was no younger son sent out from some old quiet coun-

13.

14. *Absalom, Absalom!*

Pages 9 and 13 of typescript (Catalogue No. 128)

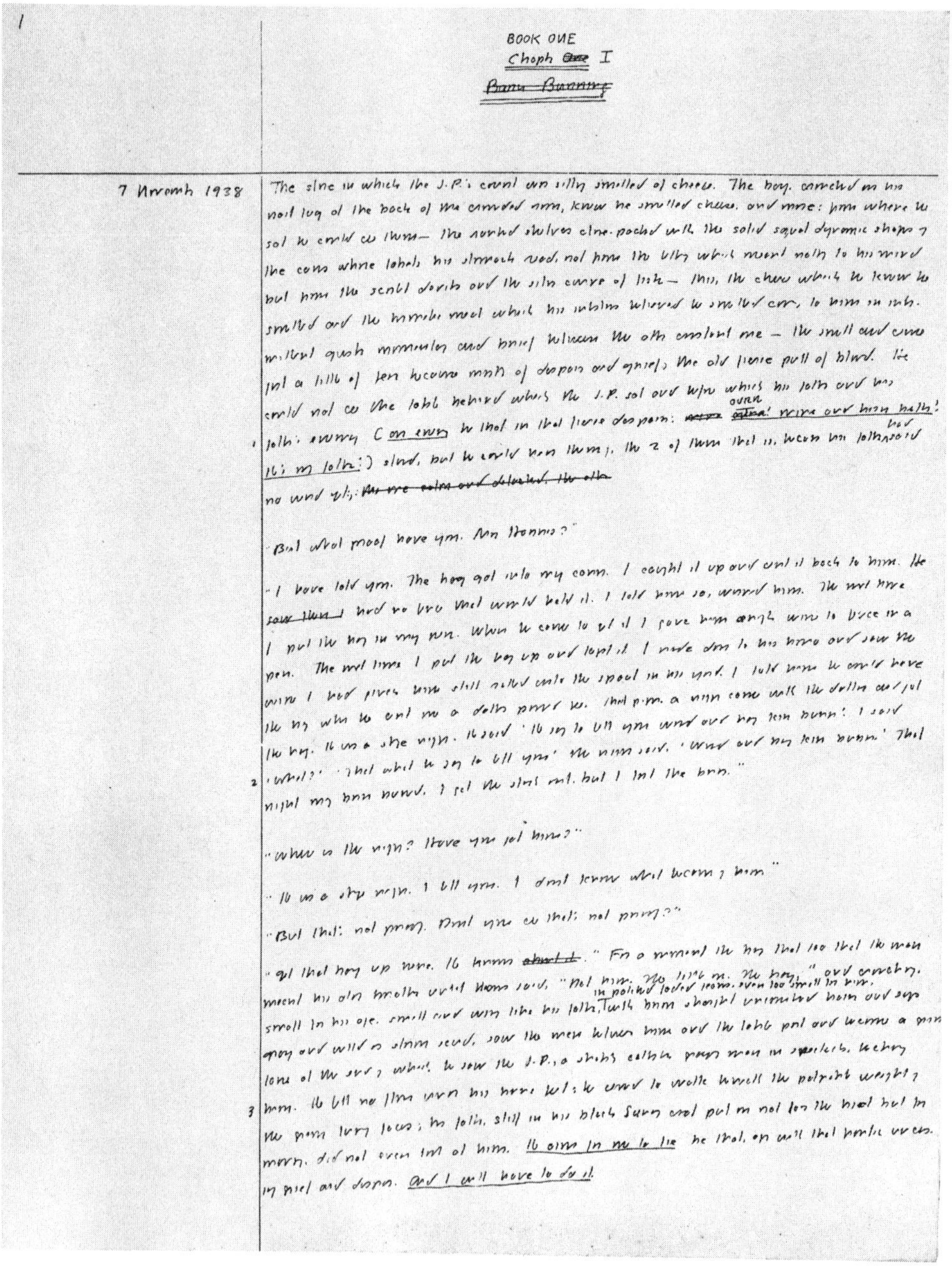


15. "Barn Burning"
Page 1 of manuscript
(Catalogue No. 160)

Page 1 of typescript (Catalogue No. 170)

When me and Uncle Buck come back to the house from
finding out Tomey's Turl had run away again, the fox and the
dogs come out of the kitchen and crossed the dogtrot and went
into the dogs' room and we could hear them running out of the
dog room into Uncle Buck's room and then we seen them cross
the dogtrot again and go into Uncle Buddy's room and then we
heard them running out of Uncle Buddy's room into the kitchen
again and this time it sounded like the whole chimbley had done
got knocked down and Uncle Buddy hollering and cussing loud as
a steamboat ~~blowing~~ and this time the fox and the dogs and three or
four sticks of firewood all come out of the kitchen together
with Uncle Buddy in the middle of them hitting at everything
in sight with another stick. It was a good race.

So me and Uncle Buck went into his room where the
fox had bayed on the mantel-shelf ~~behind the clock~~ and Uncle Buck kicked the
dogs off anf lifted the fox down by the scruff of his neck
and put him back into his box under the bed, and we went into
the kitchen where Uncle Buddy was picking the breakfast up out
of the ashes, and told him that Tomey's Turl had done run away
again.

"Od dammit, Theophilus," Uncle Buddy said. "What
in tarnation hell did you mean by turning that dam fox out
with the dogs all loose in the house?"

"Never you mind about that," Uncle Buck said. "Get
me and Bayard some breakfast. We got to get started." He's rid-
ing Old Jake. We might just barely ketch him before he reaches
Prim's.

Because we all knew where Tomey's Turl had went.

1.

16. "Was"
Page 1 of typescript (Catalogue No. 170)

---

APOTHEOSIS

AN ABSOLUTION

When Edmonds, glancing up from his
desk, saw through the window beside him the negro woman
coming up the path from the road, he did not recognise her.
It was not until he heard her toiling up the steps and then
saw her enter the commissary itself, that he realised she
~~Not with it, his right hand, his hat gone on the place in her~~
was Lucas' ~~wife~~. Because for ten years now he hardly ever
~~familiar~~
saw her, and that only from a distance when he would chance
to pass Lucas' house on his mare, to see her perhaps sitting
on the porch, her shrunken face collapsed about the reed
stem of a clay pipe, or moving about the washing-pot
and the clothes-line in the back yard as the very old move
---a small woman, almost tiny, in a perfectly clean white
headcloth and apron, whom he knew to be actually a little
older than Lucas but who looked much older, incredibly
old, who during the last ten years when she did address
him, called him by his/father's name---'marster' or 'Mister
Zack'.

When she entered at last, he did rec-
ognise her. "Why, Aunt Mollie," he said. "What are you
doing way over here? Why didn't Lucas come? You aint got
any business trying to carry anything back to your house."

"I dont want nothing," she said. "I
come to talk to you. Then he saw the myriad-wrinkled,
the tragic and despairing yet still immobile, face and he
rose from his chair and drew the other one, the straight
one with its wire-braced legs, out from behind the desk.
"Here," he said. "Sit down." But she only looked from him

1.

17. "Apotheosis"
Page 1 of typescript (Catalogue No. 171)

18. "Father Abraham"
Page 2 of manuscript
(Catalogue No. 259)

## Abraham's Children

Buck stood in the shattered doorway. He produced his carton and shook a gingersnap into his hand and tossed the carton away. The mad rushing of the animals diminished and they now trotted on high, stiff legs, tossing their rolling various eyes.

"I doubted that 'ere shell down right along," Buck said. "I reckon they thought it was bugs."

Mrs Littlejohn came onto her verande and rang a heavy bell.

"Chuck wagon," Buck said. "You boys stick around. Action begins right after breakfast." He strode across the lot. The animals watched him and slid gaudily and fluidly from his path, and the three in the wagon descended hastily and Eck caught up his son and they followed Buck closely across the lot. The fence was fairly well lined by quiet, oversized figures in patient and restful attitudes, and along the road wagons stood, the teams reversed and tethered to the wagon wheels, and saddle horses nibbled at the lower branches of the apple tree. "Action begins right after breakfast, boys," Buck repeated and he closed the gate while the spectators and the beasts watched him stonily quietly as he entered the house, the butt of his pistol hunched slightly beneath his coat. More arrivals came up and descended from their wagons and joined the group that stood or squatted along the fence, talking quietly and sparsely among themselves.

"Yere, bud------" Luck sitting on the top of the gate-

18.

**19. "Abraham's Children"**
**Page 18 of typescript (Catalogue No. 260)**

---

pretty close to the door handle with the same line through both bits and now they looked jest exactly like two fellurs
——done committed/ suicide/ hung themselves in one of these here suicide packs, with their heads snubbed up together and their tongues hanging out and their necks stretched about four foot and their legs doubled back under them like a shot rabbit until Pap jumped down and cut them outen the harness.

Yes sir. A artist. He had give them jest exactly to a inch enough of whatever it was to get them into town and off the square before it played out.

Now this here's what I mean when I said it was desperation. I can see Pap now, backed off in that corner behind Uncle Ike's plows and cultivators, with his face white and his voice shaking and his hand shaking so he couldn't hardly hand me the six bits outen his pocket. "Go to Doc Peabody's store," he says, "and git me a pint of whiskey, Harry." (Suratt turned to Doctor Peabody. "That was when hit was," he said. "You mind hit. You give me that ere hound candy."--"Yes," Doctor Peabody said. "Sholy Luug didn't hope to drive a Pat Stamper team twelve miles on one pint of whiskey."--"No, sir," Suratt said. "He drunk the whiskey hisself.")

Yes sir. Desperate. Hit wasn't even a quicksand now. Hit was a whirlpool and Pap with jest one jump left. He drunk that pint of whiskey in two drinks and he set the empty bottle careful in the corner of Uncle Ike's warehouse and we went back out to the wagon. The miles

23.

**20. "Fool About a Horse"**
**Page 23 of typescript (Catalogue No. 271)**

*Fool About a Horse*

21. "Fool About a Horse"
Page 1 of manuscript
(Catalogue No. 269)

(she exits)

**STEVENS**

(follows through the door)
Of course we are. Hasn't He been telling us that
~~for going on two thousand years?~~

*They exit.*
~~He exits.~~ The door closes in, clashes, the clash and clang
of the key as the Jailor locks it again; the three pairs of
footsteps sound and begin to fade in the outer corridor.

~~Curtain~~ *Stevens,*

BEARER    BEARER    BEARER    BEARE

*Temple, followed by ~~Gowan~~, approch the door.*

*JAILOR'S VOICE*
*(off-stage: surprised)*

*Howdy, Gowan, heres your wife now.*

*TEMPLE*
*(walking)*

*Any one ~~to save it~~ to save it. Anyone who ~~resists~~ wants it. If
there is none, I'm ~~sunk~~. We all ~~are~~ are. Doomed.
Damned.*

*STEVENS*
*(walking)*

*Of course ~~we are~~ we are. Hasn't He been telling us
that for going on two thousand years?*

*GOWAN'S VOICE*
*(offstage)*

*Temple.*

*TEMPLE*

*Coming.*

*CURTAIN*

22. *Requiem for a Nun*
Galley proof of final scene with manuscript additions
(Catalogue No. 222-d)

23. "Mule in the Yard"
First page of manuscript
(Catalogue No. 296-a)

year: the Honorable Clarence Eggleston Snopes, Member of the Mississippi Legislature---'Senator' Snopes to the people who for twenty-five years had been electing him steadily and unflaggingly to public office, first from a single Beat of our County, then from the County itself, and now (compounded by their spiritual ob at least/ political kin in the rest of the counties comprising our Congressional District) to the House of Representatives in Washington as soon as he had notified them that that was what he wanted them to do. And why not Senator, since he had as much right to the implication of Statesman now as he would when, having found his way around Congress, he would notify them to elect him to the Senate itself ---until last week, at the annual Varner's Mill picnic where by tradition our candidates always opened their campaigns, Snopes not only failed to appear on the speakers' platform, he disappeared from the scene itself even before dinner was served; and the next day word spread over the County that he had not only withdrawn from the race for Congress, he was even withdrawing from public life altogether when his present term in the State legislature was up.

He was a cadet (one of them) and, xxxxxxxxxxxx the State Capitol itself, almost a deified figurehead of a vast sprawling clan of a family or even tribe in the densely-populated southeastern part of the County, distantly kin by marriage to Uncle Billy Varner himself who was patriarch and undisputed chief of that whole section (the Snopeses had by now spread and overlapped into Jefferson, where one of them was president of the Merchants' and Farmers' Bank and was himself a local power/ xxxxxxxxxxxxxxxxxxxx in Jefferson. But that was Jefferson, and Uncle Billy Varner was absolute and supreme, emperor king arbiter and despot of every one who still lived or claimed to live in the

Frenchman's Bend section of Beat Four --- who (Snopes) as a young man had been leader of a witheriling gang of cousins and toadies which fought and drank and beat Negroes and terrified young girls until (the story ran) Uncle Billy became indicted or concluded enough to order the local P.... to appoint Snopes his constable---whereupon he his Snopeses, whole litter existence, destiny, fate, found itself

5.

24. "By the People"
Page 5 of typescript (Catalogue No. 286)

---

... With Caution And Dispatch

It was on the bulletin board when they came into the mess for lunch:

...squadron on this date will depart and proceed under arms and with caution and dispatch, for France.

By order of the General Commanding.

Whitehall
26 March, 1918

The General arrived, with an A.D.C.

There was a rush for the door. Britt, already blocking the door, stopped it. "No," he said. "There's a Staff-wallah coming. Nobody goes into town until after."

After lunch, he sat in the single armchair, the major flanking him, and the adjutant flanking him, while the Squadron sat quietly about the littered table---the juniors, the untried, gathered from the flung corners of the Empire and including two who were not even Britons---listening to Waterloo and the playing fields of Eton and here a spot which is forever England; hearing at last the rich port-winey voice in actual retrograde in a long limbo filled with horses: Fontenoy and Agincourt and Crecy and the Black Prince, and Sartoris, the Mississippian, whispering and not so sotto voce either: "What? What nigger? Is he talking about Jack Johnson?"

The General stood up. They had already drunk the King; the mess orderlies filled again and, standing again, they drank the Squadron. "You will depart

1.

25. "With Caution and Dispatch"
Page 1 of typescript (Catalogue No. 214)

"SUMMER"

The brook has now become a stream
On which long still days lie and dream
And where the lusty Summer walks
—Around his head are lifing stra[lks]—
In the shade beneath the trees
To let the cool stream fold his knees;
While I lie in the leafy shade
Until the nymphs troop down the glade,
Their limbs, that in the spring were white,
Are now burned gold by sunlight,
They as I the surge, and there they meet
Inverted selves stretched out their feet;
And they kneel languorously there
To cool and braid their short blown hair
Before they slip into the pool—
Warm gold in river liquid cool,

The sunset stains the western sky;
Night comes soon, and now I
Father toward the evening star,
A sheep bell tinkles faint and far
Then drips in silence as the sheep
More like clouds across the deep
Still dusky meadows wet with dew.
I stretch and roll and drag through
The fresh sweet grass, and the air
Is softer than my own soft hair.
I lift up my eyes the green
West is a lake on which has been
Cast a single lily——See!
In meadows stretching over me

26. *The Marble Faun*
Unnumbered page of carbon typescript (Catalogue No. 11)

Dear Anderson——

    I was with a boating party across the lake over the week end, and going up the river the pilot pointed out to us the old Jackson place. They are descendants of Old Hickory, and there is only one of them left.——Al Jackson, I wish you could know him: with your interest in people he would be a gold mine to you. The man has had a very eventful life, through no fault of his own. He is himself very retiring. It is told of him no one ever saw him in wading or swimming or undressed. Something about his feet, they say, though no one knows for certain.

    The pilot was telling me about his people. His mother at the age of seven held the tatting championship of the her parish Sunday school, and as a reward they gave her the privilege of attending every religious ceremony held at her church, with out having to go to the social ones, for a period of ninety nine years. At the age of nine she could play on a melodeon her father had snapped a boat and a clock and a pet alligator for; she could sew, cook; and the increased attendance at her church three hundred percent with some sort of a secret recipe for communion wine, including among other things, grain alcohol. The pilot's father used to go to her church. In fact the whole parish finally did. Maximally they tore down two churches for them wood to make fish-traps of, and one minister finally got a job on a ferry boat. The church gave her a bible with her name and favorite flower embossed in gold on it for this.

    Old man Jackson told her hunt that she was twelve. They say he was ravished by her prowess on the melodeon. The pilot says old man Jackson didn't have a melodeon, Old man Jackson was a character, himself. When he was eight he learned by heart one thousand verses from the new testament, bringing on an attack resembling brain fever. When they finally got a veterinary up, he said it couldn't be brain fever, though. After that he became kind of ——well, call it queer: bought library paste to eat whenever he could get it, and wore a raincoat every time he took a bath, He

27. Undated letter from Faulkner to
Sherwood Anderson, first page (Catalogue No. 17)

slept in a folding bed which he flat on the floor and closed up on him when he retired. He invented some holes bored in for air.

It seems that Jackson finally got the idea of raising sheep in that swamp of his, his belief being that wool grew like anything else, and that if sheep stood in water all the time, like trees, the fleece would be naturally more luxuriant. By the time he had about a dozen of the drowned, he made life baits out of ease for them. And then he found that the alligators were getting them.

One of the older boys (he must have had about a dozen) discovered the alligators wouldn't bother a goat with long horns, so the old man carved imitation horns about three feet across out of roots and fastened them onto his sheep. He didn't give them all horns, lest the alligators catch onto the trick. The pilot said he figured on losing so many head a year, but in this way he kept they/rate pretty low.

Soon they found that the sheep were learning to like the water, were swimming all around in it, that in about six months they never came out of the water at all. Then shearing time came, he had to borrow a motor boat to run them down with. And when they caught one and raised it out of the water, it had no legs. They had atrophied and completely disappeared.

And that was true of everyone they caught. The legs not only were gone, but that part of the sheep which was under water was covered with scales inplace of wool, and the tail had broadened and flattened like a beaver's. Within another six months they couldn't even catch one with the motor boat. They had learned to dive from watching fish; and when a year had passed Jackson saw them only when they stuck their noses up for a breath of air now and then. Soon days would pass without the water being broken by one of them. Occasionally they caught one on a hook baited with corn, but it had no wool on it at all.

28. Second page

---

got kind of discouraged. Here was all his capital swimming around under water, and he was afraid they would turn alligators before could catch any of them. Finally his second boy, Claude, the wild one that was always after women, told his father that if he would give him outright half he could catch, he would get a few of them. They agreed, and so Claude would take off his clothes and go in the water. He never got many at first, though he would occasionally hem one up under a log and get him. One of them bit him pretty badly one day, and he thought to himself: "yes, sir, I got to work fast; then things will be alligators in a year."

So he lit in, and everyday hisswimming got better and he'd get a few more. Soon he could stay under water for a half an hour at a time; but out of the water his breathing want so very good, and his legs were beginning to feel funny at the knee. He then took to staying in the water all day and all night and his folks would bring him food. He lost all use of his arms to the elbow and his legs to the knee; and the last time any of the family saw him his eyes had moved around to the side of his head and there was a faint tail sticking out of the corner of his mouth.

About a year later they heard of him again. There was a single shark appeared off the coast that kept on bothering the blonde lady bathers, especially the fat ones.

"That's Claude," said old man Jackson, "he always was hell on blondes,"

And so their sole source of income was gone. The family was in quite a bad way month for years and years, until the Prohibition law came along and saved them.

I hope you will find this story as interesting as I have.

Sincerely,

William Faulkner

29. Third page

Undated letter from Faulkner to Sherwood Anderson (Catalogue No. 17)

## 30. "Letter to a Northern Editor" (left)

William Faulkner
c/o Harold Ober Associates
40 East 49 St., New York

LETTER TO A NORTHERN EDITOR

My family has lived for generations in one same small section of north Mississippi. My great-grandfather held slaves and went to Virginia in command of a Mississippi infantry regiment in 1861. I state this simply as credentials for the sincerity and factualness of what I will try to say.

From the beginning of this present phase of the race problem in the South, I have been on record as opposing the forces in my native country which would keep the condition out of which this present evil and trouble has grown. Now I must go on record as opposing the forces outside the South which would use legal or police compulsion to eradicate that evil overnight. I was against compulsory segregation. I am just as strongly against compulsory integration. Firstly of course from principle. Secondly because I don't believe it will work.

There are more Southerners than I who believe as I do and have taken the same stand I have taken, at the same price of contumely and insult and threat from other Southerners which we foresaw and were willing to accept because we believed we were helping our native land which we love, to accept a new condition which it must accept whether it wants to or not. That is, by still being Southerners, yet not being a part of the general majority Southern point of view; by being present yet detached, committed and attainted neither by Citizens' Council nor NAACP; by being in the middle, being in position to say to any incipient irrevocality: Wait, wait now, stop and consider first.'

But where will we go if that middle becomes untenable? If we have to vacate it in order to keep from being trampled? Apart from the legal aspect, apart even from the simple incontrovertible immorality of inequality discrimination by race, there was another simply human quan-

1.

30. "Letter to a Northern Editor"
Page 1 of typescript (Catalogue No. 330-b)

## 31. "Freedom American Style" (right)

AMBASSADOR: 5 copies please, fast can be cut onion skin, SOONEST possible, please & thank you

FREEDOM AMERICAN STILL

by

William Faulkner

This was the American Dream: a sanctuary on the earth for individual man: a condition in which he could be free not only of the old established closed-corporation hierarchies of arbitrary power which had oppressed him as a mass, but free of that mass into which the hierarchies of church and state had compressed and held him individually thralled and individually impotent.

A dream simultaneous among the separate individuals of man so easier and sostered as to have no contest to match dreams and hopes among the old nations of the old world which existed as nations not on citizenship but subjectship, which endured only on the premise of size and docility of the subject mass: the individual men and women who said as with one simultaneous voice: 'We will establish a new land where man can assume that every individual man---not the mass of men but individual men---have has inalienable right to individual dignity and freedom within a fabric of individual courage and honorable work and mutual responsibility.'

Not just an idea, but a condition: a living human condition designed to be coeval with the birth of America itself, engendered created and simultaneous with the very air and word America, which at that one stroke, one instant, should cover the whole earth with one simultaneous suspiration like

1.

31. "Freedom American Style"
Page 1 of typescript (Catalogue No. 322-a)

32. The 1949 Nobel Prize for Literature, medal and scroll
(Catalogue No. 316-d)

33. Two views of the Faulkner exhibition in the
Princeton University Library

# PART TWO

*THE MANUSCRIPTS*

Introduction

## I. BOOKS

**A. PUBLISHED**

1. *Soldiers' Pay*, 1926
2. *Mosquitoes*, 1927
3. *Sartoris*, 1929
4. *The Sound and the Fury*, 1929
5. *As I Lay Dying*, 1930
6. *Sanctuary*, 1931
7. *Light in August*, 1932
8. *Pylon*, 1935
9. *Absalom, Absalom!* 1936
10. *The Unvanquished*, 1938
11. *The Wild Palms*, 1939
12. *The Hamlet*, 1940
13. *Go Down, Moses*, 1942
14. *Intruder in the Dust*, 1948
15. *Knight's Gambit*, 1949
16. *Requiem for a Nun*, 1951
17. *A Fable*, 1954
18. *Big Woods*, 1955
19. *The Town*, 1957

**B. UNPUBLISHED**

1. "Elmer"
2. "The Devil Beats His Wife" [?]

## II. SHORT STORIES

**A. PUBLISHED**

1. "Ad Astra"
2. "All the Dead Pilots"
3. "Artist at Home"
4. "Beyond"
5. "Black Music"
6. "The Brooch"
7. "Carcassonne"
8. "A Courtship" ["Crevasse" *see* "Victory"]
9. "Death Drag"
10. "Divorce in Naples"
11. "Doctor Martino"
12. "Dry September"
13. "Elly"
14. "Foxhunt"
15. "Idyll in the Desert"
16. "A Justice"
17. "Leg"
18. "Miss Zilphia Gant"
19. "Mistral"
20. "Mountain Victory"
21. "My Grandmother Millard"
22. "Pennsylvania Station"
23. "Red Leaves"
24. "A Rose for Emily"
25. "Shall Not Perish"
26. "Shingles for the Lord"
27. "That Evening Sun"
28. "The Tall Men"
29. "There Was a Queen"
30. "Thrift"
31. "Turnabout"
32. "Victory"

NOTE: The following published stories were incorporated by Faulkner into books, and are to be found with the manuscripts listed in section IA:

"Barn Burning" [*The Hamlet*]
"Delta Autumn" [*Go Down, Moses*]
"An Error in Chemistry" [*Knight's Gambit*]
"Fool about a Horse" [*The Hamlet*]
"Go Down, Moses" [*Go Down, Moses*]
"Gold Is Not Always" [*Go Down, Moses*]
"Hand upon the Waters" [*Knight's Gambit*]
"Monk" [*Knight's Gambit*]
"Mule in the Yard" [*The Town*]
"The Old People" [*Go Down, Moses*]
"Pantaloon in Black" [*Go Down, Moses*]
"Point of Law" [*Go Down, Moses*]
"Smoke" [*Knight's Gambit*]
"Tomorrow" [*Knight's Gambit*]

B. UNPUBLISHED

1. "Adolescence"
2. "The Big Shot"
3. "Love"
4. "Moonlight"
5. "Rose of Lebanon"
6. "Snow"
7. "The Wishing-Tree"
8. "With Caution and Dispatch"
9. [untitled]

NOTE: The following unpublished short stories were incorporated by Faulkner into published books, and are to be found with the manuscripts listed in section IA:

"An Absolution" [*Go Down, Moses*]
"The Fire on the Hearth" [*Go Down, Moses*]
"Knight's Gambit" [*Knight's Gambit*]
"An Odor of Verbena" [*The Unvanquished*]
"Was" [*Go Down, Moses*]

### III. VERSE

### IV. WRITING FOR MOVIES AND TELEVISION

### V. MISCELLANEOUS

# INTRODUCTION

COMPRISING more than 1500 pages of manuscript and 9700 pages of typescript, the papers which William Faulkner deposited in the Princeton University Library in March 1957 constitute by far the largest collection of Faulkner manuscript material yet known or made available for examination. Indeed, it appears highly unlikely that sufficient material now exists, outside institutional libraries, to make up half so large a collection.[1] It includes complete or nearly complete manuscript versions of five of the novels: *Sartoris, The Sound and the Fury, As I Lay Dying, Sanctu-*

[1] In June 1959 this collection was transferred to the Alderman Library of the University of Virginia, where it is now on deposit. The second largest such collection is that of the University of Texas Library. (See James B. Meriwether, *William Faulkner: An Exhibition of Manuscripts,* [Austin:] The Research Center of the University of Texas, 1959.) There are important manuscripts in several private collections, and in the New York Public Library and the libraries of Princeton and Yale universities. Up to the present time, little published use has been made of this material by literary scholars. Russell Roth, in "The Brennan Papers: Faulkner in Manuscript," *Perspective,* II (Summer 1949), pp. 219-224, presents some interesting information about Faulkner's working methods, and about drafts of two sections of *Go Down, Moses.* (Corroborative information about Faulkner's writing methods at an earlier period appears in an interview with Henry Nash Smith, in the *Dallas Morning News,* February 14, 1932, Section IV, p. 2.) Norman Holmes Pearson, in "Faulkner's Three 'Evening Suns,'" *The Yale University Library Gazette,* XXIX (October 1954), pp. 61-70, draws on manuscripts at Yale in presenting a model demonstration of the literary significance of manuscript material. But as yet we have had no full scale study of Faulkner's art, or even of any of the longer works, based upon manuscript evidence, though the depth and complexity of Faulkner's writing, as Professor Pearson shows in his article, can render such studies more than ordinarily fruitful.

In the absence or unavailability, for the purpose of such studies, of complete or nearly complete unpublished versions of Faulkner's works, it may be worthwhile to note here the scattered pages of manuscript which have been published as illustrations in various places. (An excellent example of the value of what can be done with such material is George P. Garrett, "Some Revisions in *As I Lay Dying,*" *Modern Language Notes,* LXXIII, pp. 414-417.) A page of the manuscript of *Pylon* was reproduced in the limited, signed issue of that novel in 1935. The first page of the manuscript of *Absalom, Absalom!* appears as an illustration in *The Book Collector,* IV (Winter 1955), facing p. 279, and the first page of the manuscript of *As I Lay Dying* appears in *The Paris Review,* IV (Spring 1956), pp. [32-33]. In the studies cited above, Professor Pearson reproduces a page from a manuscript of the story "That Evening Sun" and quotes from other pages, and Russell Roth quotes from typescript drafts of two sections of *Go Down, Moses.* The first page of the typescript setting copy of *The Mansion* appears as an illustration in the leaflet distributed at the Faulkner exhibition held at the University of Virginia (October 1959-January 1960). Reproductions of manuscripts, typescripts, and corrected galley proof appear in the Texas exhibition catalogue cited above, and in *The Princeton University Library Chronicle,* XVIII (Spring 1957), as well as in the present volume.

*ary*, and *Light in August*. There are substantially complete type-script versions, bound up by Faulkner himself, of *Soldiers' Pay*, *Mosquitoes*, *Sartoris*, *The Sound and the Fury*, *As I Lay Dying*, and *Sanctuary*, and there are unbound typescript versions of all the rest of his novels except *Light in August* (about a tenth missing), *The Unvanquished* (six of seven chapters missing), and *Go Down, Moses* (one chapter missing). There are manuscripts or typescripts, sometimes both, for more than thirty of Faulkner's published short stories, and eight unpublished. Verse, both published and unpublished, is similarly represented. The collection is rounded out by tearsheets from periodical printings of his short stories, and by proofsheets and other material relating to the printing of his books, particularly the later ones, including front matter, dead matter, layouts, and sample pages. (A certain number of letters and personal papers, while included in the collection which Faulkner had preserved and deposited at Princeton, are omitted from this handlist, since they pertain less to his literary career than to his private life.)

Though this collection is unusually rich in the possession of multiple versions of many pages and passages from several of the novels, and contains two or more versions of many of the novels and stories complete, it contains practically nothing that could be called a rough draft or a worksheet. Apparently Faulkner took pains to save only finished work.[2] The gaps in the manuscript holdings also invite speculation. Where is the manuscript of *Pylon*, for instance? Faulkner kept only one page. There is another at Texas, and in the University of Mississippi Library is p. 1, which he presented to a friend shortly after the novel was published. Will the rest of it turn up? What about the manuscript of *The Wild Palms*? Not enough of it is preserved among Faulkner's papers to answer the question of the extent to which the two plots were developed simultaneously. What about manuscript versions of *Soldiers' Pay* and *Mosquitoes*? There are no manuscript pages from either in the collection. Did Faulkner

[2] That Faulkner used extensive working notes on one occasion is proved by the reproduction in *Life*, XXXVII (August 9, 1954), pp. [77]-78, of the notes for *A Fable* he recorded on the wall of his study. At the Summer Seminar in American Literature at Nagano, in 1955, when questioned about his practice, Faulkner replied ". . . I have never kept notes. There have been times when I have made notes. . . . Then when I used those notes, I threw the notes away." (*Faulkner at Nagano*, ed. Robert A. Jelliffe, Tokyo: Kenkyusha, 1956, p. 102.) Two examples of worksheets in the exhibition, a note on a paraphrase of Eliot in *Requiem for a Nun* and a list of characters, and their ages, for *The Town*, were both preserved by his editor, not by Faulkner. (See items 223 and 293 of the Catalogue.)

begin them at the typewriter, as he seems to have done, as a rule, with his later books? From *Sartoris* to *The Hamlet* the collection affords ample manuscript evidence to support Henry Nash Smith's statement (in the interview cited above) that Faulkner habitually wrote first in ink, revising as he went along, and not using the typewriter until he was ready to prepare a final typescript for the publisher. He kept only a single typescript version of *Soldiers' Pay* and *Mosquitoes*; did he throw away earlier manuscript or typescript drafts?

Despite the immense interest which these papers have for the student of Faulkner's work, it should be said that they make no startling changes in the picture of Faulkner the writer which emerges from a close examination of his published writings. The great lesson which the collection as a whole provides is a better understanding of the quality of Faulkner's dedication to his craft. The writing of nearly every work represented in this collection, it is apparent, was characterized by the most rigid discipline, a discipline made equally evident at every stage in the writing, from revision involving the rearrangement of whole chapters in a novel to the almost endless process of minor stylistic polishing. But this lesson has already been taught, though not on so large a scale, by the publication of many of Faulkner's stories in several versions, which made obvious their author's concern with both major revision and minor polishing in the changes that took place between periodical and book publication.

The many changes that appear as the manuscript and typescript drafts in this collection are collated with the published texts seldom reveal radical shifts of emphasis and intention, but they often indicate substantial changes in the means Faulkner employed to work out those intentions. An example is the fourteen page typescript draft of the title story of *Go Down, Moses*. In the published book (p. 369) a character identifies himself to the census taker as Samuel Worsham Beauchamp; on the first page of the typescript, he appears as Henry Coldfield Sutpen. The decision not to involve *Go Down, Moses* so closely as this with the characters and meaning of *Absalom, Absalom!* is significant, and helps emphasize the difference in the treatment of the theme of miscegenation in the two works, though the earlier intention of connecting them more closely has its advantages too.

A more important change is evident in the process of writing *The Hamlet* which the manuscript reveals. At one time Faulkner planned to use as the opening chapter of the novel the episode which was published separately as the short story "Barn Burning." Though a shortened version of the episode is incorporated later on in the published book, it eliminates the significant figure of Colonel Sartoris Snopes. Structurally, we can guess that the decision to abandon "Barn Burning" and consequently to begin the book with what was originally planned as chapter two was made to tighten the novel, though "Barn Burning" as a prologue would be appropriate to the episodic structure of the book. However, the abandoning of Colonel Sartoris Snopes as a character represents an important change in the means that Faulkner chose to work out the themes of his novel, and a change that took place when much of the first part of the book had already been decided upon and written down in something not too far from its final form.

Nevertheless it would be a mistake, I believe, to assume too hastily from such an instance that the sort of changes in authorial tactics and strategy represented by what happened to "Barn Burning" reveal either radical shifts of intention, or the abandoning of a completed design for a book. Still less does it indicate, I think, that Faulkner was approaching the writing of the book without such a design, though Faulkner has often said, obviously with enjoyment, that sometimes he doesn't know what he plans to say when he sits down to write, or that he sometimes doesn't know how a book will end when he begins it. Plainly such a statement, like so many of the parables in which Faulkner delights to speak to a world that so often invades his privacy, has a germ of truth in it, but also a trap for the unwary. Obviously at some point in the conception of any book the author doesn't know how it will end. One is tempted to guess that Faulkner's imagination can hold a work's general design, or its basic elements, the characters and their relationships, firmly in control, allowing the author to leave to the inspiration of the actual writing much of the working out of these themes and the creation of the action that would reveal them.

The method followed in the description of these papers should be self-explanatory. Only in the case of titles have I made any change in quoting from them; there Faulkner's habit of putting titles in block capitals, perhaps underscored several times, did not seem to require more precise transcription for the purposes of this listing. In general, the descriptions are more elaborate for those items, generally manuscripts, which seemed to pose the greatest problems in identification, or in establishing the relationship of one version to another.

This handlist of the Faulkner papers by no means pretends to deal with them in final fashion. I have assumed that the first duty of such a handlist is to identify everything in the collection, and to describe it in sufficient detail to establish, where practicable, the relationship between the different versions of the same works which are included. On the whole, I feel that this goal has been achieved with reasonable success. But a more definitive account would certainly indicate in much greater detail the relationship between different versions of the same work, would identify more precisely the partial versions and brief passages which are merely listed here, and would concern itself with the difficult question of dates. Ink, watermarks, and changes in Faulkner's hand may supply clues toward solving these questions, and as other Faulkner manuscripts become available for study, many difficulties should be resolved. Another problem that needs to be examined more carefully than I have done is that of distinguishing precisely between ribbon copies, carbons, and typescripts produced by processes such as hectographing. But these appear to be tasks more properly belonging to a later time, or to extended studies of individual works or groups of works rather than of the whole collection.

## I. BOOKS

### A. PUBLISHED

1. *Soldiers' Pay* (1926)

    Bound typescript, 476 pp. Many manuscript corrections. There are 474 pages of text, numbered 1 through 473, the number 440 being given to two consecutive pages. The text is preceded by two unnumbered pages: a title page and a page with the epigraph. These pages of the text are not numbered: [38], [57], [59], [60], [131], [183], [239]. At least one page shows evidence of having been typed with a carbon. On p. 473 is this manuscript note: "New Orleans / May 1925".[3]

    There are many textual differences between this corrected typescript and the published book.

---

[3] For a reproduction of p. 151 of this typescript, see Fig. 5.

2. *Mosquitoes* (1927)

   Bound typescript, 464 pp. Many manuscript corrections. There are 461 pages of text, numbered 2 through 464, the numbers 93 and 313 being omitted though the text is complete. The first page of the text is preceded by three unnumbered pages: a title page; a page with the dedication "To Helen, Beautiful and Wise"; and a page with the epigraphic description of mosquitoes. On p. 464 is this manuscript note: "Pascagoula, Miss / 1 Sept 1926".[4]

   There are many textual differences between this corrected typescript and the published book.

3. *Sartoris* (1929)

   a. Manuscript, 237 pp. Despite gaps and duplications in the pagination, the text is continuous and appears to be complete. It is numbered as follows: 01 [the zero is crossed out], 02, 002, 003, 03, 04, 05, 1 through 30, 30 through 42 [the number 30 is given to two consecutive pages], 42a, 42b, 42c, 43 through 52, 52a, 52b, 52c, 52d, 52e, 53-131, 133, 132 through 163, 163a, 164 through 219. The title "Flags in the Dust" appears at the top of the first page.[5]

   This manuscript precedes the typescript described below, and there are many differences between the two versions.

   b. Bound carbon typescript, 594 pp. Many manuscript corrections, including a few in a hand not Faulkner's. Despite gaps and duplications in the pagination, this typescript is complete. There are 592 pages of text, preceded by an unnumbered title page; the final page of the text is also unnumbered, and one page (the first p. 513) should have been omitted when the typescript was bound, as it is an earlier version of parts of two pages (the first p. 512 and the second p. 490) of the complete typescript. The text is numbered as follows: 1 through 31, 31a, 32 through 105, 107 through 201, 212 through 265 [the number 221 is given to two pages], 270 through 280, 282 through 513 [p. 513 is superseded by pp. 512 and 490, the pages which precede and follow it], 490 through 582, final page un-

   ---

   [4] For a reproduction of p. 336 of this typescript, see Fig. 6, and for a note on this page, see Catalogue item 20.
   [5] For a reproduction of the first page of this manuscript, see Fig. 9, and for a note on this page, see Catalogue item 29.

numbered. The title *Flags in the Dust* appears on the title page, and on p. 7. On the last page of the text is this manuscript note: "Oxford, Miss / 29 September 1927".[6]

This corrected typescript is approximately a fourth longer than the published novel *Sartoris,* and there are many differences between the text of the book and the corresponding portions of the typescript.

4. *The Sound and the Fury* (1929)
   a. Manuscript, 148 pp. One page (p. 5) is missing; this version is otherwise complete, despite a gap in the pagination. The pages are numbered as follows: 1, 1a, 2, 2b, 3, 4, 6 through 15, 17 through 148. The first two pages appear to have been recently copied by Faulkner, presumably from the original first page, which is missing.[7]

      This manuscript precedes the typescript described below, and there are many differences between the two versions.
   b. Bound carbon typescript, 409 pp. Many manuscript corrections. Despite gaps and duplications in the pagination, the text is continuous and complete. The text, preceded by an unnumbered title page, is numbered as follows: 1 through 15, 15a, 15b, 15c, 15d, 17 through 57, 57a, 58 through 61, 61a, 62 through 65, 65a, 66, 67, 67a, 68 through 91, 91a, 91b, 92 through 95, 95a, 96 through 101, 101a, 102 through 116, 116a, 117 through 133, 133a, 134 through 157, 157a, 158 through 201 [the number 178 is given to two pages], 201a, 202 through 337, 339, 337, 340, 341 through 392. On p. 392 is this manuscript note: "New York, N.Y. / October 1928".

      There are many textual differences between this carbon typescript and the published book.

5. *As I Lay Dying* (1930)
   a. Manuscript, 107 pp. The pagination is continuous from 1 through 107. Some pages consist of partial leaves pasted together, or of whole sheets with inserts pasted on them. At the top of p. 1 is this note: "25 October 1929"; at the

---

[6] For a reproduction of p. 398 of this typescript, see Fig. 8.

[7] For reproductions of pp. 34 and 70 of this manuscript, see Figs. 10 and 11; for a reproduction of p. 148, see *The Princeton University Library Chronicle,* XVIII (Spring 1957), Plate III.

bottom of p. 107, "Oxford, Miss. / 11 December, 1929".[8]

This manuscript precedes the carbon typescript described below, and there are many differences between the two versions.

b. Bound carbon typescript, 266 pp. An unnumbered title page precedes the text, which is numbered 1 through 265. On p. 265 is this manuscript note: "Oxford, Missippi [*sic*] / January 12, 1930".

There are many textual differences between this carbon typescript and the published book.

6. *Sanctuary* (1931)
   a. Manuscript, 138 pp. Despite a gap in the numbering, the text is complete. The pages are numbered as follows: 1 through 8, 8a, 9 through 33, 33a, 34 through 69, 71 through 137.[9] Some pages consist of partial leaves pasted together, or of whole sheets with inserts pasted on them. On the front cover of the manila folder enclosing the manuscript is this note in Faulkner's hand: "Sanctuary. / January, 1929 —— May, 1929".

   This manuscript precedes the carbon typescript described below, and there are many differences between the two versions.

   b. Bound carbon typescript, 359 pp. A few manuscript corrections. An unnumbered title page precedes the text, which is numbered 1 through 358. On the title page is the following manuscript note: "Oxford, Miss. / January— May, 1929". On p. 358 is the following manuscript note: "Oxford, Miss. / 25 May, 1929".

   There are many differences between this carbon typescript and the galleys of the unpublished first version of *Sanctuary*, which was itself extensively rewritten before publication.

7. *Light in August* (1932)
   a. Manuscript, 188 pp. The text is continuous and complete, despite a duplication in the numbering. There is an un-

---

[8] For a reproduction of p. 107 of this manuscript, see *The Princeton University Library Chronicle*, XVIII (Spring 1957), Plate V; for a reproduction of p. 1, see *The Paris Review*, IV (Spring 1956), pp. [32-33].

[9] For a reproduction of p. 1 of this manuscript, see *The Princeton University Library Chronicle*, XVIII (Spring 1957), Plate IV; for a reproduction of p. 131, see Fig. 12; for a note on these two pages, see Catalogue item 57.

numbered title page, with the title "Dark House" crossed out and "Light in August" written above it; below it is written "Oxford, Mississippi / 17 August, 1931". The pages of the text are numbered as follows: 2, 3, 3 through 187. At the bottom of the final page is "Oxford, Miss. / 19 Feb. 1932".

This manuscript precedes the typescript described below, and there are many differences between the text of the two versions.

b. Typescript setting copy, 468 pp. Some manuscript corrections. The text is incomplete, the last page (p. 470) ending with the words "so humorless, that" which appear in the first paragraph of p. 428 of the published book, and p. 469 being missing. The text is preceded by a title page bearing the pencilled number 1, apparently not in Faulkner's hand; the text is numbered as follows: 2 through 121, 122 and 123 [one page, marked with both numbers], 124 through 468, 470 [a page missing between 468 and 470].

8. *Pylon* (1935)
   a. Manuscript, 1 page. This page is unnumbered, but represents an early version of passages which appear on pp. 9, 10, and 27 of the published book.[10]
   b. Typescript setting copy, 344 pages. The text, numbered 1 through 344, is complete, though some numbers, and a few words of the text, have been lost through damage to edges and corners of the pages.

9. *Absalom, Absalom!* (1936)
   a. Manuscript, 2 pp. These two unnumbered pages are a version of the Chronology which appears on pp. 380-381 of the published book.
   b. Typescript, 17 pages. Manuscript corrections and annotations by Faulkner and his editor. The following are the page numbers: 1, 2, 3, 8, 9, 10, 11, 14, 15, 20, 21, 22, 23, 24, 25, 31, 32. These pages, all from a version of the first chapter of the book, are consecutive where the pagination is, and show breaks where the pagination does.[11]

10 For a reproduction of this page of the manuscript, see Fig. 13.
11 For reproductions of pp. 9 and 13 of this typescript, see Fig. 14.

This version of these portions of the first chapter precedes the final version represented by the corrected typescript setting copy described below, and there are a number of minor differences between them.

c. Typescript setting copy, 463 pp. Many manuscript corrections. The text is complete, and has been consecutively repaginated by machine, 1 through 463. The original numbering is from 1 through 464, with pages 32 and 344 omitted, and 12a inserted between 11 and 12.

d. Limited edition certificate of issue statements, 35 leaves. These are extra or discarded leaves, intended to be signed and numbered by the author and tipped into the limited issue of the novel. Ten are signed or inscribed, one is numbered but not signed.

10. *The Unvanquished* (1938)
a. Manuscript, 23 pp. This is a complete version of the final chapter of the book, "An Odor of Verbena." The pages are numbered 1 through 23.

This version precedes the typescript described below, and there are many differences between them.

b. Typescript, 54 pp. Manuscript corrections. This is a complete version of the final chapter, "An Odor of Verbena." The pages are numbered as follows: 1 through 10, 10a, 10b, 10c, 11, 12, 13, 13a, 14 through 50.

There are slight differences between this typescript and the text of the published book.

11. *The Wild Palms* (1939)
a. Manuscript of "Wild Palms," 3 pp. These three unnumbered pages are versions of passages that occur in two chapters of this section of the book, its main plot. Two of them are the last two pages of a version of the first chapter of the novel (corresponding to pp. 20-22 of the published book). The third is a version of the ending of the penultimate chapter of "Wild Palms" (corresponding to pp. 227-228 of the published book).

There are many differences between the text of these three pages and the corresponding passages in the published book.

b. Manuscript of "Old Man," 16 pp. These pages are from

68

versions of passages that occur in two chapters of this section of the book, its subplot, and are numbered as follows: 92, 96, 96, 96, 97, 97, 101, 101, 102, 103, 103, 104, 142, 143, 143, 144. The first eleven of these pages represent several versions of passages that occur in the third chapter of "Old Man" (pp. 143-177 of the published book). The final four pages represent versions of the first part of this section's penultimate chapter (pp. 229-236 of the published book).

There are many differences between the text of these pages and the corresponding passages in the published book.

c. Typescript setting copy, 384 pp., plus 5 pp. front matter. Many manuscript corrections. The text is complete, and comprises 383 pages, numbered from 1 through 377, with the following six additional pages inserted: 22a, 71a, 89a, 355a, 358a, 362a. There is an unnumbered title page bearing the cancelled title "If I Forget Thee, Jerusalem," typed in block capitals, with the published title pencilled in.[12] The entire setting copy has been repaginated by machine, numbered from 1 through 389, with the five pages of front matter following the last page of the text.

12. *The Hamlet* (1940)

   a. "Abraham's Children," typescript, 3 pp. These pages (numbered 18, 19, and 29) are from early versions of the episode of the Texas ponies which occurs in Book Four, Chapter One, of *The Hamlet*. P. 29 appears to be an earlier version of the material on p. 19, which is continuous with p. 18.[13]

   b. "Fool about a Horse"

      (1) Manuscript, 10 pp. This is a complete version, the pages numbered from 1 through 10, of the short story which was incorporated into Chapter Two, part two, of Book One of *The Hamlet*.[14]

      (2) Typescript, 21 pp. Manuscript corrections. This is

---

[12] For a note on this cancelled title, see Catalogue item 151.

[13] See item 259 of the Catalogue for a more detailed discussion of the relationship of "Abraham's Children" to "Spotted Horses" and *The Hamlet*. See Fig. 19 for a reproduction of p. 18 of the typescript of "Abraham's Children," and item 261 of the Catalogue for a note on it.

[14] See Fig. 21 for a reproduction of p. 1 of this manuscript.

a later but incomplete version of the above manuscript, the pages numbered 2 through 19, 23, 28, 29.[15]

(3) Carbon typescript, 33 pp. Manuscript corrections. This is a carbon of the above typescript, but complete, and with more, and different, manuscript corrections. The pages are numbered 1 through 33.[16]

c. "Barn Burning"

(1) Manuscript, 17 pp. This complete version of the published short story bears on its first page the book and chapter headings that indicate its original position as the opening chapter of the novel. The pages are numbered 1 through 17.[17]

(2) Typescript, 32 pp. This typescript version, the pages numbered from 1 through 32, follows the manuscript above. There are minor differences between it and the published short story text in *Harper's*, CLXXIX (June 1939).

(3) Carbon typescript, 32 pp. A carbon of the above typescript.

d. Manuscript, 210 pp. This is a practically complete version of the first six and two-thirds chapters of the published novel. Despite gaps and duplications in the pagination and differences in the chapter numbers and book titles, the text is continuous, with one minor exception. Chapter one, 18 pages, numbered 1 through 18. Chapter two, 20 pages, numbered 19 through 22, 22a, 22b, 23 through 36. Chapter three, 33 pages, numbered 37 through 40, 40, 41, 41, 42, 43, 44, 44a, 44b, 45 through 55, 55 [the a of 55a is cancelled], 56 through 63, 63a. Chapter four [Book Two, Chapter One of the published novel], 28 pages, numbered 35 [this page bears two numbers, 35 and 64, both of them cancelled] through 58, 87 through 90 [pages 58 and 87 are not exactly continuous, but are nearly so; p. 58 also bears the cancelled number 87, and p. 87 also bears the cancelled number 86]. Chapter five [Book Two, Chapter Two of the published novel], 25 pages, numbered 90a, 90b, 90c, 90d, 91, 91a, 92 through 104, 104a, 104b, 104a, 104b, 104c, 104d.

15 See Fig. 20 for a reproduction of p. 23 of this typescript, and item 273 of the Catalogue for a note on p. 8.
16 See items 269 and 272 of the Catalogue for notes on this carbon typescript.
17 See Fig. 15 for a reproduction of p. 1 of this manuscript.

The following chapter should be number six, by this system. Instead, its first page is marked Book Three, Chapter One, with the cancelled title "The Peasants," and cancelled headings for Book Two, Chapter Seven, and Chapter Five. Corresponding to the first part of the first chapter of Book Three of the published novel, it has 46 pages, numbered 105 through 114, 114a, 115 through 120, 120a, 120b, 121 through 131, 131a, 132 through 146. The following chapter, marked Chapter Two, has 40 pages, numbered 147 through 167, 168 [this page is numbered 168-169, and the text is continuous with pp. 167 and 170], 170 through 187. This chapter completes the text of the manuscript through the first section of Book Three, Chapter Two of the published novel.[18]

e. Manuscript, 87 pp. These are miscellaneous pages, many of them continuous, from what appear to be a number of versions of material from the above manuscript. Most of the pages, if not all of them, appear to precede those pages of the above manuscript which include the same material. They are numbered as follows: 21, 21a, 35, 36, 41, 52, 62, 63, 64, 65, 66, 67, 112, 113, 113, 113, 113, 113, 114, 114, 114, 114, 115, 115, 116, 116, 117, 117, 118, 118, 119, 119, 120, 122, 123, 124, 124, 124, 125, 125, 125, 125, 125, 126, 126, 127, 127, 128, 128, 129, 129, 130, 130, 130, 131, 131, 131, 131, 131, 131, 131, 132, 132, 132, 133, 134, 134, 135, 136, 140, 148, 148, 148, 148, 148, 149, 149, 149, 149, 149, 150, 150, 151, 159, 161, 163, 164.

f. Typescript, 18 pp. These are versions of five passages in the published novel. The first is from the first chapter of Book Three, and occurs in two versions, each consisting of two consecutive pages numbered 316 and 317. The first of these bears at the top of both pages the job number 44283, stamped by machine. The second pair bears the same job number, and also the setting copy numbers 330 and 331. Both pairs have been cancelled, the first in red pencil, the second in black, and appear to have been part of the complete typescript copy described below, the first pair representing the original version, the

18 See items 162 and 280 of the Catalogue for notes on pp. 58 and 31 of this manuscript. For a reproduction of p. 1, see *The Princeton University Library Chronicle*, XVIII (Spring 1957), Plate VI.

second a revision which was itself replaced by the final version in the setting copy.[19]

The second passage is the beginning of the second part of the second chapter of Book Three of the published novel, and is represented by a single page, unnumbered but with the numeral 2 of the chapter section heading at the top.

The third passage, from the second part of Book One, Chapter Two of the published novel, consists of four consecutive pages, with a carbon of the fourth. The first three pages are all numbered 40; the fourth page and its carbon are unnumbered.

The fourth passage, from the second section of Book Three, Chapter One of the published novel, consists of six pages, the text consecutive despite the gaps in numbering: 266, 268, 269, 270, 272, 274.

The fifth passage is in the first section of Chapter One of Book Four of the published novel, and is represented by two pages, each a version of p. 487 in the final setting copy. The first, the earlier of the two versions, bears the job number 44283, stamped by machine. This page has been cancelled in red pencil. The second version, cancelled in black pencil, bears the same job number, and the setting copy page number 508, stamped by machine. (The third and final version of this page, in the setting copy described below, bears the same page and job numbers, 508 44283.)

g. Typescript setting copy, 604 pp., plus 8 pp. front matter. Many manuscript corrections. Despite gaps and repetitions in the pagination, the text is continuous, and complete. The pages have been renumbered by machine; the original numbering is as follows: 1 through 9, 9a, 10 through 146, [inserted fly-title for "Eula" section, unnumbered,] 147 through 214, 214a, 215 through 248, [inserted fly-title for "The Long Summer" section, unnumbered,] 249 through 267, 267a, 268 through 338, 338a, 339 through 362, 362a, 363 through 371, 371a, 372 through 374, 374a, 375, 376, 376a, 377 through 379, 379a, 379b, 380 through 414, 415 [numbered 415 and 416], 417 through 426, [inserted fly-title for "The Peasants" section, unnumbered,] 427 through 504, 504a, 505 through 536,

19 For a note on the first version, see Catalogue item 163.

535, 536 [despite the repetition, the text is continuous], 537 through 574, 576 [the text is continuous from 574 to 576], 577 through 582.[20]

13. *Go Down, Moses* (1942)
   a. "Was," typescript, 22 pp. Manuscript corrections. This is a complete, unpublished short story version of the opening chapter of the book. The pages numbered 1 through 21, with p. 3a inserted, it differs in many ways from the published version.[21]
   b. "The Fire and the Hearth"
      (1) "A Point of Law," typescript, 21 pp. Manuscript corrections. This is a complete version, the pages numbered from 1 through 21, of the story which was revised to become the first chapter of "The Fire and the Hearth" in the book. The text of this typescript differs slightly from the short story publication in *Collier's*, CV (June 22, 1941).
      (2) "Gold Is Not Always"
         (a) Typescript, 5 pp. These are unnumbered pages of a version, or versions, preceding the complete typescript described below.
         (b) Typescript, 19 pp. Manuscript corrections. This is a complete version, the pages numbered from 1 through 18 with the final page unnumbered, of the short story which was revised to become the second chapter of "The Fire and the Hearth" in the book. The text differs slightly from that published in *Atlantic*, CLXVI (November 1940).
      (3) "An Absolution" [typescript title]; also entitled "Apotheosis" [in pencil; probably in Faulkner's hand], typescript, 17 pp. Manuscript corrections. This is an earlier version of the typescript described below, "The Fire on the Hearth." It is incomplete, the pages numbered from 1 through 17, with the ending missing. Judging from the ending of "The Fire on the Hearth," only about nine typescript lines are missing.[22]

[20] For a note on a carbon of this typescript, see Catalogue item 158.
[21] For a reproduction of p. 1 of this typescript, see Fig. 16; for a note on it, see Catalogue item 170.
[22] For a reproduction of p. 1 of this typescript, see Fig. 17.

(4) "The Fire on the Hearth"

    (a) Typescript, 20 pp. Manuscript corrections. This is a complete version, the pages numbered from 1 through 20, of an unpublished short story which was revised to become the third chapter of "The Fire and the Hearth" in *Go Down, Moses*. It follows the typescript "An Absolution" described above.

    (b) Typescript, 26 pp. These are miscellaneous pages, some unnumbered, from several versions, none of them complete, of parts of the unpublished typescript "The Fire on the Hearth" described above. All of the pages appear to follow the corresponding pages of that typescript. A p. 29 of this group bears the title "The Fire and the Hearth," and on its verso appears the cancelled title "WAS / 1859".

c. "Pantaloon in Black," carbon typescript, 24 pp. Manuscript corrections. This is a complete version of the story, the pages numbered from 1 through 24. Its text differs slightly from that published in *Harper's*, CLXXXI (October 1940).

d. "The Old People," typescript, 17 pp. Manuscript corrections. This is a complete version, the pages numbered from 1 through 17, of the story. Its text differs from that published in *Harper's*, CLXXXI (September 1940).

e. "The Bear," carbon typescript, 1 p. The text of this page, which is numbered 237, appears to have been revised and replaced by the p. 237 of the final typescript setting copy described below.

f. "Delta Autumn," typescript, 18 pp. Manuscript corrections. This is a complete version of the story, the pages numbered from 1 through 17, with p. 4a inserted. The text differs slightly from that published in *Story*, XX (May-June 1942).

g. "Go Down, Moses"

    (1) Typescript, 14 pp. Manuscript corrections. This is a complete version of the story, the pages numbered from 1 through 14.

    (2) Typescript, 1 p. This is the beginning of a version of the story. Numbered p. 1, it appears to follow the version described above.

(3) Carbon typescript, 17 pp. This is a complete version of the story, the pages numbered from 1 through 17. The text appears to follow that of the complete version and the single page described above, but it differs slightly from that published in *Collier's*, CVII (January 25, 1941).

h. Genealogy of McCaslin family, manuscript, 1 p. This pencil chart presents a somewhat different version of the McCaslin family from that which appears in the published book.[23]

i. Typescript setting copy, 411 pp., plus 3 pp. front matter. Manuscript corrections. This is the complete text of the setting copy. The pages have been renumbered by machine; the original numbering is as follows: 1 through 4, 4a, 5 through 27, 27a, 28, 28a [inserted fly-title for "The Fire and the Hearth"], 29 through 54, 54a, 54b, 54c, 54d, 55 through 71, 71a, 72 through 82, 82a, 83 through 94, 94a, 95 through 131, 131a [inserted fly-title for "Pantaloon in Black"], 132 through 158, 158a [inserted fly-title for "The Old People"], 159 through 185, 185a [inserted fly-title for "The Bear"], 186 through 206, 206b [typed as "206bis"], 207 through 247, 247a, 247b, 247c, 247d, 247e, 247f [typed as "247F. 248, 249"; it is followed without a break in the text by p. 250], 250 through 253, 253b [*sic*], 254 through 298, 298a, 299 through 337, 337a [inserted fly-title for "Delta Autumn"], 338 through 370, 370a [inserted fly-title for "Go Down, Moses"], 371 through 389.[24]

j. Galley proof, 1 sheet. This is an uncorrected galley of the beginning of the book, the fly-title of "Was" and the first page of its text. It is dated January 5.

14. *Intruder in the Dust* (1948)

a. Manuscript, 8 pp. One of these is a version of the beginning of the novel. The other seven are of miscellaneous passages of dialogue between characters of the book, as if in dramatic form.

b. Typescript, 284 pp. Many manuscript corrections. These

[23] This chart is printed under Catalogue item 177.

[24] See Catalogue item 173 for a note on a cancelled title on p. 186 of this typescript setting copy, and quotation from p. 253 of Faulkner's instructions for the printing of the fourth section of "The Bear."

are pages, including carbons, of several different versions, none of them complete.

   c.   Typescript setting copy, 317 pp., plus 8 pp. front matter. Many manuscript corrections. The text is complete, and is numbered from 1 through 281, with the following thirty-six insertions: 15a, 16a, 18a, 21a, 21b, 28a, 29a, 39a, 87a, 93a, 136a, 143a, 178a, 179a, 220a, 224a, 234a, 234b, 234c, 234d, 238a, 243a, 243b, 243c, 244a, 247a, 257a, 257b, 257c, 259a, 264a, 266a, 266b, 269a, 270a, 276a. [P. 218, between pp. 217 and 220, is numbered 218-219.][25]

15. *Knight's Gambit* (1949)
   a.   "Smoke"
       (1)  Manuscript, 12 pp. The text is complete, numbered 1 through 12, and differs from the published version.
       (2)  Tear sheets from *Harper's Magazine*, CLXIV (April 1932), 9 leaves. This is the complete text, pp. [562]-578.
   b.   "Monk." See below under g., setting copy.
   c.   "Hand upon the Waters"
       (1)  Typescript, 2 pp. One page is unnumbered, the other bears the pencilled number 100 at the top, though this may not be a page number. The two pages are not continuous, and though both are versions of passages in the two typescript versions below, it is difficult to establish their precise relationship to these versions.
       (2)  Typescript, 30 pp. Manuscript corrections. This is a complete version of the story, the pages numbered from 1 through 30.
       (3)  Typescript, 30 pp. Manuscript corrections. This is a later version than the typescript listed under (2) above, but still differs from the published version. It lacks three pages of being complete. The pages are numbered from 1 through 33, with 25, 26, and 28 missing.
   d.   "Tomorrow," typescript, 20 pp. Manuscript corrections. This is a complete version of the story, the pages numbered 1 through 20. It differs slightly from the printed version, and is untitled.

[25] For a reproduction of p. 65 of this typescript, see *The Princeton University Library Chronicle*, XVIII (Spring 1957), Plate VII.

e. "An Error in Chemistry," typescript, 22 pp. Manuscript corrections. This carbon typescript differs from the published version. It is complete, the pages numbered from 1 through 22.

f. "Knight's Gambit"

(1) Typescript, 23 pp. Manuscript corrections. This complete short story is an early version of the 33,000 title story of the book. The pages are numbered 1 through 22, with 6a inserted.[26]

(2) Typescript, 50 pp. Manuscript corrections. These are miscellaneous pages, some of them carbons, from several versions, none of them complete. It is difficult to establish their precise relationship to the early short story version and the longer published version, though most of them appear to be drafts of the longer one made in revising the short story.

g. Setting copy: typescript, 162 pp.; tearsheet leaves, 42. This is the complete setting copy, comprising a typescript version of the previously unpublished title story and tearsheets (save for one page) for the other five stories from their previous published appearances:

(1) "Smoke," typescript, 1 p.; tearsheets, 19 leaves. The tearsheets are pp. 121-158 from *Doctor Martino and Other Stories* (New York, 1934). The typescript page is copied without change from the first page of the story in *Doctor Martino* (p. 120), and is continuous with pp. 121-158, comprising the complete story.

(2) "Monk," tearsheets, 5 leaves. These are pp. 16-24 of *Scribner's Magazine*, CI (May 1937).

(3) "Hand upon the Waters," tearsheets, 4 leaves. These are pp. 14, 15, 75, 76, 78, 79 of *The Saturday Evening Post*, CCXII (November 4, 1939).

(4) "Tomorrow," tearsheets, 6 leaves. These are pp. 22, 23, 32, 35, 37, 38, 39 of *The Saturday Evening Post*, CCXIII (November 23, 1940).

(5) "An Error in Chemistry," tearsheets, 8 leaves. These are pp. 5-19 of *Ellery Queen's Mystery Magazine*, VII (June 1946).

(6) "Knight's Gambit," typescript, 161 pp. Manuscript corrections. The pages are numbered from 1 through

[26] For a note on p. 22 of this typescript, see Catalogue item 202.

148, with the following 13 inserted pages: 14a, 15a, 30a, 44a, 44b, 44c, 44d, 44e, 44f, 44g, 70a, 85a, 123a.

h. Dead matter, samples, and layout for the printed book, 28 sheets.

i. Half-title leaf proofs or samples, 29 leaves.

16. *Requiem for a Nun* (1951)

a. Manuscript, 38 pp. These are miscellaneous passages from several versions. Since they do not all seem to precede the various typescript versions where they include the same material, it appears reasonable to assume that they do not represent an early, complete holograph which preceded the first typescript version, but only miscellaneous and fragmentary work done on portions of the book, perhaps when no typewriter was available. Both sides of some pages were used.

b. Typescript, 303 pp. Manuscript corrections. These are miscellaneous pages from several versions, some of them carbons.

c. Typescript setting copy, 285 pp., plus 6 pp. front matter. Manuscript corrections. The beginning of the typescript is missing (one or two pages); it is otherwise complete, despite gaps in the original pagination. It is numbered from 1 through 282, with the following extra pages inserted: 13a, 38a, 44a, 46a, 53a, 54a, 145a, 211a, 238a, 258a. Though no gap in the text results, the following page numbers are not used: 96-98, 124, 125. The entire text has been re-paginated by machine, including the front matter.

d. Bound galley proof, 93 sheets. This is a complete set of the uncorrected galleys, each sheet cut in half and the whole bound up in wrappers.

e. Galley proof, corrected, 94 sheets. Many manuscript corrections and attached sheets with typescript additions and corrections. This is a complete set of the galleys, numbered from 1 through 93, with an extra copy of 93. (One copy of 93 is corrected, the other not.)[27]

f. Front matter, typescript, 6 pp.

g. Letter from Lemuel Ayres with notes on stage adaptation, typescript, 6 pp. The letter, dated July 11, 1951, is addressed to Faulkner, and the 5 pp. of notes apparently

[27] For a reproduction of galley 93, corrected, see Fig. 22.

concern Ayres' suggestions for changes which would benefit a stage production.

17. *A Fable* (1954)
   a. Manuscript, 10 pp. These are miscellaneous, fragmentary versions of various passages.
   b. Typescript, 179 pp. Manuscript corrections. These are typescript and carbon pages from several versions.
   c. Typescript setting copy, 691 pp., plus 6 pp. front matter. Manuscript corrections. The text appears to be complete, and the pages are numbered from 1 to 653, with twenty-eight extra pages inserted.

18. *Big Woods* (1955)
   a. Setting copy: typescript, 34 pp.; tearsheet leaves, 95; galley sheets, 8; plus 17 pp. front matter and instructions. This is the complete setting copy, comprising tearsheets or galleys of the four stories included, with typescripts for the five brief pieces in italics which begin and end the book and link the stories. In a folder with a page of typescript instructions pasted onto the inside front cover.
      (1) Prelude, typescript, 3 pp. (Taken from pp. 101-105 of *Requiem for a Nun*).
      (2) "The Bear," tearsheets, 72 leaves. This is the complete text of the story, pp. 191-331 of *Go Down, Moses*, with the fly-title which precedes it. The fourth section of the story, omitted from the printing in *Big Woods*, is cancelled (pp. 254-315).
      (3) Interlude, typescript, 9 pp. (Revised from sections of the story, "Red Leaves.")
      (4) "The Old People," tearsheets, 14 leaves. This is the complete text of the story, pp. 163-187 of *Go Down, Moses*, with the fly-title which precedes it.
      (5) Interlude, typescript, 4 pp. (Revised from sections of the story, "A Justice.")
      (6) "A Bear Hunt," tearsheets, 9 leaves. Manuscript and typescript revisions. The text is pp. 63-79 of *Collected Stories*. Two typescript sheets with inserts are attached by staples.
      (7) Interlude, typescript, 6 pp. (Revised from sections of the article, "Mississippi.")

(8) "Race at Morning," galley proof, 8 sheets. These are galley proofs from the printing of the story in *The Saturday Evening Post*, CCXXVII (March 5, 1955).

(9) Epilogue, typescript, 12 pp. (Revised from the story, "Delta Autumn," *Go Down, Moses.*)

(10) Front matter, layout, and instructions, 17 pp.

b. Page proof, 72 sheets. This is the complete page proof, uncorrected.

c. Foundry proof, 214 pp., including illustrations. This is the complete foundry proof.

19. *The Town* (1957)

a. "Mule in the Yard," manuscript, 10 pp. This is a complete version, the pages numbered 1 through 10, of the short story which was incorporated into Chapter Sixteen of the novel.[28]

b. "Mule in the Yard," typescript, 10 pp. Manuscript corrections. This is a later but incomplete version of the above manuscript. The pages are numbered 1 through 4, 7 through 12 (unfinished).

c. Typescript setting copy, 488 pp., plus 10 pp. front matter. Manuscript corrections. The text is complete, and the pagination continuous, 1 through 477, with [478] unnumbered.

d. Galley proof, 119 sheets. This complete set of the galleys bears the corrections of the editor and a few replies by the author to editorial questions.[29]

e. Page proof, 123 sheets. This complete set of the page proofs was corrected by the editor but not the author.

f. Foundry proof, 361 pp. Though this set of the foundry proofs (sometimes called plate proofs) includes all the front matter of the book, the following fifteen pages are missing from the text: 151, 253, 263, 272, 278, 319, 323, 340, 342, 344, 348, 353, 357, 367, 370.

g. Specifications print sample, 4 pp. This sample consists of two conjugate leaves, for pp. 3, 4, and 5, with the specifications (dated October 30, 1956) on the verso of p. 5.

[28] For a reproduction of p. 1 of this manuscript, see Fig. 23.
[29] Two of these galleys appear as illustrations in the *Princeton University Library Chronicle*, XVIII (Spring 1957), Plate VIII.

1. "Elmer"
   a. Manuscript, 4 pp. Two are unnumbered, two represent beginnings of the novel and are both numbered 1.
   b. Typescript, 130 pp. Passages from several versions are included in the total. The pages are numbered as follows: 1-2, 1-33, 44-51, nineteen unnumbered pages, 66-94, 73-106, and five unnumbered.[30]

      Four titles are given to the various versions of the beginning of this unfinished novel: "Elmer," "Elmer and Myrtle," "Portrait of Elmer Hodge," and "Growing Pains." According to Faulkner (interview March 12, 1958), he wrote it in Paris on his trip abroad after being in New Orleans [1925], but left it unfinished—it was "funny, but not funny enough."

2. "The Devil Beats His Wife" manuscript, 3 pp. All unnumbered, but consecutive, these pages comprise a beginning to a novel or story. According to Faulkner (interview March 12, 1958), he began it in the 1920's after his return from abroad [1925], but soon abandoned it. The title was picked up by his friend Ben Wasson, who used it for a novel (New York, Harcourt, Brace, 1929).

## II. SHORT STORIES

### A. PUBLISHED

1. "Ad Astra" manuscript, 11 pp. (1-6, 6a, 7-10). [Differs from version first published in *American Caravan IV*, 1931.]

2. "All the Dead Pilots" manuscript, 10 pp. (1-10). [Differs from version published in *These 13*, 1931.]

3. "An Artist at Home" manuscript, 13 pp. (1-13). [Differs from version published, entitled "Artist at Home," in *Story*, III (Aug. 1933).]

4. "Beyond"
   a. Typescript, entitled "Beyond the Gate," 27 pp. (1-27).
   b. Manuscript, 9 pp. (1-9). [Though it differs somewhat from the version published in *Harper's*, CLXVII (Sept. 1933), this manuscript is later than the above typescript.]

[30] For a reproduction of p. 1 of this typescript, see **Fig. 7**.

5. "Black Music" manuscript, 11 pp. (1-11). [Differs from the version published in *Doctor Martino*, 1934.]

6. "The Brooch"
   a. Manuscript, 5 pp. (1-5).
   b. Carbon typescript, 15 pp. (1-15). [A manuscript note, in Faulkner's hand, on the verso of p. 7 is dated "Jan 1, 1931". This typescript appears to follow the above manuscript version and to precede the bound carbon typescript below.]
   c. Bound carbon typescript, 29 pp. (1-29). In blue folder. [Differs slightly from version published in *Scribner's*, XCIX (Jan. 1936).]

7. "Carcassonne"
   a. Typescript, 7 pp. (1-7). Manuscript corrections.
   b. Typescript, 7 pp. (1-7). [Follows the above typescript, but differs slightly from version published in *These 13*, 1931.]

8. "A Courtship" carbon typescript, 22 pp. (1-22). Manuscript corrections. [Published in *Sewanee Review*, LVI (Autumn 1948). On the verso of several pages are typescript pages from a version of the story "Shall Not Perish."]

["Crevasse" *see* "Victory"]

9. "Death Drag"
   a. Manuscript, 11 pp. (1-11).
   b. Carbon typescript, entitled "A Death-Drag," 27 pp. (1-27). [Follows the above manuscript, but differs slightly from published version below.]
   c. Tearsheets, 5 leaves. (Pp. 34-42 from *Scribner's*, XCI [Jan. 1932].)

10. "Divorce in Naples"
    a. Manuscript, 6 pp. (unnumbered, but complete). First page bears cancelled title "Equinox."
    b. Carbon typescript, 17 pp. (1-17). First page bears manuscript note "Unpublished" in Faulkner's hand. [Follows the above manuscript, but differs from version published in *These 13*, 1931.]

11. "Doctor Martino"
    a. Manuscript, 14 pp. (1-14).
    b. Manuscript, 10 pp. (1, 2, 3, 2, 3, 5, 6, 7, and two unnumbered). [Apparently follows above manuscript.]

c. Typescript, 5 pp. (27-31). [Apparently follows above manuscript, but differs from version published in *Harper's*, CLXIII (Nov. 1931).]

12. "Dry September"
    a. Manuscript, entitled "Drouth," 8 pp. (unnumbered).
    b. Carbon typescript, 19 pp. (1-10, 12-18, 18, 19 [despite gap and duplication in pagination, text is continuous and complete]). First page bears manuscript note "Scribner's" in Faulkner's hand. [Follows above manuscript, but differs slightly from published version below.]
    c. Tearsheets, 4 leaves. (Pp. 49-56 from *Scribner's*, LXXXIX [Jan. 1931].)
    d. Tearsheets of French translation by Maurice E. Coindreau, entitled "Septembre Ardent," 9 leaves. (Pp. 49-65 from *La Nouvelle Revue Francaise*, XXXVIII [Jan. 1932].)

13. "Elly"
    a. Manuscript, entitled "Selvage," 6 pp. (1-6).
    b. Typescript, entitled "Selvage," 14 pp. (1-14). Manuscript corrections. [Follows the above manuscript, and precedes the manuscript below.]
    c. Manuscript, 11 pp. (1-11). [Differs from version published in *Story*, IV (Feb. 1934).]

14. "Foxhunt"
    a. Manuscript, entitled "A Fox-Hunt," 11 pp. (unnumbered, save for p. 6).
    b. Typescript, 26 pp. (1-19, and seven unnumbered). Manuscript corrections. [Follows the above manuscript, but differs slightly from published version below.]
    c. Tearsheets, 5 leaves. (Pp. 393-402 from *Harper's*, CLXIII [Sept. 1931].)

15. "Idyll in the Desert" manuscript, 4 pp. (unnumbered). [Differs from version published in 1931 by Random House, New York.]

16. "A Justice" manuscript, 10 pp. (unnumbered). [Differs from version published in *These 13*, 1931.]

17. "The Leg"
    a. Manuscript, 10 pp. (1-10).
    b. Carbon typescript, 26 pp. (1-26). [Follows above manu-

script; published, entitled "Leg," in *Doctor Martino*, 1934.]

18. "Miss Zilphia Gant"
    a. Manuscript, 9 pp. (1-9).
    b. Typescript, 18 pp. (1-18). Manuscript corrections. In folder. [Appears to follow above manuscript, and precede carbon typescript below.]
    c. Carbon typescript, 23 pp. (1-23). [Differs slightly from version published in 1932 by the Book Club of Texas.]
    d. Library of Congress Copyright Office certificate of copyright registration for book version, 1932. [See Catalogue item 86.]

19. "Mistral"
    a. Manuscript, 17 pp. (1-17).
    b. Carbon typescript, 46 pp. (1-13, 12-44 [despite duplication in pagination, text is continuous]). [Follows above manuscript; published in *These 13*, 1931.]

20. "A Mountain Victory"
    a. Manuscript, 18 pp. (ten unnumbered pages; 9, 9a, 10, 10a, 11-13; and one unnumbered page). [The text is apparently complete, and precedes the typescript below.]
    b. Carbon typescript, 42 pp. (1-42). Manuscript corrections. [Differs slightly from the version published in *Sat. Eve. Post*, CCV (Dec. 3, 1932).]

21. "My Grandmother Millard and General Bedford Forrest and the Battle of Harrykin Creek"
    a. Typescript, 2 pp. (1-2). Incomplete.
    b. Carbon typescript, 2 pp. (1-2). [Carbon of above typescript. This version of the beginning of the story differs from that of the complete typescript below.]
    c. Carbon typescript, 42 pp. (1-42). Manuscript corrections. [Differs slightly from version published in *Story*, XXII (March-April 1943).]

22. "Pennsylvania Station"
    a. Manuscript, 8 pp. (1-8).
    b. Manuscript, 1 p. (1). [This beginning of the story differs from that of the above manuscript.]
    c. Typescript, 2 pp. (unnumbered).
    d. Typescript, 4 pp. (19-22). [These pages, and the above

two, of typescript, differ from the corresponding parts of the other versions listed here, but their relationship to them is not clear.]

    e.  Typescript, 20 pp. (1-19, last page unnumbered). Manuscript corrections. [Differs from version published in *American Mercury*, XXXI (Feb. 1934).]

23.  "Red Leaves"
    a.  Manuscript, 12 pp. (1, second page unnumbered, 3-12).
    b.  Carbon typescript, 36 pp. (1-7, eighth page unnumbered, 9-36). [Follows above manuscript, but differs from version published in *Sat. Eve. Post*, CCIII (Oct. 25, 1930).]

24.  "A Rose for Emily"
    a.  Manuscript, 6 pp. (1-6), incomplete.
    b.  Carbon typescript, 17 pp. (1, second page unnumbered, 3-16, last page unnumbered). First page bears manuscript note "Sold to Forum, 1-20-30" in Faulkner's hand. [Follows above manuscript, but still differs from published version below.]
    c.  Tearsheets, 3 leaves. (Pp. 233-238 from *Forum*, LXXXIII [April 1930].)

25.  "Shall Not Perish"
    a.  Carbon typescript, 16 pp. (1-16). Manuscript corrections. [On verso of p. 1 is part of a version of "A Courtship."]
    b.  Typescript, 4 pp. (1, 2, 19, and one unnumbered). Manuscript corrections. [Differs from the corresponding passages in the above carbon typescript.]
    c.  Carbon typescript, 11 pp. Miscellaneous pages of several versions, incomplete. [All versions listed here appear to differ from that published in *Story*, XXIII (July-Aug. 1943).]

26.  "Shingles for the Lord" carbon typescript, 21 pp. (1-21). [Differs somewhat from version published in *Sat. Eve. Post*, CCXV (Feb. 13, 1943).]

27.  "That Evening Sun" carbon typescript, 26 pp. (1-26). The first page bears the original title "—That Evening Sun Go Down" with the last two words cancelled, and the remaining three words written in again in ink, in Faulkner's hand. Above the title Faulkner has written and cancelled the name "Forum" and added the name "Mercury". [Differs somewhat

from version published in *American Mercury*, XXII (March 1931).]

28. "The Tall Men" carbon typescript, 18 pp. (1-18). [Published in *Sat. Eve. Post*, CCXIII (May 31, 1941).]

29. "There Was a Queen"
    a. Manuscript, entitled "An Empress Passed," and with cancelled title "Through the Window," 8 pp. (1-8).
    b. Typescript, 25 pp. (1-5, 5a, 6-24). Manuscript corrections. [Follows above manuscript, but differs somewhat from version published in *Scribner's*, XCIII (Jan. 1933).]
    c. Carbon typescript, 25 pp. [Carbon of above typescript.]

30. "Thrift"
    a. Manuscript, 5 pp. (1-5), incomplete.
    b. Typescript, 18 pp. (24-41), incomplete. [This ending of the story follows the corresponding passages in the above manuscript, but differs from the ending of the version published in *Sat. Eve. Post*, CCIII (Sept. 6, 1930).}

31. "Turn About" manuscript, 16 pp. (first page unnumbered, 2-16). [Differs from version published in *Sat. Eve. Post*, CCIV (March 5, 1932).]

32. "Victory"
    a. Manuscript, 9 pp. Miscellaneous pages, only one (p. 1) numbered, incomplete.
    b. Typescript, 56 pp. (1-41, 43-57), incomplete. Manuscript corrections. [Precedes typescript below. The episode on pp. 22-41 of this typescript constitutes a version of the story "Crevasse," published in *These 13*, 1931. It is incomplete, but would apparently be completed by the missing p. 42. On p. 22 the title "Crevasse" is written in, apparently by Faulkner.]
    c. Typescript, 49 pp. (3-51), incomplete. [Follows above typescript, but differs from version published in *These 13*, 1931. Pp. 25-33 constitute the "Crevasse" episode, which is complete here, though untitled.]

### B. UNPUBLISHED

1. "Adolescence" typescript, 26 pp. (1-26). According to Faulkner (interview March 12, 1958), it was written in the early 1920's.

2. "The Big Shot" typescript, 37 pp. (1-4, 4a, 5-36). Manuscript corrections. Faulkner had submitted it to five magazines by mid-April, 1930 (see Appendix).

3. "Love"
   a. Manuscript, 13 pp. (1-13). Apparently complete, this version differs from the incomplete manuscript and the typescript below.
   b. Manuscript, 5 pp. (1, 3, 6, 7, and 1). These miscellaneous pages may be from more than one version.
   c. Typescript, 49 pp. (1-47, and two unnumbered). Incomplete. According to Faulkner (interview March 12, 1958), it was written about 1921[?].

4. "Moonlight" carbon typescript, 16 pp. (1-16). Incomplete. According to Faulkner (interview March 12, 1958), it was written around 1919 or 1920 or 1921 and is "about the first short story I ever wrote."

5. "Rose of Lebanon" manuscript, 9 pp. (all unnumbered), incomplete [?]. Faulkner submitted it to three magazines in 1930 and 1931 (see Appendix).

6. "Snow"
   a. Typescript, 2 pp. (13a, 13b). Manuscript corrections. These two pages precede the corresponding passages in the complete carbon typescript below.
   b. Carbon typescript, 18 pp. (1-13, 13a, 13b, 14-16). According to his agent's records, Faulkner submitted this story in 1942.

7. "The Wishing-Tree" typescript, 47 pp. (1-47). Manuscript corrections. Faulkner wrote this children's story in the 1920's for the daughter of a friend (see Catalogue item 211).

8. "With Caution and Dispatch"
   a. Typescript, 2 pp. (1, 10). It is not clear what their relationship is to the corresponding passages of the typescript below.
   b. Typescript, 47 pp. (1-47), incomplete. Manuscript corrections. According to Faulkner (interview March 12, 1958), this story dates from about the time of "Turn About" (1932). But on the versos of nine pages of the setting copy of *The Hamlet* (pp. 530-536, 535-536 [*sic*]) are pages from what is presumably a later version (see

Catalogue item 213). According to his agent's records, Faulkner submitted this story to him early in 1940.[31]

9. [untitled] typescript, 23 pp. (1-23). This obviously early story is related to Faulkner's sketch "The Kid Learns," in the New Orleans *Times-Picayune* Sunday magazine, May 31, 1925, p. 2.

## III. VERSE

### A. PUBLISHED

1. "Cathay," typescript, 1 p. Text differs slightly from that published in *The Mississippian*, November 12, 1919, p. 8.[32]

2. "April," typescript, 2 pp. Text identical with that published in *Contempo*, I (February 1, 1932), p. 2. Above the title on the first page is the number 9, in ink.

3. "I Will Not Weep for Youth," typescript, 1 p. Manuscript corrections. The text, as corrected, is identical with that published in *Contempo*, I (February 1, 1932), p. 1. The title appears to have been written in pencil in a hand not Faulkner's; though it has been erased, it is still faintly legible. Below the title is the number 1.

4. ["Knew I Love Once,"] typescript, 1 p. Manuscript corrections. The text, as corrected, is identical with that published in *Contempo*, I (February 1, 1932), p. 1.[33]

5. "My Epitaph," typescript, 1 p. The text is identical with that published in *Contempo*, I (February 1, 1932), p. 2. (Also published, revised, as *A Green Bough*, XLIV.)

6. "Spring," typescript, 1 p. The text is identical with that published in *Contempo*, I (February 1, 1932), p. 2. (Also published, revised, as *A Green Bough*, XXXVI.) It is dated at the bottom of the page in Faulkner's hand "13 December, 1924". Above the title has been pencilled, probably not in Faulkner's hand, the number 14.

[31] For a reproduction of p. 1 of this typescript, see Fig. 25.
[32] For a reproduction of this typescript, see Fig. 3.
[33] A revised version of this poem appeared in Faulkner's second book of verse, *A Green Bough*, New York, 1933. The forty-four poems of this collection are numbered but untitled; this poem appears as number XXXIII. (Subsequent references to this collection will appear in the text.)

7. "To a Virgin," typescript, 1 p. The text is identical with that published in *Contempo*, I (February 1, 1932), p. 2. (Also published, revised, as *A Green Bough*, XXXIX.)

8. "Twilight," typescript, 1 p. The text is identical with that published in *Contempo*, I (February 1, 1932), p. 1. (Also published, revised, as *A Green Bough*, X.) The title appears to have been written in pencil, in a hand not Faulkner's; though it has been erased, it is still faintly legible. Below the title is the number 5.

9. "Vision in Spring," typescript, 3 pp. The text is identical with that published in *Contempo*, I (February 1, 1932), p. 1, entitled "Visions in Spring," save for the presence of an accent mark over the word "hushèd" in line nineteen of the typescript. Above the title is the number 2, in ink.

10. ["Winter Is Gone,"] typescript, 1 p. The text is identical with that published in *Contempo*, I (February 1, 1932), p. 2. It is possible that the title was once pencilled in; several words at the head of the text have been erased and are illegible. Below the erasure is the number 3.

11. "A Child Looks from His Window," typescript, 1 p. The text is identical with that published in *Contempo*, II (May 25, 1932), p. 3, save that the published text is italicized.

12. "Marriage," typescript, 4 pp. The text differs slightly from that published as *A Green Bough*, II. At the top of the first page is the number 8, in ink. At the bottoms of the four pages, in order, the numbers 9, 10, 11, and 12, each in parentheses, have been erased, but remain legible.

13. "Philosophy," typescript, 2 pp. The text differs slightly from that published as *A Green Bough*, V. There is one manuscript correction, apparently not in Faulkner's hand. At the bottom of the first page is the number 21; at the bottom of the second, the number 22; both numbers are in parentheses, and both have been erased, but are still legible.

14. ["Man Comes, Man Goes,"] typescript, 1 p. The text differs slightly from that published as *A Green Bough*, VI. (The title supplied here, from the first line, was used for the publication of the poem in *The New Republic*, LXXIV [May

3, 1933], p. 338.) At the bottom of the page the number 1, in parentheses, has been erased, but is still legible.

15. ["Night Piece,"] typescript, 2 pp. The text differs in a few details from that published as *A Green Bough*, VII. (The title supplied here was used for the publication of the poem in *The New Republic*, LXXIV [April 12, 1933], p. 253.) There is one manuscript correction, apparently not in Faulkner's hand. On the verso of the second page, not in Faulkner's hand, is the pencilled note "And [sic] of Section". At the top of the first page the number XXVIII was apparently typed, then the last I erased to make the number XXVII, and that number finally cancelled in ink.

16. [untitled,] typescript, 1 p. The text differs slightly from that published as *A Green Bough*, IX. At the top of the page appears the number 4.

17. [untitled,] typescript, 1 p. The text as published in *A Green Bough*, XI, omits the second stanza of this typescript version, and differs in other details. At the top of the page appears the number 7.

18. [untitled,] typescript, 1 p. The text differs slightly from that published as *A Green Bough*, XII. At the top of the page appears the number 6.

19. [untitled,] typescript, 1 p. The text differs slightly from that published as *A Green Bough*, XIII. At the top of the page appears the number 8.

20. "Puck and Death," typescript, 1 p. The text differs slightly from that published as *A Green Bough*, XVI. At the bottom of the page the number 7, in parentheses, has been erased, but is still legible.

21. "On Seeing the Winged Victory for the First Time," typescript, 1 p. The text differs slightly from that published as *A Green Bough*, XVII.

22. "La Lune ne Grade Aucune Rancune," typescript, 1 p. The text is identical, save for the omission of capitals, with that published as *A Green Bough*, XXXII. At the bottom of the page appears a typed inscription by Faulkner for Sam Gilmore.[34]

[34] For a reproduction of this page, see Fig. 4. The verb in the title is presumably spelled incorrectly; the expression *garder rancune* means to owe a grudge.

23. "Nativity," typescript, 1 p. The text differs slightly from that published as *A Green Bough*, XXXIV. One pencilled change in Faulkner's hand ("to swell" for "within", line 11) is incorporated into the published text.

24. "Cleopatra," typescript, 1 p. The text as published in *A Green Bough*, XXXVII, differs somewhat, including the change of "Cleopatra" to "Lilith" in line 9. At the bottom of the page it is dated in ink, in Faulkner's hand, "9 December 1924".

25. "The Flowers That Died," typescript, 1 p. The text is identical with that published in *Contempo*, III (June 25, 1933), p. 1, save that the published text is italicized. One manuscript revision in Faulkner's hand ("day is born" for "it is morn", line 16) is incorporated into the published text. The title appears to have been written in pencil, in a hand not Faulkner's, and then erased; it is still faintly legible.

### B. UNPUBLISHED

1. "Adolescence," typescript, 1 p. Twenty-eight lines, in seven stanzas. First line, "Within this garden close, where afternoon".

2. "The Dancer," typescript, 1 p. Twenty lines, in five stanzas. First line, "I am Youth, so swift, so white, so slim,". Beneath the title is the dedication "to V. de G. F." Above the title, in ink, is the number 1. At the bottom of the page the number 4, in parentheses, has been erased, but is still legible.

3. "Eunice," typescript, 3 pp. Sixty-eight lines, in seventeen stanzas. First line, "Is this the house where Eunice lived,". The pencilled corrections on the last page appear not to be in Faulkner's hand. At the bottoms of the three pages, in order, the numbers 17, 18, and 19, each in parentheses, have been erased, but remain legible.

4. "The Shepherd's Love," typescript, 1 p. Twenty lines, in five stanzas. First line, "O come, sweet love, and let us keep".

5. "To Elise," typescript, 1 p. Sixteen lines, in four stanzas. First line, "Where has flown the spring we knew together?" Above the title, in ink, probably not in Faulkner's hand, is the word *Dedication*. At the bottom of the page is typed "5 December, 1924".

6. [untitled,] typescript, 1 p. Sixteen lines, in four stanzas. First line, "Shall I recall this tree, when I am old?" Above the text appears the number 1.

7. [untitled,] typescript, 1 p. Twelve lines, in three stanzas. First line, "Sweet will it be to us who sleep".

8. [untitled,] typescript, 1 p. Sixteen lines, in four stanzas. First line, "Where I am dead the clover loved of bees". The second stanza has been cancelled. There is a one-word correction in Faulkner's hand. At the bottom is typed "William Faulkner / New Orleans / 10 February 1925".

## IV. WRITING FOR MOVIES AND TELEVISION

1. *The Big Sleep* manuscript, 1 p. This page of dialogue was identified by Faulkner (interview March 12, 1958).

2. "Continuous Performance" carbon typescript, 38 pp. (1-30, 30a, 31-37). An unidentified screen treatment. Cary Grant is noted as a possibility for casting.

3. "Old Man"
   a. Typescript and carbon typescript, 22 pp. (1-16, 16a, 16b, 17-20). Manuscript corrections. On the versos of some of the pages appear typescript pages and passages from versions of Faulkner's article "Mississippi," and from his television script from the story "Shall Not Perish."
   b. Carbon typescript, 26 pp. (first page unnumbered, 2-26). Follows above version. Manuscript corrections.
   c. Carbon typescript letter, 1 p. Dated April 16, 1953, from Saxe Commins to Martin Jurow of the William Morris Agency, the letter describes this "full synopsis . . . for a working script" (*i.e.,* treatment) made by Faulkner from the "Old Man" section of his 1939 novel, *The Wild Palms.* (Apparently this treatment was made for the purpose of television, rather than movie, performance.)

4. "One Way to Catch a Horse" carbon typescript, 36 pp. (1-35, last page unnumbered). Manuscript corrections. An unidentified treatment (the hero is Ernest Trueblood).

5. "Revolt in the Earth" carbon typescript, 62 pp. (1-62). This is a treatment of Faulkner's 1936 novel *Absalom, Absalom!*

by Faulkner and Dudley Murphy. Attached is a Warner Brothers house telegram concerning it, dated January 6, 1943.

6. [untitled science fiction treatment] typescript and carbon typescript, 2 pp. This incomplete treatment is unidentified (characters who appear are Zweistein and Dale), but dated by two accompanying letters from Faulkner to Howard Hawks. The first, dated June 18, 1948, is 1 p. typescript, unsigned; the second, dated June 29, 1948, is 2 pp. carbon typescript, unsigned.

7. [untitled script] typescript, 31 pp. (29-30, 56-83, 113). This unidentified script (characters who appear are Sarastro, Anna, Rico, and David) may date from the early 1940's.

## V. MISCELLANEOUS

1. [untitled,] introduction to *The Sound and the Fury* [?], typescript, 4 pp. (2-5). Internal evidence suggests that this piece was written no earlier than 1932 and no later than 1934. It discusses the writing of the first seven of his novels, particularly *The Sound and the Fury*, and may quite possibly have been intended for the Random House edition of *The Sound and the Fury* which was announced for publication, with an introduction by Faulkner, in 1933, but was never brought out.

2. The Viking *Portable Faulkner*
   a. Appendix on Compson family, carbon typescript, 12 pp. (1-2, 4-13), incomplete.
   b. "Dilsey" section, typescript, 35 pp. (first page unnumbered, 2-35).

3. [untitled,] commencement address, manuscript, 2 pp. This is a version of the address Faulkner made to the graduating class of University High School, Oxford, Miss., May 28, 1951. It was printed in the *Oxford Eagle*, May 31, 1951, p. 1.

PART THREE

*THE ENGLISH EDITIONS*

# Introduction

## I. Published in England:

1. *Soldiers' Pay* 1930
2. *The Sound and the Fury* 1931
3. *Sanctuary* 1931
4. *Sartoris* 1932
5. *Light in August* 1933
6. *These Thirteen* 1933
7. *Doctor Martino* 1934
8. *Pylon* 1935
9. *As I Lay Dying* 1935
10. *Absalom, Absalom!* 1937
11. *The Unvanquished* 1938
12. *The Wild Palms* 1939
13. *The Hamlet* 1940
14. *Go Down, Moses* 1942
15. *Intruder in the Dust* 1949
16. *Knight's Gambit* 1951
17. *Collected Stories* 1951
18. *Requiem for a Nun* 1953
19. *A Fable* 1955
20. *Faulkner's County* 1955
21. *The Town* 1958
22. Collected Short Stories, Vol. I 1958
23. Collected Short Stories, Vol. II 1958
24. Collected Short Stories, Vol. III 1959
25. *New Orleans Sketches* 1959
26. *The Mansion* 1961

## II. Published in Other Countries:

A. FRANCE

B. GERMANY

C. JAPAN

D. SWEDEN

# INTRODUCTION

FAULKNER'S text is becoming the subject of sufficiently close critical scrutiny to make worth while at this time a fairly detailed study of the English editions of his works. In this bibliographical listing I have therefore been primarily concerned with the printing history of the English text, and I have tried to provide sufficient description to identify each edition, impression, and issue I have encountered. Final solution of some of the problems described here—chiefly those concerning the so-called Chatto and Windus "cheap editions"—will have to await the passage of time and the examination of many more copies of several of the books, and the present listing should be regarded as a preliminary description rather than an attempt to cover the ground in any final fashion. A more definitive treatment of the subject, in addition to answering the questions raised here, would properly concern itself with variations between the English and American texts, by collation of the impressions and editions which I have tried to determine here.

In preparation for this listing I examined, in the summer of 1958, all copies of Faulkner's books to be found in four of the British copyright depositories: the British Museum, the Bodleian, the Library of Cambridge University, and the Scottish National Library. All four had complete or nearly complete sets of the first English editions issued through 1955. Also examined were the copies of the books to be found in the libraries of Trinity College, Dublin; Queen's College, Belfast; the University of Glasgow; and the University of Edinburgh. In addition, the file copies in the office of Chatto and Windus, London, were examined. In this country, a few copies were found in the libraries of Princeton, Yale, and Harvard, and more in the private collections of the individuals mentioned below. In every case, a total of at least six copies were seen of each of the "first editions" described in the primary bibliographical listings provided, save for the dust jackets. These were missing from all the copies in the British libraries, of course, and from many seen elswhere, so that in many cases I saw only one copy of the jacket described, and in one case have seen none at all. For all the subsequent or variant states, issues, impressions, and editions listed, I have seen at least two copies unless otherwise noted.

Where I have listed a later impression or edition as "not examined," the information given was taken from the annual volumes of the *English Catalogue of Books*. Prices and dates of publication were sometimes taken from the same source. In every case, the date of publication and number of copies of the first impression were supplied by Chatto and Windus. I have also given the acquisition date which the Scottish National Library so helpfully provides for its books, as a piece of evidence which supports the claims of these copyright deposit copies for primacy in the descriptions. This evidence may prove particularly helpful in the case of those books which Chatto and Windus, in the 1930's, issued in their so-called "cheap editions," where it is obvious in some cases that they were merely issuing unsold copies of the original (and probably only) impression, perhaps newly bound up, perhaps with only the dust jacket to indicate their newly lowered status.

A few Faulkner books which have been published in English in non-English-speaking countries are listed separately at the end of this section.

To the staffs of the various British libraries where I worked, particularly those of the British Museum, the Bodleian, and the Scottish National Library, I am indebted for many courtesies. My chief obligation in Britain, however, is to Mr. Bertram Rota, upon whose patience I imposed more often than I care to think, and whose advice frequently pointed the way toward the solution of problems beyond the capacities of my bibliographical inexperience. Mr. Anthony Brett-James and Miss Anne Grint, of Chatto and Windus, were likewise subjected to repeated impositions upon their busy schedules, and I should like to thank them especially for their assistance.[1] But perhaps my greatest debt in Britain, measured by hours and tolerance expended, is to my wife, who spent an inordinate amount of what was supposed to be a vacation in transcribing title-pages and doing other harmless-seeming drudgery in libraries.

In this country, for helpful correspondence and for permitting me to examine their books, I am indebted to three collectors, Carl Petersen, James Bloom, and particularly to Linton Massey, who kindly placed at my disposal his English editions at a time that was most inconvenient to him.

[1] After I had received the galley proof of this book, Mr. Gordon Price-Stevens was kind enough to check a number of details for me in British libraries.

I. Published in England:

## 1. *Soldiers' Pay* 1930

SOLDIERS' / PAY / *By* / William Faulkner / WITH A PREFACE
BY / Richard Hughes / LONDON / Chatto and Windus / 1930

Green cloth, stamped in gold on spine. Top edges stained green.
Bottom edges rough-trimmed. 7 7/16 X 4 3/4 inches. Dust
jacket white, lettered in black and decorated in red.

[A]⁶ B-X⁸ Y⁴ [Z]². Pp. [i-ii] blank; [iii] half-title; [iv] publisher's
statement of intent to publish three other books by author;
[v] title-page, as above; [vi] copyright page; [vii-viii] epigraph,
verso blank; ix-xi Preface by Richard Hughes; [xii] blank;
[1]-326 text; [327-328] colophon, verso blank; [329-332] ads.

Publication date, 20 June, 1930. (Acq. date, SNL copy, 23
June.) 2000 copies. 7*s.* 6*d.*

*Later impressions and editions*:

Second impression, September 1930. (So states on copyright
page.) 7*s.* 6*d.*

Centaur Library (Chatto and Windus "cheap edition"), February 1932. 3*s.* 6*d.* The only copy I have examined is one of
the second impression (see above entry), but with a Centaur
Library label pasted on the spine of the dust jacket. Additional evidence that this "cheap edition" consisted merely
of unsold copies of the second impression is supplied by the
publisher's advertisement in the 1935 *As I Lay Dying*, which
states that the second impression of *Soldiers' Pay* may be
obtained for either 7*s.* 6*d.* or 3*s.* 6*d.*

Penguin edition, Harmondsworth, Penguin Books Limited,
January 1938. 310 pp. 6*d.* Includes the Hughes Preface.

New Phoenix Library, Chatto and Windus, March 1951, 326
pp. 5*s.* Text reproduced by photo-offset from the original
Chatto and Windus setting, but without the Hughes Preface.

NOTE: Within a few weeks of publication, the price was raised to 6*s.*, and
the book was issued with a dust jacket bearing the new price.

"Uniform Edition," Chatto and Windus, 1957. 326 pp. 9*s.* 6*d.*
Reproduced by photo-offset, without the Hughes Preface.

## 2. *The Sound and the Fury* 1931

THE SOUND / AND THE FURY / WILLIAM FAULKNER / WITH AN INTRODUCTION BY / RICHARD HUGHES / CHATTO AND WINDUS, LONDON / 1931

> Black cloth, stamped in red on spine. Top edges stained red. Bottom edges rough-trimmed. 7 3/8 X 4 7/8 inches. Dust jacket white, lettered and decorated in red and black.

> [A]⁶ B-X⁸ Y²[Z]². Pp. [i-ii] blank; [iii] half-title; [iv] list of books by author; [v] title-page, as above; [vi] copyright page; vii-ix Introduction by Richard Hughes; [x] blank; [xi-xii] Contents, verso blank; 1-321 text; [322] colophon; [323-326] ads; [327-328] blank.

> Publication date, 16 April, 1931. (Acq. date, SNL copy, 18 April.) 2000 copies. 7s. 6d.

> NOTE: In all copies examined of this issue in black cloth, the two conjugate leaves of ads (signature [Z]² in the above collation) have been inserted between the two leaves of signature Y. The ads are missing from two copies seen of what appears to be a later binding-up of sheets from the first impression. These two copies, otherwise apparently identical to the issue in black cloth, are bound in tan cloth, stamped in red on spine, top edges unstained, and bottom edges trimmed. Both are in dust jackets apparently identical to that of the only copy with dust jacket I have seen of the issue in black cloth, but the price has been removed from the jacket of one. It is possible that the removal of the price in this copy indicates that it was issued in the Centaur Library and consequently sold at a lower price.

*Later impressions and editions*:

> Centaur Library, Chatto and Windus, March 1933. 3s. 6d. Not examined, but see above note.

> "Uniform Edition," Chatto and Windus, 1954. 321 pp. 10s. 6d. Text reproduced by photo-offset from the original Chatto and Windus setting.

> Four Square edition, London, Landsborough Publications Limited, April 1959. 223 pp. 2s. 6d.

## 3. *Sanctuary* 1931

SANCTUARY / *By* / William Faulkner / LONDON / Chatto and Windus / 1931

> Red cloth, stamped in gold on spine. Top edges stained gray. Bottom edges rough-trimmed. 7 3/8 X 4 7/8 inches. Dust jacket light gray, lettered in red and blue and decorated in blue.

[A]² B-U⁸ X⁶ [Y]². Pp. [i] half-title; [ii] list of books by author; [iii] title-page, as above; [iv] copyright page; 1-316 text; [317-320] ads. (Colophon at foot of 316.)

Publication date, 10 September, 1931. (Acq. date, SNL copy, 14 Sept.) 2000 copies. 7s. 6d.

NOTE: I have seen a copy in rose cloth, stamped in black on spine, the top edges unstained, and without the ads. There is no indication that the sheets are other than those of the first impression; nor, if so, whether this copy represents an earlier state of the binding or a later one.

*Later impressions and editions*:

Phoenix Library (Chatto and Windus "cheap edition"), February 1933. 315 pp. 3s. 6d. Text reproduced by photo-offset from the original Chatto and Windus setting (omitting the number of the final page).

"Uniform Edition," Chatto and Windus, February 1952. 254 pp. 8s. 6d. Printed in Sweden. A 1957 impression is printed in England.

Penguin edition, Harmondsworth, Penguin Books Ltd., February 1953. 252 pp. 2s.

# 4. *Sartoris* 1932

A Novel / *SARTORIS* / by / WILLIAM FAULKNER / 1932 / CHATTO & WINDUS / LONDON

Blue cloth, stamped in gold on spine. Top edges stained blue. Bottom edges rough-trimmed. 7 3/8 X 4 7/8 inches. Dust jacket white, lettered in blue and black, and decorated in blue.

[A]⁸ B-Z⁸ AA¹⁰ [BB]². Pp. [i] half-title; [ii] list of books by author; [iii] title-page, as above; [iv] copyright page; [v] dedication; [vi] Contents; 1-[380] text; [381-382] colophon, verso blank; [383-386] ads.

Publication date, 18 February, 1932. (Acq. date, SNL copy, 24 Feb.) 2000 copies. 7s. 6d. Text reproduced by photo-offset from the American setting (New York, Harcourt, Brace, 1929).

NOTE: I have seen only two copies of the book in which the two conjugate leaves of ads appeared as described above, *i.e.*, properly inserted at the end, between the final leaf of signature AA (the colophon and its verso) and the back free end paper. In six other copies, including the copyright deposit copies at the Scottish National Library, the Bodleian, and the British Museum, the ads were inserted between the last page of the text and the colophon. This binding variant was noted in the fall, 1932 catalogue of the Casanova Bookshop, Milwaukee, which stated that in "most" copies the ads were correctly inserted following the colophon. There seems little point in attempting to assign priority to either variant, despite the fact that all three copyright deposit copies examined were the same in this respect, as the variation might have taken place either accidentally or on purpose at any time during the period when the sheets were being bound up.

*Later impressions*:

Centaur Library, Chatto and Windus, September 1933. 3*s.* 6*d.*

NOTE: The only copy I have examined appears to consist of sheets of the first impression, bound in tan cloth, the top edges unstained, and with the dust jacket having a Centaur Library label pasted on the spine. The original price has been cut from the flap of the dust jacket, and the label gives the price as 3*s.* 6*d.* The ads (inserted after the colophon) mention *As I Lay Dying*, which was not published until 1935. A Chatto and Windus file copy, similarly bound, has a label pasted to its dust jacket identifying it as a "Cheap Edition" but not Centaur Library, and with the price 4*s.* 6*d.*

"Uniform Edition," Chatto and Windus, 1954. 379 pp. 10*s.* 6*d.* Text reproduced by photo-offset.

## 5. *Light in August* 1933

LIGHT IN / AUGUST / *William* / *Faulkner* / 1933 / CHATTO & WINDUS / LONDON

> Brown cloth, stamped in gold on spine. Top edges stained brown. Bottom edges rough-trimmed. 8 1/8 X 5 1/4 inches. Dust jacket white, lettered and decorated in black.

> [A]⁸ B-Z⁸ AA-FF⁸ GG¹⁰. Pp. [i] half-title; [ii] list of books by author; [iii] title-page, as above; [iv] copyright page; 1-480 text. (Colophon at foot of p. 480.)

> Publication date, 26 January, 1933. (Acq. date, SNL copy, 8 Feb.) 2500 copies. 8*s.* 6*d.* Text reproduced from the American setting (New York, Smith and Haas, 1932) by photo-offset.

*Later impressions and editions*:

Phoenix Library (Chatto and Windus "cheap edition"), November 1934. 480 pp. 3*s.* 6*d.*
"Uniform Edition," Chatto and Windus, July 1952. 479 pp. 12*s.* 6*d.* Text reproduced by photo-offset (omitting the number from the final page).

Penguin edition, Harmondsworth, Penguin Books Ltd., Nov. 1960. 380 pp. Not examined.

## 6. *These Thirteen* 1933

THESE THIRTEEN / STORIES / *by* / William Faulkner / 1933 / CHATTO & WINDUS / LONDON

Blue cloth, stamped in gold on spine. Top edges stained green. 7 7/16 X 4 3/4 inches. Dust jacket white, lettered and decorated in black and green.

[A]⁸ B-Z⁸ [AA]². (The final two conjugate leaves of ads are inserted between the last page of text and the blank last leaf of gathering Z in all six copies so far examined.) Pp. [i] half-title; [ii] list of books by author; [iii] title-page as above; [iv] copyright page; [v-vi] dedication, verso blank; [vii-viii] Contents, verso blank; [1-2] fly-title, verso blank; 3-[358] text; [359-362] ads; [363-364] blank. (Colophon at foot of p. [358].)

Publication date, 21 September, 1933. (Acq. date, SNL copy, 28 Sept.) 1500 copies. 7*s*. 6*d*. Text reproduced from the American setting (New York, Cape and Smith, 1931) by photo-offset.

*Contents*: the contents are the same as in the original American text.

*Later impression*:

Chatto and Windus "cheap edition," October 1938. 3*s*. 6*d*. Not examined.

[See also No. 23, Vol. II of the Collected Short Stories, 1958.]

## 7. *Doctor Martino* 1934

DOCTOR MARTINO / *and other stories* / *By* / William Faulkner / London / CHATTO & WINDUS / 1934

Orange cloth, stamped in gold on spine. Top edges stained red. Bottom edges rough-trimmed. 7 3/8 X 4 3/4 inches. Dust jacket white, lettered in red.

[A]⁸ B-Z⁸ AA⁸ [BB]². (The final 2 conjugate leaves of ads are inserted between the last two leaves of signature [BB], *i.e.*

between the last page of the text and the blank final leaf.) Pp. [i-ii] blank; [iii] half-title; [iv] list of books by author; [v] title-page, as above; [vi] copyright page; [vii-viii] Contents, verso blank; [ix-x] acknowledgments, verso blank; [1]-371 text; [372] blank; [373-376] ads; [377-378] blank. (Colophon at foot of p. 371.)

Publication date, September, 1934. (Acq. date, SNL copy, 19 Sept.) 1500 copies. 7s. 6d. Text reproduced by photo-offset from the American setting (New York, Smith and Haas, 1934).

*Contents*: the contents are the same as in the original American text.

NOTE: The copyright deposit copy at the British Museum is actually a copy of the original American edition (New York, 1934), with a printed slip bearing the name of the English publisher pasted, on the title-page, over the American.

*Later impression*:

Chatto and Windus "cheap edition," September 1934. Not examined.
[See also No. 24, Vol. III of the Collected Short Stories, 1959.]

## 8. *Pylon* 1935

PYLON / *A Novel* / BY / WILLIAM FAULKNER / 1935 / CHATTO & WINDUS / LONDON

Rose-brown cloth, stamped in white on spine. Top edges stained rose. Bottom edges rough-trimmed. 7 3/8 X 4 3/4 inches. Dust jacket white, lettered and decorated in blue and black.

[A]⁴ B-X⁸ [Y]². Pp. [i-ii] blank; [iii] half-title; [iv] list of books by author; [v] title-page, as above; [vi] copyright page; vii-[viii] Contents, verso blank; 1-[319] text; [320] blank; [321-324] ads. (Colophon at foot of p. [319].)

Publication date, March 25, 1935. (Acq. date, SNL copy, 9 April.) 2900 copies. 7s. 6d.

*Later impressions and editions*:

Centaur Library (Chatto and Windus "cheap edition"), September 1936. 3s. 6d.

NOTE: The one copy I have examined, in the library of Mr. Faulkner, appeared identical to the first edition save in the following respects: the binding was a darker reddish-brown, the top edges were unstained, the bottom edges were trimmed, and on the spine of the dust jacket was pasted a Centaur Library label, with the price 3s. 6d. It is highly questionable whether the cloth, the stain, and the bottom trim are points which determine if the book were issued in the Centaur Library, since the only direct evidence—the altered dust jacket—is not an integral part of the book. A copy in the Massey collection lacks the staining and has the bottom edges trimmed, but the cloth is of a lighter hue than the Faulkner copy, the dust jacket bears no Centaur Library label, and the final two conjugate leaves of ads are missing. Conceivably both the Faulkner and Massey copies represent sheets of the first impression, bound up later than the original issue represented by the copyright deposit copies, the one issued in Centaur Library when the decision was made to get rid of unsold copies by lowering the price, and the other, which was possibly bound up at the same time, either sold earlier at the original price, or possibly sold at the lower price but without the identifying label. It is also possible that it once bore such a label which has been now lost. The printing history noted on the copyright page of the 1950 Holiday Library edition makes no mention of a second impression of the original edition, additional evidence that the "cheap edition" consisted of sheets or copies from the first impression.

Holiday Library edition, John Lehmann, October 1950, 230 pp. 6s.

New Phoenix Library, Chatto and Windus, 1954, 230 pp. 6s. Text apparently printed from the same plates as the Holiday Library edition.

"Uniform Edition," Chatto and Windus, 1955. 230 pp. 8s. 6d. Text apparently printed from the same plates as the two preceding entries.

## 9. *As I Lay Dying* 1935

AS I / LAY DYING / By / William Faulkner / LONDON / Chatto & Windus / 1935

Blue cloth, lettered in white on spine. Top edges stained blue. Bottom edges rough-trimmed. 7 3/8 X 4 3/4 inches. Dust jacket white, lettered in blue.

[A]⁴ B-Q⁸ R⁴ [S]². Pp. [i-ii] blank; [iii] half-title; [iv] list of books by author; [v] title-page, as above; [vi] copyright page; [vii-viii] dedication, verso blank; 1-248 text; [249-252] ads. (Colophon at foot of p. 248.)

Publication date, 26 September, 1935. (Acq. date, SNL copy, 8 Oct.) 1500 copies. 7s. 6d.

*Later impressions:*

Chatto and Windus "cheap edition," October 1938. 3*s*. 6*d*. Not examined.

"Uniform Edition," Chatto and Windus, May 1952. 248 pp. 8*s*. 6*d*. Text reproduced from the original Chatto and Windus setting by photo-offset.

## 10. *Absalom, Absalom!* 1937

*William Faulkner | Absalom, Absalom! [in red] | Chatto & Windus | London*

[on copyright page:] *Copyright, 1936, by William Faulkner*

Cream cloth, lettered in red and decorated in red and black on front cover and spine. Top edges stained red. 8 1/16 X 5 1/4 inches. No copy in dust jacket yet examined, but two copies in the library of Mr. Faulkner had what appeared to be jacket flaps, which were held inside the covers by glassine wrappers.

[1-24]⁸. Pp. [1] half-title; [2] list of books by author; [3] title-page, as above; [4] copyright page, including the above (identical to original American issue); [5-6] fly-title, verso blank; 7-384 text (including appended Chronology and Genealogy); between final leaf of last signature and the back free endpaper is a tipped-in leaf, folded, with a map of Yoknapatawpha County.

Publication date, 11 February, 1937. (Acq. date, SNL copy, 12 Feb.) 1750 copies (sheets imported from America). 8*s*. 6*d*.

*Later impressions:*

Chatto and Windus "cheap edition," February 1938. 3*s*. 6*d*.

NOTE: A copy in the Massey collection, in other respects apparently identical to the copyright deposit copies described above, lacks the staining on the top edges, and may possibly represent a later binding-up of the sheets which was issued at a lower price. On the other hand, it may represent a binding variant which was produced at the same time or even before the copyright deposit copies. A file copy in the Chatto and Windus Library also lacks the top staining, but as the front cover bears no title or ornaments, it is quite likely to represent only an advance copy sent to the publisher by the binder for approval.

"Uniform Edition," Chatto and Windus, September 1960. 384 pp. 15s. Text reproduced from the original setting by photo-offset. Not examined.

## 11. *The Unvanquished* 1938

THE / UNVANQUISHED / [*swelled rule*] / William Faulkner / LONDON / CHATTO & WINDUS / 1938

Pale blue cloth, with pale blue lettering showing against irregular black ground on front cover and spine. Top edges stained purple. Bottom edges rough-trimmed. 7 1/2 X 4 3/4 inches. No copy in dust jacket yet examined.

[A]⁴ B-X⁸. Pp. [i-ii] blank; [i] half-title; [ii] list of books by author; [iii] title-page, as above; [iv] copyright page; v-[vi] Contents, verso blank; 1-319 text; [320] colophon.

Publication date, 12 May, 1938. (Acq. date, SNL copy, 20 May.) 1750 copies. 7s. 6d.

*Later impressions and editions*:

Penguin edition, Harmondsworth, Penguin Books Ltd., May 1955. 191 pp. 2s. 6d.

"Uniform Edition," Chatto and Windus, September 1960. 319 pp. 12s. 6d. Text reproduced from the original Chatto and Windus setting by photo-offset.

## 12. *The Wild Palms* 1939

THE / WILD PALMS / By / *William Faulkner* / 1939 / CHATTO & WINDUS / LONDON

Vari-toned cloth, separated by narrow band of dark green, the upper part white and blue mixture lettered in green on spine, the lower part green lettered in white on spine. Top edges stained green. Bottom edges rough-trimmed. 7 3/8 X 4 3/4 inches. Dust jacket green and yellow, lettered in yellow and green.

[A]² B-U⁸ X⁶. Pp. [i] half-title; [ii] list of books by author; [iii] title-page, as above; [iv] copyright page; 1-315 text; [316] colophon.

Publication date, 16 March, 1939. (Acq. date, SNL copy, 29 March.) 2000 copies. 7s. 6d.

"Uniform Edition," Chatto and Windus, February 1952. 314 pp. 8*s*. 6*d*. Printed in Sweden. The text is reproduced from the original Chatto and Windus setting by photo-offset (omitting the number of the final page).

## 13. *The Hamlet* 1940

THE HAMLET / A NOVEL BY / *William Faulkner* / 1940 / CHATTO & WINDUS / LONDON

Yellow cloth, stamped in green on spine. Top edges stained yellow. Bottom edges rough-trimmed. 7 3/8 X 4 7/8 inches. Dust jacket yellow, lettered and decorated in green.

[A]⁴ B-Y⁸. Pp. [i] half-title; [ii] list of books by author; [iii] title-page, as above; [iv] copyright page; [v-vi] dedication, verso blank; vii-[viii] Contents, verso blank; [1-2] fly-title, verso blank; 3-333 text; [334] blank; [335-336] colophon, verso blank.

Publication date, 12 September, 1940. (Acq. date, SNL copy, 28 Sept.) 2000 copies. 8*s*. 6*d*.

*Later impression*:

"Uniform Edition," Chatto and Windus, January 1958. 333 pp. 12*s*. 6*d*. Reproduced by photo-offset from the original English setting.

## 14. *Go Down, Moses* 1942

GO DOWN, MOSES / And Other Stories / *by* / WILLIAM FAULKNER / 1942 / Chatto & Windus / LONDON [*the whole enclosed in chain design between two thin lines with a third line, thicker, at the outer edge*]

Green cloth, stamped in white on spine. 8 X 5 1/4 inches. Dust jacket pinkish-white, lettered in dark green.

[A]⁸ B-R⁸. Pp. [1] notice that book conforms to War Economy Standard; [2] list of books by author; [3] title-page, as above; [4] copyright page; [5] Contents; [6] dedication; 7-[269] text; [270] colophon; [271-272] blank.

Publication date, 8 October, 1942. (Acq. date, SNL copy, 20 Oct.) 2500 copies. 9*s*.

Penguin edition, Harmondsworth, Penguin Books Ltd., 1960. 288 pp. 3*s*. 6*d*.

"Uniform Edition," Chatto and Windus, September 1960. 268 pp. 12*s*. 6*d*. Text reproduced from the original Chatto and Windus setting by photo-offset.

## 15. *Intruder in the Dust* 1949

INTRUDER / IN THE DUST / *A Novel by* / William Faulkner / 1949 / CHATTO & WINDUS / LONDON

Blue cloth, stamped in gold on spine. Top edges stained blue-green. 8 1/8 X 5 3/8 inches. Dust jacket white, lettered in black, and decorated in yellow, green, blue, and black.

[A]⁸ B-P⁸ Q⁶. Pp. [i] half-title; [ii] list of books by author; [iii] title-page, as above; [iv] copyright page; [1-2] fly-title, verso blank; 3-247 text; [248] colophon.

Publication date, 29 September, 1949. (Acq. date, SNL copy, 24 Oct.) 2000 copies. Text reproduced from the American setting (New York, Random House, 1948) by photo-offset. 9*s*. 6*d*.

*Later edition*:

Penguin edition, Harmondsworth, Penguin Books Ltd., Nov. 1960. 237 pp. 3*s*. 6*d*.

## 16. *Knight's Gambit* 1951

KNIGHT'S / GAMBIT / Six Stories by / WILLIAM FAULKNER / 1951 / CHATTO & WINDUS / LONDON

Blue cloth, stamped in gold on spine. Top edges stained light blue. 7 7/8 X 5 inches. Dust jacket white, lettered in black, decorated in blue, gray, and black, lettered in gray against black ground, lettered in black against gray ground, and with white lettering showing against blue and gray grounds.

[1]⁸ 2-14⁸. The front and back endpapers are the pasted-down first leaf of the first signature and last leaf of the last signature, and are not included in the following collation. Pp. [1-2] blank; [3] half-title; [4] list of books by author; [5] title-page, as above; [6] copyright page; [7-8] Contents, verso blank; 9-218 text; [219-220] blank.

Publication date, 16 April, 1951. (Acq. date, SNL copy, 5 May.) 4000 copies. 9s. 6d. Recommended by the Book Society.

*Contents*: the contents are the same as in the original American text.

## 17. *Collected Stories* 1951

*Collected Stories of* / WILLIAM FAULKNER / 1951 / CHATTO & WINDUS / LONDON [*the first two lines against a blue ground*]

Blue cloth, stamped in gold on spine. Top edges stained light blue. 8 1/4 X 5 1/2 inches. Dust jacket white, lettered in blue, and with white lettering showing against blue ground.

[1]⁸ [2-29]¹⁶. Pp. [i] half-title; [ii] list of books by author; [iii] title-page, as above; [iv] copyright page; [v-vi] Contents; [1-2] fly-title, verso blank; 3-900 text; [901-906] blank.

Publication date, 18 October, 1951. (Acq. date, SNL copy, 30 Oct.) 1526 copies (sheets imported from America). 25s.

*Contents*: the contents are the same as in the original American text.

*Later impressions*: See Nos. 22, 23, and 24, Vols. I, II, and III of the Collected Short Stories.

## 18. *Requiem for a Nun* 1953

WILLIAM FAULKNER / [*ornamented rule*] / *Requiem for a Nun* / 1953 / CHATTO & WINDUS / LONDON

Pale blue cloth, stamped in gold on spine. 7 1/4 X 4 7/8 inches. Dust jacket white, lettered in black and with white lettering showing against black ground, and decorated in yellow and black.

[A]⁸ B-Q⁸. Pp. [1] half-title; [2] list of books by author; [3] title-page, as above; [4] copyright page; [5-6] Contents, verso blank; [7-8] fly-title, verso blank; 9-251 text; [252] blank; [253] colophon; [254-256] blank.

Publication date, 9 February, 1953. (Acq. date, SNL copy, 18 Feb.) 5500 copies. 11s. 6d.

*Later edition*:

Penguin edition, Harmondsworth, Penguin Books Ltd., 1960. 239 pp. 3s. 6d.

# 19. *A Fable* 1955

A / FABLE / *By* / *William Faulkner* / 1955 / CHATTO & WINDUS / LONDON

Red cloth, stamped in gold on spine. 7 3/4 X 5 1/8 inches. Dust jacket white, lettered in black and red; and lettered in black and with white lettering and decorations showing against red ground.

[A]¹⁶ B-M¹⁶ N⁴. Pp. [1] half-title; [2] list of works by author; [3] title-page, as above; [4] copyright page; [5-6] dedication, verso blank; [7-8] acknowledgments, verso blank; 9-[392] text. (Colophon at foot of p. [392].)

Publication date, 9 June, 1955. (Acq. date, SNL copy, 23 Aug.) 13,160 copies. 15s. Recommended by the Book Society.

# 20. *Faulkner's County* 1955

Faulkner's County / *Tales of* / *Yoknapatawpha County* / *by* / WILLIAM FAULKNER / 1955 / CHATTO & WINDUS / LONDON

Green cloth, stamped on spine in gold and in gold against brown ground. 7 3/4 X 5 inches. Dust jacket off-white, lettered in green and red.

[1-14]¹⁶ [15]¹² [16]¹⁶. Pp. [i-ii] half-title, verso blank; [iii] title-page, as above; [iv] copyright page; [v-vi] Contents, verso blank; [vii-viii] Nobel Prize address; [1-2] fly-title, verso blank; 3-494 text; [495-496] blank.

Publication date, 11 July, 1955. 5000 copies. 15s.

*Contents*: contains the Nobel Prize address; *As I Lay Dying*; "The Bear" (from *Go Down, Moses*); "Spotted Horses" (from *The Hamlet*); "A Rose for Emily"; "Barn Burning"; "Dry September"; "That Evening Sun"; "Turnabout"; "Shingles for the Lord"; "A Justice"; "Wash"; "Percy Grimm" (episode from *Light in August*); and "The Courthouse" (Act I, with its narrative prologue, from *Requiem for a Nun*).

# 21. *The Town* 1958

THE TOWN / [*ornament*] / William Faulkner / 1958 / CHATTO AND WINDUS / LONDON

Orange-brown cloth, stamped in gold on spine. 7 3/4 X 5 3/16 inches. Dust jacket cream, lettered and decorated in brown and black.

[A]¹⁶ B-K¹⁶. Pp. [1] publisher's note; [2] list of books by author; [3] title-page, as above; [4] copyright page; [5-6] dedication, verso blank; [7]-319 text; [320] colophon.

Publication date, 30 January, 1958. 10,000 copies. 16s. Recommended by the Book Society.

## 22. Collected Short Stories, Vol. I 1958

UNCLE WILLY / AND OTHER STORIES / Volume One of the / Collected Short Stories / of / WILLIAM FAULKNER / 1958 / CHATTO & WINDUS / LONDON

Blue cloth, stamped in gold on spine. 7 3/4 X 5 1/8 inches. Dust jacket white, lettered and decorated in blue and red, and with white lettering showing against red and blue grounds.

[A]⁸ B-U⁸. Pp. [1-2] blank; [3] half-title; [4] list of books by author; [5] title-page, as above; [6] copyright page; [7-8] Contents, verso blank; 9-320 text.

Publication date, 24 March, 1958. 6000 copies. 15s.

*Contents*: contains "Shingles for the Lord," "The Tall Men," "A Bear Hunt," "Two Soldiers," "Shall Not Perish," "Centaur in Brass," "Uncle Willy," "Mule in the Yard," "That Will Be Fine," "A Courtship," "Pennsylvania Station," "Artist at Home," "The Brooch," "My Grandmother Millard and General Bedford Forrest and the Battle of Harrykin Creek," and "Golden Land."

## 23. Collected Short Stories, Vol. II 1958

THESE THIRTEEN / Volume Two of the / Collected Short Stories / of / WILLIAM FAULKNER / 1958 / CHATTO & WINDUS / LONDON

Blue cloth, stamped in gold on spine. 7 11/16 X 5 inches. Dust jacket white, lettered and decorated in purple and orange, and with white lettering showing against purple and orange grounds.

[A]⁸ B-I¹⁶. Pp. [1-2] blank; [3] half-title; [4] list of works by author; [5] title-page, as above; [6] copyright page; [7-8] Contents, verso blank; 9-272 text.

Publication date, 18 September, 1958. 15s. Text reproduced by photo-offset from the *Collected Stories*.

*Contents*: the contents are the same as in the original English issue (1933).

## 24. Collected Short Stories, Vol. III 1959

DR MARTINO / AND OTHER STORIES / Volume Three of the / Collected Short Stories / of / WILLIAM FAULKNER / 1958 / CHATTO & WINDUS / LONDON

Blue cloth, stamped in gold on spine. 7 11/16 X 5 1/8 inches. Dust jacket white, lettered and decorated in green and red, and with white lettering showing against green and red grounds.

[A]¹⁶ B-H¹⁶ [I]¹⁶ K¹⁶. Pp. [1-2] blank; [3] half-title; [4] list of works by author; [5] title-page, as above; [6] copyright page; [7-8] Contents, verso blank; [9]-320 text.

Publication date, 5 February, 1959. 15s. Text reproduced by photo-offset from the *Collected Stories*.

*Contents*: the contents are the same as in the original English issue (1934), save that "Lo!" and "Barn Burning" replace "The Hound" and "Smoke," which had in the meantime been incorporated into *The Hamlet* and *Knight's Gambit*, respectively.

## 25. *New Orleans Sketches* 1959

NEW ORLEANS / SKETCHES / WILLIAM FAULKNER / INTRODUCTION BY CARVEL COLLINS / SIDGWICK AND JACKSON LIMITED / LONDON

[on copyright page:] *First published in this edition 1959*

Issued simultaneously in both black and tan boards (with imitation cloth grain), stamped in gold on spine. 7 1/4 X 4 7/8 inches. Dust jacket white, lettered in black, and lettered in white and decorated in black against yellow ground.

[1]¹⁶ 2-4¹⁶ [5]¹⁶ 6-7¹⁶. Pp. [1-2] half-title, verso blank; [3] title-page, as above; [4] copyright page, including above; [5-6]

Contents; [7-8] fly-title, verso blank; 9-34 introduction; [35-36] fly-title, verso blank; 37-223 text; [224] blank.

Publication date, 15 May, 1959. 15*s*. Text reproduced by photo-offset from the Rutgers University Press edition.

## 26. *The Mansion* 1961

The Mansion / [*ornament*] / William Faulkner / 1961 / CHATTO AND WINDUS / LONDON

Orange boards (imitation cloth grain), stamped in gold on spine. Top edges stained orange. 7 5/8 X 5 1/8 inches. Dust jacket white, lettered in black and green; lettered in blue and black against black, blue, and green grounds, and with white lettering showing against blue and green grounds.

A-M¹⁶ N⁸. Pp. [1] publisher's note; [2] list of works by author; [3] title-page, as above; [4] copyright page; [5-6] dedication, verso blank; [7-8] Contents, verso blank; [9-10] author's note, verso blank; [11-12] fly-title, verso blank; 13-399 text; [400] blank.

Publication date, 12 January, 1961. 21*s*.

NOTE: I have examined only two copies of this book.

II. Published in Other Countries:

### A. FRANCE

*Sanctuary*. Paris: Crosby Continental Editions, 1932. 308 pp. Wrappers. [Only three copies examined.]

### B. GERMANY

*Pylon*. Hamburg, Paris, Bologna: Albatross Verlag, 1935. 243 pp. Wrappers, with dust jacket. [Only one copy examined.]

*The Unvanquished*. Leipzig, Paris, Bologna: Albatross Verlag, 1938. 252 pp. Wrappers, with dust jacket. [Only one copy examined.]

*The Unvanquished*. Bielefeld, Berlin, Hannover: Velhagen & Klasing, [1957]. 47 pp. Wrappers. No. 22 in a series of English and American readings edited by Friedrich Lange. With a foreword and notes. (Excerpts from chapters one, three, and four of the book.) [Only one copy examined.]

*The Bear.* Paderborn: Verlag Ferdinand Schöningh, 1958. 15 pp. Wrappers. No. 134 in a series of English-language readings. With an afterword and notes by Alex Niederstenbruch. (Brief excerpts from the 1942 version in *Go Down, Moses.*) [Only two copies examined.]

*The Bear.* Verden/Aller: Silva-Verlag, 1959. 96 pp. Wrappers. No. 24 in a series of English-language school texts. With an Introduction and Notes by Paul Fussell. (Text reprinted from the 1955 version in *Big Woods.*)

## C. JAPAN

*A Rose for Emily and Other Stories.* Tokyo: Kairyudo, 1956. 141 pp. Wrappers, with dust jacket. No. 5 in Kairyudo's Mentor Library. Edited, with an introduction and notes, by Kenzaburo Ōhashi. (Contains "A Rose for Emily," "That Evening Sun," "Dry September," and "Red Leaves.") [Only one copy examined.]

*The Unvanquished.* Tokyo: Kairyudo, 1957. 114 pp. Wrappers, with dust jacket. No. 7 in Kairyudo's Mentor Library. Edited, with an introduction and notes, by Katsuji Takamura. (Contains only chapters three and seven from the book.) [Only one copy examined.]

*W. Faulkner's Short Stories and Speeches.* Tokyo: Kaibunsha, 1957. 66 pp. Wrappers, with dust jacket. Edited, with an introduction and notes, by Shuichi Motoda. (Contains "A Rose for Emily," the Nobel Prize Address, "To the Youth of Japan," and "Wash.") [Only two copies examined.]

## D. SWEDEN

*The Wild Palms.* Stockholm, London: Continental Book Company, 1945. 314 pp. Wrappers, with dust jacket. Vol. 68 in the Zephyr Books Library of British and American authors. [Only two copies examined.]

*Sanctuary.* Stockholm, London: Continental Book Company, 1947. 254 pp. Wrappers, with dust jacket. Vol. 120 in the Zephyr Books Library of British and American authors. [Only two copies examined.]

PART FOUR

*THE TRANSLATIONS*

Introduction

I. List of Books by Faulkner Which Have Been Translated

II. Check List of Translations

# INTRODUCTION

THIS check list of Faulkner translations I offer unhappily, and with apologies. The unhappiness can be attributed to the fact that though such a list was needed, for several years I have been hoping that someone else would undertake it, and no one has proved foolish enough to do so. The apologies are for the fact that the list is quite certainly both incomplete and inaccurate.

When I began, in the spring of 1956, to compile a check list of Faulkner's writings, I quickly (and, I now know, correctly) decided that to include the translations would add more to the labor than to the value of the project. Translations are an index to an author's popularity, they are vital to the study of literary influences, they may just possibly shed light upon obscure passages in the original,[1] and they may well include valuable introductions—if written by the translator, at any rate, one is assured of reading criticism by someone who has a closer knowledge of the text than do most critics who have written about Faulkner. But no bibliography of translations can conform to even the most lenient standards of bibliographic completeness, much less accuracy, unless the compiler has an extraordinary combination of linguistic competence and the time and means for sufficient travel to examine multiple copies of many translations.

This check list, then, is offered, with all its deficiencies in completeness and accuracy, merely as a contribution toward a bibliography of Faulkner translations. The twenty-nine countries where translations have been published are listed alphabetically; under each country, the main entry for each translation appears alphabetically according to the original English title. For some countries the dual rendering of original and translated title may seem superfluous, but I hope that the practice will justify itself on the whole. As a table of contents and cross reference to these main entries, a preliminary table lists alphabetically the titles of all Faulkner's books which have been translated, each followed by a chronological list of the countries where translations have appeared. Unfortunately, where two or more translations ap-

---

[1] An example is the French translation of *The Sound and the Fury* by Maurice E. Coindreau. As Professor Coindreau indicates in his Preface, he worked closely with Faulkner himself upon the translation. I should add, however, that this is the only case which has come to my attention where Faulkner has taken any part in the process of translating his books.

peared the same year, I have not obtained sufficient data to determine the proper chronological order, and therefore within each year, the order is merely alphabetical.

The main entry for each translation includes the original title, the translated title (occasionally in somewhat shortened form), the name of the translator, the place and date of publication, the pagination, and notice of the presence of additional matter like introductions and illustrations. Since I have been able to examine only about half the translations listed, and of those examined was able to see only one copy of the majority, it was not possible to adhere to any general standard of description which might have made it easier for the user of this list to distinguish between various impressions or issues by the presence or absence of certain information on the title page. Therefore there is no certainty that a date of publication or name of translator or even name of publisher, as given here, appears upon the title-page or any other page of the translation described. Further, though I have given, where possible, the number of the last numbered page of each book, it is fairly certain that in some of the cases where I have relied upon information supplied by others, a method of description has been followed which supplied inferred numbers. For such discrepancies in the format, as well as the errors, I ask the reader's indulgence, and welcome his corrections.

No attempt has been made to list impressions subsequent to the first, or the binding variants and different issues of the original editions described. Gallimard, for example, has commonly published its translations of Faulkner into French in multiple issues, and several countries have released what appear to be the same sheets in both wrappers and in cloth—whether simultaneously or not I do not know. Nor have I attempted to include translations which appeared in foreign periodicals, or in anthologies of work by several authors. These problems call for final resolution, I believe, by individuals working within the countries of origin of the translations.[2] I have noted later edi-

[2] For a fine example of what can be done along such lines, see Stanley D. Woodworth's list of periodical appearances of Faulkner translations in his *William Faulkner en France (1931-1952)*, Paris, 1959. I know of no other such listing. However, as libraries in eight countries (Argentina, Belgium, Holland, Hungary, Poland, Portugal, Russia, and Sweden) were kind enough to include information about periodical and anthology appearances in their replies to my questions about books, I have deposited this correspondence in the Faulkner Collection of the Princeton University Library, where it can be consulted by anyone who wishes to pursue the subject beyond the scope of the present check list.

tions—*i.e.*, new settings-up of type—whenever possible, but have noted later impressions of each edition only when there was evidence of a significant change—addition or omission of an introduction, or a change in publisher or place of publication that might cause confusion.

In all, Faulkner has written twenty-eight books published in this country, counting as books the two separately published short stories (*Idyll in the Desert* and *Miss Zilphia Gant*), and the episode in *A Fable* published earlier as *Notes on a Horsethief*. Of this total, twenty-three have been translated: all but *The Marble Faun* (his first book, a volume of verse), *Notes on a Horsethief*, *Idyll in the Desert, Big Woods*, and the recently published *The Mansion*. Several of these gaps are likely to be soon filled: the translation rights to *Big Woods* have been secured in Japan, for *Idyll in the Desert* in Italy, and for *The Mansion* in Italy, Sweden, and Switzerland.

These translations have appeared in twenty-nine countries. As might be expected, France leads with a total of twenty books translated—I count here only those translations which were original books by Faulkner, not the various combinations and collections made by foreign publishers without regard for the original form of the works. Italy follows with seventeen. Surprisingly enough, Argentina is a close third, tied with Germany, at fifteen. To turn to the works translated, as might also be expected, *Sanctuary* leads in number of translations, with sixteen countries and thirteen languages. (Germany and Switzerland commonly share the same German translation. Argentina and Spain have occasionally shared the same translation, more often used different ones. Portugal and Brazil share a language but not, so far, any Faulkner translations.) Unexpectedly, *The Wild Palms* follows, with thirteen countries. *Light in August* appears in twelve. Many of the books have appeared in from four to eight countries, and indeed the spread of translations is a remarkable one. Translations of *A Fable* and *As I Lay Dying*, for instance, have appeared in a total of nine countries each, but both novels have appeared in only four of them. It might be tempting to speculate upon what national variations in literary taste account for such discrepancies, but the passage of even a small amount of time is apt to change the evidence radically. The records of Faulkner's publishers reveal that permissions have been obtained, some of them for many years, for many more books than have been translated, and the discrepancy between the date when permission was acquired and the date when the translation appeared for not a few of the published books indicates how soon the picture may change.

I have of necessity depended to an unusual degree upon the efforts of others in compiling this list. I am grateful to four collectors who made available to me their Faulkner translations, or corresponded with me about them: Carl Petersen, H. Richard Archer, James Bloom, and Linton Massey. Albert Erskine and Emmanuel Harper of Random House, Inc., Faulkner's publisher, made available records and many copies of the more recent translations. Mrs. Marguerite Cohn, of the House of Books, called attention to several recent translations I might otherwise have missed. Joe C. Rees, of the University of North Carolina Library School, did much of the preliminary work of consulting the annual volumes of the *Index Translationum* and the various national bibliographies, and assembling the data from other sources as it was added to the list. At the Princeton University Library, I am indebted to Alexander D. Wainwright, Noburu Hiraga, and Miss Katharine S. Pearce for their assistance in identifying and transliterating Japanese, Yugoslavian, and Russian names and titles.

But my heaviest obligation is to these scholars and librarians in various foreign countries: Miss Laura Martinez of the Biblioteca Nacional in Buenos Aires; Dr. F. Rennhofer of the Österreichische Nationalbibliothek in Vienna; L. Danckaert, Librarian of the Bibliothèque Royale in Brussels; Miss Celuta Moreira Gomes of the Biblioteca Nacional in Rio de Janeiro; Ernesto Galliano of the Biblioteca Nacional in Santiago; Mrs. Lis Rigun of the Det Kgl. Bibliotek in Copenhagen; H. Sauget of the Société des Amis de la Bibliothèque Nationale et des Grandes Bibliothèques de France; H. Höhne and Dr. Schaaf of the Deutsche Bücherei in Leipzig; Miss M. van Laarhoven of the Koninklijke Bibliotheek in The Hague; Dr. Alice Goriupp of the Bibliotheque Nationale Széchényi in Budapest; Mansuino Carlo of Florence, Italy; I. Hatsukade of the National Diet Library in Tokyo; Dr. Manuel Alcalá of the Biblioteca Nacional in Mexico City; Erling Grønland of the Universitetsbiblioteket in Oslo; Dr. Bogdan Horodyski, Director of the Biblioteka Narodowa in Warsaw; Luísa Maria de Castro e Azevedo of the Biblioteca Nacional in Lisbon; V. Cândea and Professor Gh. Vlădescu-Răcoasa of the Academiei Republicii Populare Romîne in Bucharest; I. Rudo-

126

mino, Director of the Library of Foreign Literatures, Moscow; Justo Garcia Morales of the Biblioteca Nacional in Madrid; Olof von Feilitzen of the Kungl. Biblioteket in Stockholm; Cevat Çapan of the Department of English, University of Istanbul; the Director of the Schweizerische Landesbibliothek in Berne; and Cedomir Minderovic of the Narodna Biblioteka in Belgrade. To my requests for information they responded patiently and carefully, though the demand for a complete list of translations into their languages was an imposition and the following correspondence often even more so. I can only thank them again, and acknowledge that this list would not have been possible without their assistance.

## I. *List of Books by Faulkner Which Have Been Translated*

*Absalom, Absalom!*, 1936: Germany (1938); Argentina (1950); France (1953); Italy (1954); Japan (1958); Poland (1959).

*As I Lay Dying*, 1930: France (1934); Argentina (1942); Sweden (1948); Finland (1952); Denmark (1954); Spain (1954); Holland (1955); Italy (1958); Japan (1959).

*Collected Stories*, 1950: Poland (1958).    See also under *Doctor Martino* and *These 13*.

*Doctor Martino and Other Stories*, 1934: France (1948).

*A Fable*, 1954: Germany and Switzerland (1955); Mexico (1955); Spain (1955); Argentina (1956); Brazil (1956); Chile (1956); France (1958); Japan (1960).

*Go Down, Moses*, 1942: Italy (1947); Germany* and Switzerland* (1953); France (1955); Spain (1955).

*A Green Bough*, 1933: France (1955); Germany* and Switzerland* (1957).

*The Hamlet*, 1940: Italy (1942); Argentina (1947); Spain (1953); Germany and Switzerland (1957); France (1959).

*Intruder in the Dust*, 1948: Denmark (1950); Sweden (1950); Argentina (1951); Belgium and Holland (1951); Germany and Switzerland (1951); Italy (1951); Japan (1951); France (1952); Portugal (1952); Yugoslavia (1953); Czechoslovakia (1958).

*Knight's Gambit*, 1949: Argentina (1951); France* (1951); Japan (1951); Denmark (1952).

*Light in August*, 1932: Norway (1934); France (1935); Germany (1935); Czechoslovakia (1936); Holland (1938); Italy (1939);

---

* Substantially the same, but part of contents omitted in translation.

127

Argentina (1942); Sweden (1944); Denmark (1946); Brazil (1948); Yugoslavia (Slovenian, 1952; Serbo-Croatian, 1953); Poland (1959).

*Miss Zilphia Gant*, 1932: Italy (1959).

*Mosquitoes*, 1927: France (1948); Argentina (1956); Italy (1957); Spain (1959).

*Pylon*, 1935: Germany (1936); Italy (1937); France (1946); Spain (1947); Denmark (1952); Japan (1954).

*Requiem for a Nun*, 1951: Argentina (1952); Sweden (1952); Italy (1955); France (acting version, 1956; original version, 1957); Germany and Switzerland (1956; acting version, Germany only, 1956); Brazil (acting version, 1958); Portugal (1958).

*Sanctuary*, 1931: France (1933); Spain (1934); Czechoslovakia (1935); Denmark (1942); Italy (1943); Argentina (1945); Brazil (1948); Japan (1950); Holland (1951); Norway (1951); Sweden (1951); Switzerland (1951); Germany (1953); Yugoslavia (1953); Poland (1957); Portugal (1958).

*Sartoris*, 1929: France (1937); Italy (1946); Argentina (1953); Sweden (1955); Portugal (1958).

*Soldiers' Pay*, 1926: Norway (1932); France (1948); Japan (1951); Argentina (1953); Italy (1953); Spain (1954); Japan (1957); Germany (1958).

*The Sound and the Fury*, 1929: France (1938); Argentina (1947); Italy (1947); Japan (1954); Germany and Switzerland (1956); Yugoslavia (1958).

*These 13*, 1931: France (1939); Italy (1948); Argentina (1944* and 1956).

*The Town*, 1957: Germany and Switzerland (1958); Sweden (1958); Yugoslavia (1959); Spain (1960).

*The Unvanquished*, 1938: Holland (1938); Italy (1948); Sweden (1948); France (1949); Spain (1951); Germany and Switzerland (1954); Iran (1956); Norway (1957); Czechoslovakia (1958); Portugal (1960).

*The Wild Palms*, 1939: Denmark (1939); Argentina (1940); Finland (1947); Sweden (1949); Japan (1950); France (1952); Italy (1956); Germany and Switzerland (1957); Korea (1958); Poland (1958); Yugoslavia (1959); Czechoslovakia (1960).

## II. *Check List of Translations*

## ARGENTINA

### Absalom, Absalom!

*¡Absalón, Absalón!* tr. by Beatriz Florencia Nelson. Buenos Aires, Emecé, 1950. 409 pp. With a short prefatory note by the translator.

### As I Lay Dying

*Mientras yo agonizo,* tr. by Max Dickmann. Buenos Aires, Santiago Rueda, 1942. 267 pp. With a preface by the translator.

### A Fable

*Una fábula,* tr. by Antonio Ribera. Buenos Aires, Jackson, 1956. 365 pp. With a preface by Agustín Bartra.

### The Hamlet

*El villorrio,* tr. by Raquel W. de Ortiz. Buenos Aires, Futuro, 1947. 312 pp.

### Intruder in the Dust

*Intruso en el polvo,* tr. by Aída Aisenson. Buenos Aires, Losada, 1951. 222 pp.

### Knight's Gambit

*Gambito de caballo,* tr. by Lucrecia Moreno de Sáenz. Buenos Aires, Emecé, 1951. 263 pp.

### Light in August

*Luz de Agosto,* tr. by Pedro Lecuona. Buenos Aires, Sur, 1942. 434 pp. Also Buenos Aires, Goyanarte, 1957, 353 pp.

### Mosquitoes

*Mosquitos,* tr. by Jerónimo Córdoba. Buenos Aires, Siglo Veinte, 1956. 318 pp.

### Requiem for a Nun

*Réquiem para una mujer,* tr. by Jorge Zalamea. Buenos Aires, Emecé, 1952. 225 pp.

### Sanctuary

*Santuario,* tr. by Lino Novás Calvo. Buenos Aires, Espasa-Calpe, 1945. 217 pp. With a preface by Antonio Marichalar.

### Sartoris

*Sartoris,* tr. by Francisco Gurza. Buenos Aires, Schapire, 1953. 340 pp.

## SOLDIERS' PAY

*La paga de los soldados,* tr. by Francisco Gurza. Buenos Aires, Schapire, 1953. 323 pp.

## THE SOUND AND THE FURY

*El sonido y la furia,* tr. by Floreal Mazía. Buenos Aires, Futuro, 1947. 230 pp.

## THESE 13

*Victoria y otros relatos,* tr. by José Blaya Lozano. Buenos Aires, Corinto, 1944. 316 pp. Contains twelve of the thirteen stories, omitting "Carcassonne."

*Estos trece,* tr. by Aurora Bernárdez. Buenos Aires, Losada, 1956. 265 pp.

## THE WILD PALMS

*Las palmeras salvajes,* tr. by Jorge Luis Borges. Buenos Aires, Sudamericana, 1940. 365 pp.

# BELGIUM

## INTRUDER IN THE DUST

*Ongenode gast,* tr. into Dutch by Apie Prins. Amsterdam and Antwerp, Wereld-Bibliotheek, 1951. 237 pp. (Published simultaneously in Belgium and Holland.)

# BRAZIL

## A FABLE

*Uma fábula,* tr. by Olívia Krähenbühl. São Paulo and Rio de Janeiro, Mérito, 1956. 410 pp. With a preface by the translator.

## LIGHT IN AUGUST

*Luz de Agôsto,* tr. by Berenice Xavier. Rio de Janeiro, Porto Alegre, Globo, 1948. 348 pp.

## REQUIEM FOR A NUN

*Oração para uma negra,* tr. by Guilherme Figueiredo. Rio de Janeiro, Agir, 1958. 159 pp. (Translated from the Camus adaptation.)

## SANCTUARY

*Santuário,* tr. by Lígia Junqueira Smith. São Paulo, Instituto Progresso, 1948. 300 pp.

## CHILE

### A Fable

*Una Fábula*, tr. by Antonio Ribera. Santiago, Circulo Literario, 1956. 365 pp. With an introduction by Agustín Bartra.

## CZECHOSLOVAKIA

### Intruder in the Dust

*Neodpočívej v pokoji*, tr. by Jiří Valja. Prague, Naše Vojsko, 1958. 177 pp. With an afterword by Dr. Libuše Bubeníková.

### Light in August

*Srpnové Světlo*, tr. by Vilém Werner. Prague, Nakladatelské družstvo Máje, 1936. 357 pp.

### Sanctuary

*Svatyné*, tr. by Z. Wattersonova. Prague, Kvasnicka a Hampl, 1935. 268 pp.

### The Unvanquished

*Nepřemoženi,* tr. by Josef Schwarz. Prague, Naše Vojsko, 1958. 167 pp.

### The Wild Palms

*Divoké palmy*, tr. by Jiří Valja. Prague, Mladá Fronta, 1960. 288 pp. With illustrations by Vladimír Fuka, and an afterword by the translator.

### twenty stories

*Růže pro Emilii*, tr. by Josef Schwarz and Zdeněk Urbánek. Prague, Státní Nakladatelství, 1958. 383 pp. Contains an afterword by Vítězslav Kocourek, "Lo!," "Mountain Victory," "Wash," "Barn Burning," "A Rose for Emily," "That Will Be Fine," "That Evening Sun," "Dry September," "A Bear Hunt," "Elly," "The Brooch," "Pennsylvania Station," "Golden Land," "Crevasse," "Ad Astra," "Victory," "Turnabout," "The Tall Men," "Two Soldiers," and "Shall Not Perish."

## DENMARK

### As I Lay Dying

*I min sidste time*, tr. by Gunnar Juel-Jørgensen. Copenhagen, Carit Andersen, 1954. 172 pp.

#### Intruder in the Dust

*Ubuden gaest i støvet*, tr. by Mogens Boisen. Copenhagen, Aschehoug, 1950. 277 pp.

#### Knight's Gambit

*Høje ret!*, tr. by Georg Gjedde. Copenhagen, Wangel, 1952. 240 pp.

#### Light in August

*Lys i August*, tr. by Sven Møller Kristensen. Copenhagen, Athenaeum, 1946. 456 pp.

#### Pylon

*Trekanten*, tr. by Peter Toubro. Copenhagen, Fønss, 1952. 231 pp. (I am informed that the original issue bore no date, and that later in 1952, Fønss Forlag was taken over by Winthers Forlag, which reissued the book the same year.)

#### Sanctuary

*Det allerhelligste*, tr. by Sven Møller Kristensen. Copenhagen, Athenaeum, 1942. 272 pp.

#### The Wild Palms

*De vilde palmer*, tr. by Niels Haislund and Sven Møller Kristensen. Copenhagen, Athenaeum, 1939. 308 pp. Also Copenhagen, Gyldendal, 1959, 237 pp., with an introduction by Harald Engberg.

#### The Nobel Prize address

*William Faulkners Nobelpristale*, tr. by Kay Nielsen. Copenhagen, Aschehoug, 1951. (Two leaves, without pagination.)

#### "The Bear" (from Go Down, Moses)

*Bjørnen*, tr. by Ole Storm. Copenhagen, Gyldendal, 1957. 154 pp. With a preface by the translator.

## FINLAND

#### As I Lay Dying

*Kun tein kuolemaa*, tr. by Alex. Matson. Helsinki, Kustannusosakeyhtiö Tammi, 1952. 261 pp. With a preface by the translator.

#### The Wild Palms

*Villipalmut*, tr. by Alex. Matson. Helsinki, Kustannusosakeyhtiö Tammi, 1947. 307 pp. With a preface by the translator.

# FRANCE

## ABSALOM, ABSALOM!

*Absalon! Absalon!*, tr. by R.-N. Raimbault and Ch.-P. Vorce. Paris, Gallimard, 1953. 331 pp.

## AS I LAY DYING

*Tandis que j'agonise*, tr. by Maurice E. Coindreau. Paris, Gallimard, 1934. 270 pp. With a preface by Valery Larbaud. Also Paris, Éditions Jean Boisseau, 1946. 225 pp., with engravings by Pierre Courtin, and without the preface.

## DOCTOR MARTINO

*Le Docteur Martino et autres histoires*, tr. by R.-N. Raimbault and Ch.-P. Vorce. Paris, Gallimard, 1948. 335 pp.

## A FABLE

*Parabole*, tr. by R.-N. Raimbault. Paris, Gallimard, 1958. 481 pp.

## GO DOWN, MOSES

*Descends, Moïse*, tr. by R.-N. Raimbault. Paris, Gallimard, 1955. 318 pp.

## A GREEN BOUGH

*Le rameau vert*, tr. by R.-N. Raimbault. Paris, Gallimard, 1955. 220 pp. With parallel English and French texts.

## THE HAMLET

*Le hameau*, tr. by René Hilleret. Paris, Gallimard, 1959. 400 pp.

## INTRUDER IN THE DUST

*L'intrus*, tr. by R.-N. Raimbault. Paris, Gallimard, 1952. 301 pp.

## KNIGHT'S GAMBIT

*Le gambit du cavalier*, tr. by André du Bouchet. Paris, Gallimard, 1951. 263 pp. Omits the story "Smoke."

## LIGHT IN AUGUST

*Lumière d'août*, tr. by Maurice E. Coindreau. Paris, Gallimard, 1935. 421 pp. Preface by the translator.

## MOSQUITOES

*Moustiques*, tr. by Pierre Desgroupes. Paris, Éditions de Minuit, 1948. 388 pp. With an introduction by Raymond Queneau.

## PYLON

*Pylone,* tr. by R.-N. Raimbault and Mme. Germaine Louis-Rousselet. Paris, Gallimard, 1946. 270 pp. Of three copies of the first impression I have examined, two have contained an unattached errata slip correcting an error on p. 244, line 27.

## REQUIEM FOR A NUN

*Requiem pour une nonne,* tr. by Maurice E. Coindreau. Paris, Gallimard, 1957. 314 pp. With a preface by Albert Camus.

(acting version)

————, tr. and adapted by Albert Camus. Paris, Gallimard, 1956. 196 pp.

## SANCTUARY

*Sanctuaire,* tr. by R.-N. Raimbault and Henri Delgove. Paris, Gallimard, 1933. 308 pp. With a preface by André Malraux. Also Gallimard, 1958?, 436 pp., in their series Le Livre de Poche.

## SARTORIS

*Sartoris,* tr. by R.-N. Raimbault and Henri Delgove. Paris, Gallimard, 1937. 335 pp.

## SOLDIERS' PAY

*Monnaie de singe,* tr. by Maxime Gaucher. Grenoble and Paris, Arthaud, 1948. 363 pp. With a preface by the translator.

## THE SOUND AND THE FURY

*Le bruit et la fureur,* tr. by Maurice E. Coindreau. Paris, Gallimard, 1938. 309 pp. With a preface by the translator. Also Gallimard, 1959, in their series Le Livre de Poche.

## THESE 13

*Treize histoires,* tr. by R.-N. Raimbault, Ch.-P. Vorce, and Maurice E. Coindreau. Paris, Gallimard, 1939. 280 pp. With a preface by R.-N. Raimbault.

## THE UNVANQUISHED

*L'invaincu,* tr. by R.-N. Raimbault and Ch.-P. Vorce. Paris, Gallimard, 1949. 280 pp.

## THE WILD PALMS

*Les palmiers sauvages,* tr. by Maurice E. Coindreau. Paris, Gallimard, 1952. 348 pp. With a preface by the translator.

anthology

*Jefferson, Mississippi*, edited by Michel Mohrt. Paris, Le Club du meilleur livre (by arrangement with Gallimard), 1956. 458 pp. With illustrations by Jacques Noël. Contains a map (based upon that in the American edition of *Absalom, Absalom!*) of Jefferson and Yoknapatawpha County, an introduction by the editor, and translations of seven short stories and excerpts from seven books. These selections, all but one of which had previously appeared, are grouped in six sections, each with a brief introduction by the editor: "Le Tribunal," containing "A Name for the City" from *Requiem for a Nun*; "Sutpen," containing an excerpt from *Absalom, Absalom!*, and "Wash" from *Doctor Martino*; "Les Sartoris," containing excerpts from *Sartoris* and *The Unvanquished*, and "All the Dead Pilots" and "There Was a Queen"; "Les Compson," containing "A Justice," "That Evening Sun," and excerpts from *The Sound and the Fury* (including the Appendix, tr. by Maurice E. Coindreau, published here for the first time); "Les McCaslin," containing "The Bear" from *Go Down, Moses*; and "Deux Portraits de Femmes," containing "A Rose for Emily" and "Dry September."

## GERMANY

### ABSALOM, ABSALOM!

*Absalom, Absalom!*, tr. by Hermann Stresau. Berlin, Rowohlt, 1938. 373 pp. Also Stuttgart, Hamburg, and Baden-Baden, Rowohlt, 1948. 373 pp. Also Hamburg, Rowohlt, 1956, 373 pp.

### A FABLE

*Eine Legende*, tr. by Kurt Heinrich Hansen. Stuttgart, Scherz & Goverts, 1955. 509 pp. (Published simultaneously in Switzerland.)

### GO DOWN, MOSES (see also "The Bear")

*Das verworfene Erbe*, tr. by Hermann Stresau. Stuttgart and Hamburg, Scherz & Goverts, 1953. 358 pp. This translation omits "Pantaloon in Black," and includes a genealogy of the McCaslin family. (Published simultaneously in Switzerland.)

### A GREEN BOUGH

*Ein grüner Zweig*, tr. by Hans Hennecke. Stuttgart, Goverts, 1957. 80 pp. Contains twenty-five of the forty-four poems of the original, with parallel English and German texts, and an afterword by the translator. (Published earlier in the same year in Switzerland.)

### The Hamlet (see also "Spotted Horses")

*Das Dorf*, tr. by Helmut M. Braem and Elisabeth Kaiser. Stuttgart, Goverts, 1957. 413 pp. (Published simultaneously in Switzerland.)

### Intruder in the Dust

*Griff in den Staub*, tr. by Harry Kahn. Stuttgart and Hamburg, Scherz & Goverts, 1951. 275 pp. (Published simultaneously in Switzerland.) Also Darmstadt, Das goldene Vlies, [no date; 1954 or 1955?,] 184 pp.

### Light in August

*Licht in August*, tr. by Franz Fein. Berlin, Rowohlt, 1935. 455 pp. Other editions of this translation are: Hamburg and Stuttgart, Rowohlt, 1949, 95 pp. (a paperback without wrappers, the format resembling a newspaper, 11 x 15 inches), illustrated by John A. Krause and Wilhelm M. Busch; Stuttgart, Hamburg, and Baden-Baden, Rowohlt, 1949, 455 pp.; Berlin and Darmstadt, Deutsche Buch-Gemeinschaft, 1951, 406 pp.; Hamburg, Rowohlt, 1955, 365 pp.; Berlin, Volk & Welt, 1957, 508 pp.

### Pylon

*Wendemark*, tr. by Georg Goyert. Berlin, Rowohlt, 1936. 295 pp. Also Hamburg, Rowohlt, 1951, 222 pp.

### Requiem for a Nun

*Requiem für eine Nonne*, tr. by Robert Schnorr. Stuttgart, Scherz & Goverts, 1956. 316 pp. (Published simultaneously in Switzerland.) Also Darmstadt, Moderner Buch-Club, 1958, 271 pp.

### (acting version)

————, tr. and adapted by Robert Schnorr. Frankfurt, Fischer, 1956. 171 pp. This translation, reproduced from typewritten copy, was available for acting purposes only and not for general sale.

### Sanctuary

*Die Freistatt*, tr. by Herberth E. Herlitschka. Cologne and Berlin, Kiepenheuer & Witsch, 1953. 218 pp. (Published in Switzerland in 1951.) Also Frankfurt, Das goldene Vlies, 1955, 218 pp. (includes the Modern Library introduction).

*Soldatenlohn*, tr. by Susanna Rademacher. Hamburg, Rowohlt, 1958. 242 pp.

## THE SOUND AND THE FURY

*Schall und Wahn*, tr. by Helmut M. Braem and Elisabeth Kaiser. Stuttgart, Scherz & Goverts, 1956. 336 pp. (Published simultaneously in Switzerland.)

## THE TOWN

*Die Stadt*, tr. by Elisabeth Schnack. Stuttgart, Goverts, 1958. 387 pp. (Published simultaneously in Switzerland.)

## THE UNVANQUISHED

*Die Unbesiegten*, tr. by Erich Franzen. Stuttgart, Scherz & Goverts, 1954. 274 pp. With a preface by the translator. (Published simultaneously in Switzerland.) Also Frankfurt and Hamburg, Fischer, 1957, 210 pp.

## THE WILD PALMS

*Wilde Palmen und Der Strom*, tr. by Helmut M. Braem and Elisabeth Kaiser. Stuttgart, Scherz & Goverts, 1957. 321 pp. (Published simultaneously in Switzerland.)

## "The Bear" (from GO DOWN, MOSES)

*Der Bär*, tr. by Hermann Stresau. Frankfurt and Vienna, Forum, 1955. 169 pp. (Published simultaneously in Switzerland.) Also Berlin and Frankfurt, Suhrkamp, 1960, 180 pp.

## "Mountain Victory"

*Sieg in den Bergen*, tr. by Hans Hennecke. Munich, Langen & Müller, 1956. 67 pp. With an afterword by the translator.

## "Spotted Horses" (episode from THE HAMLET)

*Scheckige Mustangs*, tr. by Kurt Alboldt. Wiesbaden, Insel, 1956. 76 pp.

### three stories

*Abendsonne: Drei Erzählungen*, tr. by Erich Franzen. Munich, Piper, 1956. 76 pp. Contains "That Evening Sun," "Red Leaves," and "Dry September."

### two stories

*Meine Grossmutter Millard und die Schlacht am Harrykin-Bach;*

*Schwarzer Harlekin*, tr. by Elisabeth Schnack and Hermann Stresau. Stuttgart, Reclam, 1958. 91 pp. Contains "My Grandmother Millard and General Bedford Forrest and the Battle of Harrykin Creek," and "Pantaloon in Black" (from *Go Down, Moses*), with an afterword by Helmut M. Braem.

## GREECE

### "Smoke" and Other Stories

*Kapnos kai alla diégémata*, tr. by Bas. L. Kazantzés. Athens, Eklekta, [no date]. 128 pp. Contains an introduction by the translator, and "Smoke," "Tomorrow," "Knight's Gambit," and "Hand upon the Waters" from *Knight's Gambit*.

## HOLLAND

### As I Lay Dying

*Uitvaart in Mississippi*, tr. by Apie Prins and John Vandenbergh. Amsterdam, Bezige Bij, 1955. 197 pp.

### Intruder in the Dust

*Ongenode gast*, tr. by Apie Prins. Amsterdam and Antwerp, Wereld-Bibliotheek, 1951. 237 pp. (Published simultaneously in Holland and Belgium.)

### Light in August

*Het licht in Augustus*, tr. by I. E. Prins-Willekes Macdonald. Rotterdam, Van Staal & Co., 1938. 476 pp. With an introduction by Theun de Vries.

*Geboorte in Augustus*, tr. by I. E. Prins-Willekes Macdonald. Amsterdam, Querido, 1951. 365 pp. (Translation originally published in 1938 as *Het licht in Augustus*.)

### Sanctuary

*Grijze zomer*, tr. by Johan van Keulen. The Hague, Oisterwijk, 1951. 201 pp. Later impressions, with 208 pp., contain an introduction by the translator.

### The Unvanquished

*De familie Sartoris*, [name of translator not indicated]. Haarlem, Spaarnestad, 1938. 318 pp. With illustrations by Edward Shenton.

138

"Go Down, Moses" and "The Old People"
(from Go Down, Moses)
*Het Oude Volk*, tr. by Hans Edinga. Delft, W. Gaade, 1957. 76 pp. With a preface by the translator.

## HUNGARY

"The Bear" (from Go Down, Moses)
*A medve*, tr. by Viktor János. Budapest, Európa Könyvkiadó, 1959. 201 pp. With a genealogy of the McCaslin family, p. [203].

## ICELAND

### stories
*Smásögur*, tr. by Kristján Karlsson, Reykjavik, Almenna Boka-félagid, 1956. 140 pp. Contains a foreword, and "Dry September," "Elly," "That Evening Sun," "Wash," "A Rose for Emily," and "A Justice."

## IRAN

### The Unvanquished
*Taskhīr nā pazīr*, tr. into Persian by Parvīz Dāryūsh. Teheran, Amīr Kabīr, 1956. 296 pp.

## ITALY

### Absalom, Absalom!
*Assalonne, Assalonne!*, tr. by Glauco Cambon. Milan and Verona, Mondadori, 1954. 449 pp. With a preface by the translator, and illustrations by Bianca de Feo.

### As I Lay Dying
*Mentre Morivo*, tr. by Giulio de Angelis. Milan and Verona, Mondadori, 1958. 242 pp.

### Go Down, Moses
*Scendi, Mosè*, tr. by Edoardo Bizzarri. Milan and Verona, Mondadori, 1947. 386 pp.

### The Hamlet
*Il Borgo*, tr. by Cesare Pavese. Milan and Verona, Mondadori, 1942. 420 pp.

### Intruder in the Dust

*Non si Fruga nella Polvere*, tr. by Fernanda Pivano. Milan and Verona, Mondadori, 1951. 309 pp. With an introduction by the translator.

### Light in August

*Luce d'Agosto*, tr. by Elio Vittorini. Milan and Verona, Mondadori, 1939. 484 pp. (Also Mondadori, 1954, 505 pp.)

### Miss Zilphia Gant

*La pallida Zilphia Gant*, tr. by Fernanda Pivano. Milan, Il Saggiatore, 1959. 45 pp. With a preface by the translator.

### Mosquitoes

*Zanzare*, tr. by Giulio de Angelis. Milan and Verona, Mondadori, 1957. 374 pp.

### Pylon

*Oggi si Vola*, tr. by Lorenzo Gigli. Milan and Verona, Mondadori, 1937. 287 pp. (I have seen a 1947 copy of this translation with 276 pp.)

### Requiem for a Nun

*Requiem per una Monaca*, tr. by Fernanda Pivano. Milan and Verona, Mondadori, 1955. 228 pp.

### Sanctuary

*Santuario*, tr. by Aldo Scagnetti. Milan and Rome, Jandi Sapi, 1943. 327 pp.

————, tr. by Paola Ojetti Zamattio. Milan and Verona, Mondadori, 1946. 368 pp. With an introduction by the translator, and illustrations by Renato Guttuso. (Also Mondadori, 1958, 327 pp., without the illustrations.)

### Sartoris

*Sartoris*, tr. by Filiberto Storoni. Milan and Rome, Jandi Sapi, 1946. 350 pp.

————, tr. by Maria Stella Ferrari. Milan, Garzanti, 1955. 450 pp.

### Soldiers' Pay

*La Paga del Soldato*, tr. by Massimo Alvaro. Milan, Garzanti, 1953. 379 pp.

### The Sound and the Fury

*L'Urlo e il Furore*, tr. by Augusto Dauphiné. Milan and Verona, Mondadori, 1947. 261 pp.

## These 13
*Questi Tredici*, tr. by Francesco Lo Bue. Turin, Lattes, 1948. 323 pp. With an introduction by the translator.

## The Unvanquished
*Gli Invitti*, tr. by Alberto Marmont. Milan and Verona, Mondadori, 1948. 226 pp.

## The Wild Palms
*Palme Selvagge*, tr. by Bruno Fonzi. Milan and Verona, Mondadori, 1956. 335 pp.

## anthology (The Portable Faulkner)
*664 Pagine di William Faulkner*, tr. by Edoardo Bizzarri, Augusto Dauphiné, Alberto Marmont, Cesare Pavese, Fernanda Pivano, and Elio Vittorini. Milan, Il Saggiatore, 1959. 652 pp. With an introduction and notes by Malcolm Cowley. The contents are the same as in the Viking *Portable Faulkner* (New York, 1946), with the addition of two excerpts from *Requiem for a Nun*.

## New Orleans sketches
*New Orleans*, tr. by Cesare Salmaggi. Milan, Il Saggiatore, 1959. 71 pp. Contains an abridged version of Carvel Collins' introduction to his edition of these sketches (Rutgers Univ. Press, 1958), and six of the sixteen sketches: "Out of Nazareth," "The Kingdom of God," "The Kid Learns," "The Liar," "Country Mice," and "Yo Ho and Two Bottles of Rum."

# JAPAN

## Absalom, Absalom!
### (and other works)
*Gendai Amerika Bungaku Zenshu . . .* , tr. by Junzaburo Nishiwaki, *et al.* Tokyo, Arechi Shuppansha, 1958. 478 pp. (No. 8 in the series, Collection of Contemporary American Literature.) Contains *Absalom, Absalom!*, "The Bear," "A Rose for Emily," and "That Evening Sun."

## As I Lay Dying
### (and other works)
[Works by Faulkner and Hemingway,] tr. by Kenzo Ohashi, *et al.* Tokyo, Chikuma, 1959. 473 pp. Contains *As I Lay Dying, Pylon*, and "Mississippi" by Faulkner, with Hemingway's *A Farewell to Arms*.

## A Fable

*Guwa*, tr. by Tomoji Abe. Tokyo, Iwanami, 1960. 473 pp.

## Intruder in the Dust

*Bojō eno chinnyūsha*, tr. by Shōzō Katō. Tokyo, Hayakawa Shobō, 1951. 273 pp.

## Knight's Gambit

*Kishi no kansei*, tr. by Yasuo Ōkubo. Tokyo, Yukeisha, 1951. 360 pp. Also Tokyo, Shin'eisha, 1957, 255 pp.

## Pylon

*Sora no yūwaku*, tr. by Kenzo Ohashi. Tokyo, Dabiddosha, 1954. 263 pp. See also above, under *As I Lay Dying*.

## Sanctuary

*Tsumi no saidan*, tr. by Masami Nishikawa and Naotarō Tatsunokuchi. Tokyo, Getsuyō Shobō, 1950. 330 pp. Also Tokyo, Shinchōsha, 1955, 427 pp.

## Soldiers' Pay

*Heishi no kyūyo*, tr. by Saburo Yamaya. Tokyo, Hayakawa Shobō, 1951. 410 pp. Also published in 1957 in two volumes, 250 and 269 pp.

*Heishi no moratta hōshū*, tr. by Ichirō Nishizaki. Tokyo, Jiji Tsushinsha, 1956. 319 pp.

## The Sound and the Fury; five stories

*Hibiki to Ikari*, tr. by Masao Takahashi. Tokyo, Mikasa Shobō, 1954. 461 pp. Contains, in addition to the novel, the stories "A Rose for Emily," "Doctor Martino," "Red Leaves," "The Unvanquished" [?], and "That Evening Sun."

## The Wild Palms

*Yasei no jōnetsu*, tr. by Yasuo Ōkubo. Tokyo, Hibiya Shuppansha, 1950. 414 pp. Also Tokyo, Mikasa Shobō, 1951, 312 pp.

### five stories

*Emily no bara; Ryōken*, tr. by Masao Takahashi and Kichinosuke Ōhashi. Tokyo, Eihōsha, 1956. 190 pp. Contains "A Rose for Emily," "Crevasse," "The Hound," "Pantaloon in Black," and "Eula."

### six stories

*Tampenshū*, tr. by Naotarō Tatsunokuchi. Tokyo, Shinchōsha,

1955. 168 pp. Contains "Jealousy," "A Rose for Emily," "Dry September," "That Evening Sun," "Barn Burning," and "Wash."

eight stories

*Emily no bara*, tr. by Naotarō Tatsunokuchi. Tokyo, Cosmopolitansha, 1952. 344 pp. Contains "A Rose for Emily," "That Evening Sun," "Dry September," "An Odor of Verbena," "Delta Autumn." "Barn Burning," "Turnabout," and "The Hound."

## KOREA

### THE WILD PALMS

*Yasaeng eui zongyeol. Beommungak*. Seoul, Bak Seung Hun, 1958. 323 pp.

## LEBANON

five stories

*Dukhān wa qiṣaṣ ukhrā*, tr. into Arabic by Ādil Hāmid. Beirut, Dār al-Kitāb, 1957. 168 pp. Contains "Smoke," "Monk," "Hand upon the Waters," "Tomorrow," and "An Error in Chemistry" (all but the title story from *Knight's Gambit*), with a preface by the translator.

## MEXICO

### A FABLE

*Una Fábula*, tr. by Antonio Ribera. Mexico City, Editorial Cumbre, 1955. 365 pp. With an introduction by Agustí [*sic*] Bartra.

## NORWAY

### LIGHT IN AUGUST

*Mørk August*, tr. by Sigurd Hoel. Oslo, Gyldendal, 1934. 442 pp. (Also 1951, 426 pp.)

### SANCTUARY

*Det aller helligste*, tr. by Leo Strøm. Oslo, Gyldendal, 1951. 289 pp. With a foreword by Sigurd Hoel, and the Modern Library introduction.

### SOLDIERS' PAY

*Soldatens sold*, tr. by Hans Heiberg. Oslo, Gyldendal, 1932.

### THE UNVANQUISHED

*De ubeseirede*, tr. by Leo Strøm. Oslo, Gyldendal, 1957. 206 pp.

fourteen stories

*Noveller,* tr. by Leo Strøm. Oslo, Gyldendal, 1951. 261 pp. Contains a preface by the translator, "Was," "Barn Burning," "Two Soldiers," "Dry September," "All the Dead Pilots," "That Evening Sun," "Red Leaves," "A Justice," "A Courtship," "Ad Astra," "Wash," "Honor," "Doctor Martino," and "Carcassonne."

## POLAND

### Absalom, Absalom!

*Absalomie, Absalomie,* tr. by Zofia Kierszys. Warsaw, Państwowy Instytut Wydawniczy, 1959. 528 pp. With an afterword by the translator.

### Collected Stories

*Opowiadania,* tr. by Zofia Kierszys, Ewa Zycieńska, and Jan Zakrzewski. Warsaw, Państwowy Instytut Wydawniczy, 1958. 2 vols. 470, 605 pp. Vol. I contains the first twenty stories of the original edition, Vol. II contains the remaining twenty-two.

### Light in August

*Światłość w Sierpniu,* tr. by Maciej Słomczyński. Warsaw, Czytelnik, 1959. 509 pp.

### Sanctuary

*Azyl,* tr. by Zofia Kierszys. Warsaw, Państwowy Instytut Wydawniczy, 1957. 317 pp.

### The Wild Palms

*Dzikie Palmy; Stary,* tr. by Kalina Wojciechowska. Warsaw, Czytelnik, 1958. 410 pp. With an afterword by the translator. The two parts of the novel are printed separately, instead of alternately, chapter by chapter, as in the original.

## PORTUGAL

### Intruder in the Dust

*O Mundo não Perdoa,* tr. by Antônio de Sousa. Lisbon, Publicações Europa-America, 1952. 356 pp. With a prefatory note by the publisher.

### Requiem for a Nun

*Requiem por uma Freira,* tr. by Luis de Sousa Rebelo. Lisbon, Minerva (Coleccao Folio), 1958. 297 pp. With an introduction by the translator.

## SANCTUARY

*Santuário*, tr. by Marília de Vasconcelos. Lisbon, Minerva, 1958. 277 pp.

## SARTORIS

*Sartoris*, tr. by Carlos Vieira. Lisbon, Ulisseia, 1958. 422 pp. With a translation of the introduction by Robert Cantwell from the Signet edition (New York, 1953).

## THE UNVANQUISHED

*Os Invencidos*, tr. by Abel Marques Ribeiro. Lisbon, Minerva, 1960. 285 pp.

## "Old Man" (from THE WILD PALMS)

*O Homem e O Rio*, tr. by Luis de Sousa Rebelo. Lisbon, Portugalia, n.d. [1959 or 1960?]. 200 pp. With a preface by the translator. (No. 1 in the series, O Livro de Bolso.)

## six stories

*Antologia do Conto Moderno: William Faulkner*, tr. by Victor Palla. Coimbra, Atlântida-Livraria, 1948. 201 pp. Contains a preface by the translator, "That Evening Sun," "Elly," "Two Soldiers," "The Old People," "The Bear," and "Delta Autumn."

## RUMANIA

### five stories

*Victorie*, tr. by Margareta Sterian. Bucharest, Editura de stat pentru literatura si arta, 1957. 169 pp. Contains "Victory," "Dry September," "A Rose for Emily," "Red Leaves," and "A Justice." A 4 pp. publisher's note precedes the text.

## RUSSIA

### seven stories

*Sem' rasskazov*, tr. by I. Kashkin, O. Kholmskaya, R. Raĭm-Kovaleva, M. Bekker, and M. Bogoslovskaya. Moscow, Izdatel'stvo inostrannoĭ literatury, 1958. 177 pp. Contains an afterword by I. Kashkin, and "Barn Burning," "A Justice," "Red Leaves," "That Evening Sun," "Smoke," "Percy Grimm" [episode from *Light in August*], and "Victory."

# SPAIN

## As I Lay Dying

*Mientras agonizo*, tr. by Agustín Caballero Robredo and Arturo del Hoyo. Madrid, Aguilar, 1954. 243 pp. With an introduction by the translators.

## A Fable

*Una Fábula*, tr. by Antonio Ribera. Barcelona, Exito, 1955. 373 pp.

## Go Down, Moses

*¡Desciende, Moisés!*, tr. by Ana-María de Foronda. Barcelona, Caralt, 1955. 296 pp. With a prefatory note by the translator.

## The Hamlet

*El Villorrio*, tr. by J. Napoletano Torre and P. Carbó Amiguet. Barcelona, Caralt, 1953. 328 pp. (In three copies examined of what appears to be the first impression, the last page number is 283, but this is in error for 328.)

## Mosquitoes

*Mosquitos*, tr. by Domingo Manfredi. Barcelona, Caralt, 1959. 256 pp.

## Pylon

*Pylon*, tr. by Julio Fernández-Yáñez. Barcelona, Caralt, 1947. 221 pp.

## Sanctuary

*Santuario*, tr. by Lino Novás Calvo. Madrid, Espasa-Calpe, 1934. 269 pp. With a preface by Antonio Marichalar.

## Soldiers' Pay

*La Paga de los Soldados* [name of translator not indicated]. Barcelona, Caralt, 1954. 303 pp.

## The Town

*En la Ciudad*, tr. by Ramon Hernandez. Barcelona and Buenos Aires, Plaza & Janes, 1960. 351 pp. (Though the imprint lists both the Spanish and the Argentine branches of the publisher, the only two copies I have examined were issued by the Spanish branch.)

## The Unvanquished

*Los invictos*, tr. by Alberto Vilá de Avilés. Barcelona, Caralt, 1951. 222 pp.

*Obras escogidas*, Vol. I, tr. by Agustín Caballero Robredo, Arturo del Hoyo, Julio Fernández-Yáñez, Alberto Vilá de Avilés, J. Napoletano Torre, P. Carbó Amiguet, and Ana-María de Foronda. Madrid, Aguilar, 1956. 1266 pp. Contains a preface by Agustín Caballero Robredo; the Nobel Prize address; *Mientras agonizo; Pylon; Los invictos; El Villorrio;* and *¡Desciende, Moisés!*

NOTE: The firm of Caralt have announced their intention of bringing out an *Obras completas* of Faulkner, of which the first volume, bound in leather, will contain *La Paga de los Soldados; Mosquitos; El Villorrio;* and *¡Desciende, Moisés!* Each work will be illustrated by a different artist.

# SWEDEN

## As I Lay Dying

*Medan jag låg och dog*, tr. by Mårten Edlund. Stockholm, Bonnier, 1948. 205 pp.

## Intruder in the Dust

*Inkräktare i stoftet*, tr. by Th. Warburton. Stockholm, Bonnier, 1950. 202 pp.

## Light in August

*Ljus i augusti*, tr. by Erik Lindegren. Stockholm, Bonnier, 1944. 387 pp.

## Requiem for a Nun

*Själamässa för en nunna*, tr. by Mårten Edlund. Stockholm, Bonnier, 1952. 272 pp.

## Sanctuary

*Det allra heligaste*, tr. by Mårten Edlund. Stockholm, Bonnier, 1951. 236 pp.

## Sartoris

*Sartoris*, tr. by Th. Warburton. Stockholm, Bonnier, 1955. 285 pp.

## The Town

*Staden*, tr. by Pelle Fritz-Crone. Stockholm, Bonnier, 1958. 345 pp.

## The Unvanquished

*De obesegrade*, tr. by Håkan Norlén. Stockholm, Folket i Bild, 1948. 267 pp. With an introduction by Thorsten Jonsson.

## THE WILD PALMS

*De vilda palmerna*, tr. by Mårten Edlund. Stockholm, Bonnier, 1949. 260 pp.

### "The Bear" (from GO DOWN, MOSES)

*Björnen*, tr. by Olov Jonason. Stockholm, Rabén & Sjögren, 1959. 186 pp. With a foreword by the translator, and a genealogy.

## SWITZERLAND

### A FABLE

*Eine Legende*, tr. by Kurt Heinrich Hansen. Zurich, Fretz & Wasmuth, 1955. 509 pp. (Published simultaneously in Germany.)

### GO DOWN, MOSES
### (see also "Was")

*Das verworfene Erbe*, tr. by Hermann Stresau. Zurich, Fretz & Wasmuth, 1953. 358 pp. This translation omits "Pantaloon in Black," and includes a genealogy of the McCaslin family. (Published simultaneously in Germany.)

### A GREEN BOUGH

*Ein grüner Zweig*, tr. by Hans Hennecke. Zurich, Fretz & Wasmuth, 1957. 80 pp. Contains twenty-five of the forty-four poems of the original, with parallel English and German texts, and an afterword by the translator. (Published later in the same year in Germany.)

### THE HAMLET

*Das Dorf*, tr. by Helmut M. Braem and Elisabeth Kaiser. Zurich, Fretz & Wasmuth, 1957. 413 pp. (Published simultaneously in Germany.)

### INTRUDER IN THE DUST

*Griff in den Staub*, tr. by Harry Kahn. Zurich, Fretz & Wasmuth, 1951. 275 pp. (Published simultaneously in Germany.)

### REQUIEM FOR A NUN

*Requiem für eine Nonne*, tr. by Robert Schnorr. Zurich, Fretz & Wasmuth, 1956. 316 pp. (Published simultaneously in Germany.)

### SANCTUARY

*Die Freistatt*, tr. by Herberth E. Herlitschka. Zurich, Artemis, 1951. 279 pp. Includes the Modern Library introduction. Also

1953, 218 pp. (1953 edition also published in Germany in that year.)

### THE SOUND AND THE FURY

*Schall und Wahn,* tr. by Helmut M. Braem and Elisabeth Kaiser. Zurich, Fretz & Wasmuth, 1956. 336 pp. (Published simultaneously in Germany.)

### THE TOWN

*Die Stadt,* tr. by Elisabeth Schnack. Zurich, Fretz & Wasmuth, 1958. 387 pp. (Published simultaneously in Germany.)

### THE UNVANQUISHED

*Die Unbesiegten,* tr. by Erich Franzen. Zurich, Fretz & Wasmuth, 1954. 274 pp. With a preface by the translator. (Published simultaneously in Germany.)

### THE WILD PALMS

*Wilde Palmen und Der Strom,* tr. by Helmut M. Braem and Elisabeth Kaiser. Zurich, Fretz & Wasmuth, 1957. 321 pp. (Published simultaneously in Germany.)

### "Was" (from GO DOWN, MOSES)

*Jagdglück,* tr. by Elisabeth Schnack. Zurich, Arche, 1956. 46 pp. With an afterword by the translator.

## TURKEY

### four stories

*Doktor Martino,* tr. by Bilge Karasu. Istanbul, Yenilik Yayinevi, 1956. 79 pp. Contains "Go Down, Moses," "Elly," "Carcassonne," and "Doctor Martino."

### five stories

*Duman,* tr. by Talât Halman. Istanbul, Varlik Yayinevi, 1952. 124 pp. Contains "Smoke," "Hand upon the Waters," "Tomorrow," "An Error in Chemistry," and "Monk" (all save the title story from *Knight's Gambit*).

### anthology

*Kirmizi Yapraklar,* tr. by Ulkü Tamer. Istanbul, Ataç Kitapevi, 1959. Contains the Nobel Prize address and four stories: "That Evening Sun," "Dry September," "Red Leaves," and "A Justice."

# YUGOSLAVIA

## INTRUDER IN THE DUST

*Uljez u prašinu*, tr. into Serbo-Croatian by Svetozar Brkić. Belgrade, Novo pokoljenje, 1953. 234 pp.

## LIGHT IN AUGUST

*Svetloba v Avgustu*, tr. into Slovenian by Mira Mihelič. Ljubljana, Cankarjeva založba, 1952. 457 pp.
*Svjetlo u Augustu*, tr. into Serbo-Croatian by Šime Balen. Zagreb, Zora, 1953. 370 pp.

## SANCTUARY

*Svetilište*, tr. into Serbo-Croatian (Cyrillic alphabet) by Milica Mihajlović. Novi Sad, Bratstvo jedinstvo, 1953. 325 pp.

## THE SOUND AND THE FURY

*Krik i bijes*, tr. into Serbo-Croatian by Stjepan Krešić. Zagreb, Naprijed, 1958. 352 pp. Includes the Modern Library Appendix, and an introduction by the translator.

## THE TOWN

*Grad*, tr. into Serbo-Croatian by Branko Brusar. Zagreb, Mladost, 1959. 403 pp. With an afterword by the translator.

## THE WILD PALMS

*Divlje palme*, tr. into Serbo-Croatian by Herbert Grün. Ljubljana, Državna založba Slovenije, 1959. 278 pp.

## "The Bear" (from GO DOWN, MOSES)

*Medved*, tr. into Serbo-Croatian (Cyrillic alphabet) by Aleksandar Nejgebauer. Novi Sad, Matica srpska, 1954. 125 pp.

## "Knight's Gambit" (from KNIGHT'S GAMBIT)

*Konjički gambit*, tr. into Serbo-Croatian (Cyrillic alphabet) by Božidar Marković. Belgrade, Prosveta, 1954. 149 pp. Contains the title story only from *Knight's Gambit*, and an afterword, presumably by the translator.

## two stories

*Ruža za Emily; Sušni Septembar*, tr. into Serbo-Croatian by Ivan Slamnig and Antun Šoljan. Zagreb, Sloga, 1957. 42 pp. Contains "A Rose for Emily" and "Dry September."

# PART FIVE

## MOTION PICTURES AND TELEVISION

# INTRODUCTION

FAULKNER's career as a writer for the screen has been a long one. His professional connection with Hollywood began in 1933 with the MGM *Today We Live*, based on his short story "Turn About," and adapted for the screen by Faulkner himself, among others. Though this is the only movie based on his own writings which Faulkner has had a hand in adapting, five of his novels have been produced as motion pictures, and for a span of twenty years, off and on, he worked as a writer in Hollywood. In 1953 he similarly made his debut as a television writer by helping adapt one of his own stories, "The Brooch," and since that date there have been performances of an original Faulkner television play, and of eleven more adaptations from his stories or novels, one made by Faulkner himself.

To compile a list of Faulkner's works that have been adapted for movies or TV presents few problems, and the only scripts which he did for TV received wide publicity. But his own work for Hollywood is another matter. He has said that he has received film credit for work he did not do, and has not received credit for work which he did. The whole question of credits and attributions in film writing is a complex and, to the outsider, often insoluble one. A writer's part in a film may be anything from a small collaborative part in a screenplay to the writing of the entire script. He may do a treatment (that is, a preliminary outline of a script, perhaps with some dialogue) of a property (that is, a novel or play or other source for the script), or he may be assigned to the revision of someone else's treatment or screenplay. Whatever part he plays, even in the writing of the final screenplay used in the actual production of the movie, is unlikely to be reliably recorded in any detail anywhere that it is available for such a purpose as this check list. In short, there is likely to be very little point in attempting to determine anything about a film writer from the spoken dialogue of a movie or even from the script itself, save for the remote possibility of certain knowledge that the writer is the sole author of the final script.

Because of these factors, much of the information presented here about Faulkner's writing for Hollywood is speculative, with a high possibility of inaccuracy. But it still seems proper to me to attempt to assemble what is known about the subject, though

155

the reliability of the data may be open to question. No trace of Faulkner's hand may remain in a film, yet to record the fact or even the possibility that he worked on it may not only point the way toward eventual proof but also can help round out our picture of Faulkner—not Faulkner the artist and pioneer in fiction, but Faulkner the hardworking twentieth-century literary craftsman engaged in the business of making a living by his writing.

Most of the basic facts about the films provided in sections I and II of this listing were taken from three sources: the Library of Congress Copyright Office *Catalogue of Copyright Entries . . . : Motion Pictures, 1912-1939* (Washington, 1951), and its supplement for 1940-1949 (Washington, 1953); the biennial, later annual, volumes of the *Motion Picture Almanac* (published in New York by Quigley); and the annual volumes of the *Film Daily Year Book of Motion Pictures* (published in New York by the *Film Daily*). But for the attribution to Faulkner of most of the items listed in Ib. and Ic. I am indebted to George Sidney, who has kindly permitted me to make use here of his unpublished doctoral dissertation, "Faulkner in Hollywood: A Study of His Career as a Scenarist" (University of New Mexico, 1959). With few exceptions, all of them noted, the list of Faulkner's writing for the movies for which he did not receive screen credit is based on Dr. Sidney's valuable study.

Undocumented information concerning television adaptations is taken from the daily or weekly schedules, announcements, and advertisements of the Radio and Television programs in the *New York Times*, or the weekly listings of the *TV Guide* published by Triangle Publications, Inc., where they can be referred to by the date of the broadcast. Miss Anne Louise Davis of Harold Ober Associates was kind enough to supply me with a list of many of the titles and dates of performances.

## I. FAULKNER'S WRITING FOR
## MOTION PICTURES

a. *Pictures for which Faulkner received screen credit*:

1. *Today We Live*, released 28 April, 1933. Metro-Goldwyn-Mayer Corp. Producer and director, Howard Hawks. Story and dialogue, William Faulkner. Screenplay, Edith Fitzgerald

156

and Dwight Taylor. Cast includes Joan Crawford, Gary Cooper, and Robert Young. [Based on the Faulkner short story "Turn About." Faulkner did original treatment of the story.]

2. *Road to Glory*, released 4 September, 1936. Twentieth Century-Fox Film Corp. Director, Howard Hawks. Screenplay, Joel Sayre and William Faulkner.[1] Cast includes Fredric March, Warner Baxter, and Lionel Barrymore. [Based on the novel *Wooden Crosses* by Roland Dorgelès, New York, 1921.]

3. *Slave Ship*, released 2 July, 1937. Twentieth Century-Fox Film Corp. Director, Tay Garnett. Story, William Faulkner.[2] Screenplay, Sam Hellman, Lamar Trotti, and Gladys Lehman. Cast includes Wallace Beery and Warner Baxter. [Based on the novel *The Last Slaver*, by George S. King, New York, 1933.]

4. *To Have and Have Not*, released 20 January, 1945. Warner Brothers Pictures, Inc. Director, Howard Hawks. Screenplay, Jules Furthman and William Faulkner. Cast includes Humphrey Bogart and Lauren Bacall. [Based on the novel by Ernest Hemingway, New York, 1937.]

5. *The Big Sleep*, released 31 August, 1946. Warner Brothers Pictures, Inc. Director, Howard Hawks. Screenplay, William Faulkner, Leigh Brackett, and Jules Furthman. Cast includes Humphrey Bogart and Lauren Bacall. [Based on the novel by Raymond Chandler, New York, 1939.]

6. *Land of the Pharaohs*, released July 2, 1955. Continental Co., released by Warner Brothers Pictures, Inc. Producer and director, Howard Hawks. Screenplay, William Faulkner, Harry Kurnitz, and Harold Jack Bloom. Cast includes Jack Hawkins and Joan Collins.

[1] According to Sidney, p. 44, the final version of the screenplay was done by Nunnally Johnson, who "threw out much of what they had written, . . . at the same time insisting that Faulkner and Sayre receive screen credit." Sidney thinks (p. 42n.) that Faulkner may have written a treatment of it.

[2] Sidney concludes, p. 85 in the dissertation cited above, that "the attribution . . . to Faulkner is inexplicable and probably incorrect," basing his decision on records at the Twentieth Century-Fox offices which show no evidence that Faulkner worked on this property until the final credits were released. However, Sidney thinks that Faulkner may possibly have written a treatment of *The Last Slaver* (see pp. 42n. and 84).

b. *Pictures on which Faulkner worked for which he did not receive screen credit:*

NOTE: Included in this highly speculative listing are pictures in which Faulkner is supposed to have had a share in the finished production, and those for which he is supposed to have done work which was discarded before production.

1. *Lazy River*, released 7 March, 1934. Metro-Goldwyn-Mayer Corp. Producer, Lucien Hubbard. Director, George B. Seitz. Screenplay, Lucien Hubbard. Cast includes Jean Parker and Robert Young. [Faulkner did some work on the screenplay.]

2. *Banjo on My Knee*, released 4 Dec., 1936. Twentieth Century-Fox Film Corp. Director, John Cromwell. Screenplay, Nunnally Johnson. Cast includes Barbara Stanwyck and Joel McCrea. [Faulkner wrote a part of a discarded screenplay.[3]]

3. *Four Men and a Prayer*, released 29 April, 1938. Twentieth Century-Fox Film Corp. Director, John Ford. Screenplay, Richard Sherman, Sonya Levien, and Walter Ferris. Cast includes Loretta Young and Richard Greene. [Faulkner was assigned to this screenplay, but apparently did not complete the assignment.[4]]

4. *Submarine Patrol*, released 25 Nov., 1938. Twentieth Century-Fox Film Corp. Associate producer, Gene Markey. Director, John Ford. Screenplay, Rian James, Darrell Ware, and Jack Yellen. Cast includes Richard Greene and Nancy Kelly. [Based on the book *The Splinter Fleet of the Otranto Barrage*, by Ray Millholland, Indianapolis and New York, 1936. Faulkner's screenplay, done in collaboration with Katherine Scola, was never used.]

5. *Gunga Din*, released 17 Feb., 1939. RKO Radio Pictures, Inc. Producer, George Stevens. Author, Rudyard Kipling. Screenplay, Ben Hecht, Charles MacArthur, Joel Sayre, Fred Guiol. Cast includes Cary Grant, Victor McLagen, and Douglas Fairbanks, Jr.[5]

6. *Drums along the Mohawk*, released 10 Nov., 1939. Twentieth Century-Fox Film Corp. Director, John Ford. Screen-

---

[3] Sidney, pp. 161-165, quotes part of Faulkner's unused sequence.

[4] Sidney, pp. 41-42.

[5] A friend of Faulkner who had at one time been his literary agent is responsible for the statement, made in August 1937, that Faulkner had done work on this film, before going on to *Drums along the Mohawk*. (Information provided by Mr. H. Richard Archer, January 30, 1960.)

play, Lamar Trotti and Sonya Levien. Cast includes Henry Fonda and Claudette Colbert. [Based on the novel by Walter Edmonds, Boston, 1936. Faulkner's original treatment was never used.[6]]

7. *The Southerner*, released 10 Aug., 1945. United Artists. Producers, David Loew and Robert Hakim. Director, Jean Renoir. Author, George Sessions Perry. Screenplay, Jean Renoir. Adaptation, Hugo Butler. Cast includes Zachary Scott and Betty Field. [Based on the novel, *Hold Autumn in Your Hand*, by George Sessions Perry, New York, 1941.[7]]

8. *Stallion Road*, released 12 April, 1947. Warner Brothers Pictures, Inc. Producer, Alex Gottlieb. Director, James V. Kern. Screenplay, Stephen Longstreet. Cast includes Ronald Reagan, Alexis Smith, and Zachary Scott. [Based on the novel of the same name by Stephen Longstreet, New York, 1945. Faulkner is supposed to have done some work on this property between June and September, 1945.]

9. *The Left Hand of God*, released September, 1955. Twentieth Century-Fox Film Corp. Producer, Buddy Adler. Director, Edward Dmytryk. Screenplay, Alfred Hayes. Cast includes Humphrey Bogart and Gene Tierney. [Based on the novel by William E. Barrett, New York, 1951.[8]]

NOTE: Sidney, p. 48, states that according to the Twentieth Century-Fox files, Faulkner did some work for Universal, where he did a treatment of *Sutter's Gold* (released 9 April, 1936). But Universal, according to Sidney, denies the affiliation. While at Warner, between July 1942 and September 1945, Faulkner may well have had a hand in the following films, Sidney feels (p. 47), though proof is lacking: *Background to Danger* (released 25 June, 1943); *God Is My Copilot* (7 April, 1945); *Mildred Pierce* (20 Dec., 1945); *Deep Valley* (29 Aug., 1947); and *The Adventures of Don Juan* (29 Jan., 1949).

[6] Sidney, pp. 113-151, quotes this treatment in full.

[7] According to Zachary Scott, Faulkner wrote the screenplay for this film, but could not receive credit because of contractual obligations. (Information provided in interview with Mr. Scott, January 23, 1958. See also p. 47.)

[8] Apparently Faulkner did a screenplay based on this novel for Howard Hawks in 1951, which was not used. Hedda Hopper, in her column of March 24, 1951 (*Chicago Daily Tribune*, Part 2, p. 2), quotes Hawks as saying that Faulkner's script is "terrific." A collector has shown me a copy of Faulkner's script reproduced from typewritten copy, 170 pp., with the cover-title THE LEFT HAND OF GOD / Screen Play / by / William Faulkner / FIRST DRAFT CONTINUITY / January 24, 1952.

*c. Unproduced properties upon which Faulkner worked*:

For Metro-Goldwyn-Mayer, between May 1932 and May 1933:

1. "Man Servant"  Faulkner wrote original screenplay.
2. "Faulkner Story #2"  Faulkner wrote original screenplay.
3. "Honor"  Faulkner wrote original screenplay, based on his short story.
4. "Latin American Kingdom"  Faulkner wrote original screenplay.
5. "War Birds"  Faulkner wrote original screenplay, based on his novel *Sartoris* (New York, 1929) and stories "Ad Astra" and "All the Dead Pilots" (both 1931).
6. "Flying the Mail"  Faulkner wrote original treatment.
7. "Turn to the Right"  Faulkner wrote original treatment.

For Twentieth Century-Fox, between November 1935 and August 1937:

8. "The Giant Swing"  Faulkner was assigned to this screenplay but apparently turned in nothing on it.

For Warner Bros. Pictures, Inc., between July, 1942 and September, 1945:

9. "The DeGaulle Story"  Faulkner wrote original screenplay.
10. "The Life and Death of a Bomber"  Faulkner wrote original treatment.
11. "Country Lawyer"  Faulkner wrote original treatment of the novel by Bellamy Partridge (New York, 1939).
12. "Battle Cry"  Faulkner did some work on this collaborative screenplay.[9]
13. "The Amazing Dr. Clitterhouse"  Faulkner rewrote the screenplay for a remake of the 1938 film adapted from the Barré Lyndon play of the same name. Faulkner's revision was tentatively entitled "Fog over London."
14. "Revolt in the Earth"  Faulkner and Dudley Murphy collaborated upon this treatment of *Absalom, Absalom!*, which exists in Faulkner's collection of his manuscripts. (See p. 92.)

[9] This completed but unproduced screenplay has no connection with the 1955 Warner Brothers film based on the novel by Leon Uris (New York, 1953).

*Note*: Sidney, p. 48n., states that according to the Twentieth Century-Fox files, Faulkner in the 1930's did some work for Paramount, where he collaborated on a screenplay entitled "Bride of the Bayou." But Paramount, according to Sidney, denies the affiliation. Sidney also feels (p. 47) that Faulkner may well have had a hand in an unproduced rewriting, for Warner in the 1940's, of the 1936 *Petrified Forest*. For Faulkner manuscripts relating to his Hollywood career which cannot be dated or more precisely identified, see pp. 92/93.

## II. MOTION PICTURES ADAPTED FROM FAULKNER'S WRITINGS

1. *Today We Live.* (See under Ia.)

2. *The Story of Temple Drake*, released 12 May, 1933. Paramount Productions, Inc. Director, Stephen Roberts. Screenplay, Oliver H. P. Garrett.[10] Cast includes Miriam Hopkins and Jack LaRue. [Based on the novel *Sanctuary*, New York, 1931.]

3. *Intruder in the Dust*, released 3 Feb., 1950. Metro-Goldwyn-Mayer Corp. Producer and director, Clarence Brown. Screenplay, Ben Maddow. Cast includes David Brian, Claude Jarman, Jr., and Juano Hernandez. [Based on the novel of the same name, New York, 1948.]

4. *The Tarnished Angels,* released January, 1958. Universal. Producer, Albert Zugsmith. Director, Douglas Sirk. Screenplay, George Zuckerman. Cast includes Rock Hudson and Robert Stack. [Based on the novel *Pylon*, New York, 1935.]

5. *The Long Hot Summer*, released March, 1958. Twentieth Century-Fox. Producer, Jerry Wald. Director, Martin Ritt. Screenplay, Irving Ravetch and Harriet Frank, Jr. Cast includes Paul Newman, Joanne Woodward, and Orson Welles. [Based on the novel *The Hamlet*, New York, 1940.]

6. *The Sound and the Fury*, released March 1959. Twentieth Century-Fox. Producer, Jerry Wald. Director, Martin Ritt.

10 A shooting script in the Paramount files, however, bears the name of Maurice Watkins as co-author. See p. 48.

Screenplay by Irving Ravetch and Harriet Frank, Jr. Cast includes Yul Brynner and Joanne Woodward. [Based on the novel of the same name, New York, 1929.]

NOTE: Several other Faulkner novels have been bought by Hollywood, including *The Unvanquished, Light in August,* and *Requiem for a Nun.*

## III. FAULKNER'S WRITING FOR TELEVISION

1. *The Brooch,* telecast 2 April, 1953. Lux Video Theatre. Adapted by William Faulkner, Ed Rice, and Richard Mc-Donogh from Faulkner's short story of the same name. Cast includes Dan Duryea, Sally Forrest, and Mildred Natwick.

NOTE: Although the advertising for "The Brooch" credited only Faulkner with the adaptation (see ad in the *New York Times,* 2 April, 1953, p. 38), both Rice, who was an editor for the Lux Video Theatre, and McDonogh, who was a producer-editor on the show, collaborated with him on the final script. (Information in a letter from Edward B. Roberts, 17 May, 1960.)

2. *"Shall Not Perish,"* telecast 11 Feb., 1954. CBS, Video Theatre. Adapted by Faulkner from his short story of the same name. Cast includes Fay Bainter and Raymond Burr.

3. *The Graduation Dress,* telecast 30 Oct., 1960. CBS, General Electric Theatre. Original television play by Faulkner. Cast includes Hugh O'Brian and Stella Stevens.

## IV. TELEVISION PLAYS ADAPTED FROM FAULKNER'S WRITINGS

1. *The Brooch.* (See under III.)

2. *Shall Not Perish.* (See under III.)

3. *Smoke,* telecast 4 May, 1954. CBS, Suspense. Adapted by Gore Vidal from Faulkner's story of the same name. Producer, Martin Manulis. Director, Robert Mulligan. Cast includes E. G. Marshall, George Mitchell, Pat Hingle, and Bart Burns. Winner of the 1954 Mystery Writers of America Award for the year's best television play.[11]

4. *Barn Burning,* telecast 17 Aug., 1954. CBS, Suspense. Adapted by Gore Vidal from Faulkner's story of the same

name. Producer, David Heilweil. Director, Robert Mulligan. Cast includes E. G. Marshall, Charles Taylor, Peter Cookson, and Beatrice Straight.[11]

5. *An Error in Chemistry*, telecast 2 Dec., 1954. CBS, Climax. Adapted from Faulkner's story of the same name. Cast includes Edmund O'Brien.

6. *Wild Stallion*, telecast 7 July, 1955. CBS, Climax. Adapted from Faulkner's long story, "Knight's Gambit." Cast includes Paul Henreid, Evelyn Keyes, and Mary Astor.

7. *The Sound and the Fury*, telecast 6 Dec., 1955. NBC, Playwrights '56. Producer, Fred Coe. Director, Vincent J. Donehue. Adapted by Frank W. Durkee, Jr., from Faulkner's novel of the same name (New York, 1929). Cast includes Franchot Tone, Lillian Gish, and Ethel Waters.

8. *As I Lay Dying*, telecast 7 Oct., 1956. CBS, Camera Three. Adapted by John McGiffert from Faulkner's novel of the same name. Cast includes Mildred Dunnock.

9. *Ad Astra*, telecast 7 Sept., 1958. CBS, Camera Three. Adapted from Faulkner's story of the same name. Host, James Macandrew. Cast includes George Voskavek.

10. *The Tall Men*, telecast 14 Sept., 1958. CBS, Camera Three. Adapted from Faulkner's story of the same name. Host, James Macandrew. Narrator, Richard Shepard.

11. *The Old Man*, telecast 20 Nov., 1958. CBS, Playhouse 90. Adapted by Horton Foote from the section entitled "Old Man" of Faulkner's novel, *The Wild Palms*. Producer, Fred Coe. Director, John Frankenheimer. Art director, Walter Scott Herndon. Cast includes Sterling Hayden and Geraldine Page. (Re-telecast 10 Sept., 1959.)

12. *Tomorrow*, telecast 7 March, 1960. CBS, Playhouse 90. Adapted by Horton Foote from Faulkner's story of the same name. Producer, Herbert Brodkin. Director, Robert Mulligan. Cast includes Richard Boone, Kim Stanley, and Charles Bickford.

[11] The scripts of *Smoke* and *Barn Burning* were published in *Visit to a Small Planet and Other Television Plays*, by Gore Vidal (Boston: Little, Brown, 1956), from which some of the information given in this listing was derived. See also p. 48.

APPENDIX

*FAULKNER'S SHORT STORY SENDING*

*SCHEDULE*

# INTRODUCTION

FOR a period of approximately two years during the early part of his career Faulkner kept on a sheet of cardboard a record of his attempts to place his short stories. Under fifteen headings—twelve magazines, an annual, and the names of two friends who served him occasionally as literary agents—he listed in his tiny, neat handwriting the titles of his stories as he sent them out, encircling them when they were accepted, crossing the titles out when they were rejected. For most of the stories Faulkner added the date—presumably the date when it was originally sent, not when it was accepted or rejected.

The earliest date that appears on the schedule is January 23, 1930; the latest is January 9, 1932. Of a total of 129 entries, twenty-nine are undated, mostly at the beginning and the end of the record. From the rate at which he was sending out the stories, it is probable that the undated entries cover only a few weeks' time, and that the whole schedule covers a two-year period that began about the first of January, 1930.

Despite the relatively brief period it covers, the schedule is an extremely interesting source of information concerning an important part of Faulkner's literary career, and it is fortunate that he preserved it among his manuscripts. By the end of 1929, Faulkner had published four novels and written two more (the first version of *Sanctuary* and *As I Lay Dying*), but had made little money from them. He had published no stories. But at that time, barring the luck of producing a novel which would be a real commercial success, the best way of making a living from his writing would be the sale of short stories to magazines. (It is likely that Faulkner received more, on the average, from the sale of each of the four stories accepted by the *Saturday Evening Post* during the period covered by this schedule, than he did from any of his first five novels.) The luck of a commercial success, of course, came with his sixth novel, the revised *Sanctuary*. It was published in February 1931, a date that almost exactly divides in half the record of Faulkner's activity as a writer of short stories that is afforded by this schedule. A little over a year after the success of *Sanctuary*, he first went to Hollywood, which for the next decade and a half was to give him the opportunity to make the money, in short stints of writing for the films, to return home and write books.

Only five Faulkner short stories were published during the year that began with the appearance of "A Rose for Emily" in *Forum* (April, 1930) and ended with the success of *Sanctuary*, and a persistent legend has it that Faulkner collected rejection slips before *Sanctuary* for stories that he afterward sold, at fat prices, to the same editors who had previously rejected them. The legend, though it perhaps has a germ of truth, is not borne out by the statistics afforded by the sending schedule. It lists a total of forty-four separate titles, not counting minor or obvious variations. Of these forty-four, two can be proved to be alternate titles of other stories on the list. Of the forty-two remaining titles, twenty were published or accepted for publication during this two-year period, and ten were published later. Six titles are unpublished and are not known to survive; two others are unpublished but still exist in manuscript. Of the remaining four, two ("Dead Pilots" and "Point of Honor") may have been published under slightly different names, or may be unpublished and have disappeared; one ("Aria Con Amore") was marked accepted but was not published, at least under that title; one ("Peasants") was not marked accepted but may quite possibly have been published under a different name. This is an impressive list of stories, in number, even if a good many were written before 1930, and impressive too is the proportion known to have been published: thirty of the forty-two.

But if only five had actually appeared before the publication of *Sanctuary*, eight had been accepted, and Faulkner marked only eight acceptances during the year following. (Several stories were published for the first time in the collection *These 13* in September 1931, but these were not recorded on the sending schedule.) *Sanctuary* may have helped the sale of Faulkner's stories, but there is little evidence that it did so in the first ten or twelve months after its publication. Of course, it may have raised prices somewhat. But again this is doubtful, because the highest prices for fiction being paid by a magazine at that time were generally paid by the *Saturday Evening Post*, a fact that is reflected in the number of stories Faulkner submitted to it, according to the schedule: thirty-two separate submissions, with five acceptances. (One story, "Smoke," was submitted three times, presumably with some revision each time; two others were submitted twice.) But all five acceptances preceded the publication of *Sanctuary*, though Faulkner tried them with six stories afterward.

After the *Post,* Faulkner's favorite target was *Scribner's,* which also paid fairly well: twenty-six submissions, again including several more than once, with three acceptances. Third highest number, sixteen, went to the *American Mercury,* which accepted four.

In the two tables below the information from the sending schedule is recorded and annotated. The second table presents the entries just as Faulkner made them in the columns of the schedule, though for convenience I have rearranged the columns alphabetically. The only information from the schedule omitted, in this table, is the brief address that Faulkner gave for most of the fifteen periodicals or persons. I have also expanded and normalized the titles for clarity (*i.e.,* MERCURY to *American Mercury*). Below the column headings the only changes made were those made necessary by the change of manuscript to type, which are explained in footnotes, and in the omission of the neat, generally one-line cancellation which Faulkner used to indicate the rejection of a story. All entries are presumed to be cancelled unless there is a bracketed indication to the contrary.

In the first table the titles which appear on the sending schedule are arranged alphabetically. Where a story appeared by more than one title, the entry appears under the main or final one, with the alternate appearing in smaller type only as a cross-reference. All titles are given just as they appear on the schedule; where, for convenience of reference or clarity, it seemed helpful, I have inserted, in reduced type and in brackets, the better-known title, with a cross-reference to the main entry. In the annotations under the main entries, I have tried to bring together the available evidence concerning the story, though many gaps remain to be filled.

## I. ALPHABETICAL LIST OF STORIES:

"Ad Astra" *Am. Merc.* March 5, 1930; *American Caravan\** March 25, 1930.
> Publ. in *American Caravan IV*, New York, 1931.

["All the Dead Pilots" *see* "Dead Pilots"]

"Aria Con Amore" *Sat. Eve. Post* Feb. 2, 1931; *Scribner's\** Feb. 13, 1931.
> Though Faulkner encircled the title to indicate its acceptance by *Scribner's,* and though it does not appear again on the sending schedule,

---

\* An asterisk indicates that Faulkner encircled the title of the story on the sending schedule to show that it had been accepted.

*Scribner's* published no story by this title, by any author, and Faulkner has published no story by this title, anywhere. Nor do his unpublished manuscripts that I have seen afford any help. A possibly relevant piece of evidence is the fact that during the period covered by this sending schedule Faulkner published one story in *Scribner's*, "Spotted Horses" in the June 1931 issue, which appears by that name nowhere on the schedule. It might be tempting to speculate that "Aria Con Amore" was the original title, that it was accepted by *Scribner's* after being submitted in February 1931, and that it was published under the title "Spotted Horses" the following June. However, the title "Aria Con Amore" is a most unlikely one for "Spotted Horses." The title "Peasants" would be far more fitting, as Faulkner gives the title "The Peasants" to the section of *The Hamlet* in which he incorporated the final version of the story. "Peasants" appears, and is cancelled as rejected, in the *Scribner's* column of the schedule; possibly Faulkner erred in marking the one story as accepted, the other as rejected. Possibly he revised and resubmitted "Peasants" later, without recording the fact, and it was accepted and published as "Spotted Horses." Certainly "Peasants" and "Aria Con Amore" appear to be the only possibilities for the missing entry for "Spotted Horses" under *Scribner's*. But lacking further evidence we can only speculate.

"Artist at Home" *Sat. Eve. Post* March 16, 1931; *Scribner's* June 6, 1931; Ben Wasson [uncancelled; undated, but after June 5, 1931].
> Publ. in *Story*, III (Aug. 1933).

["Beyond" *see* "Beyond the gate"]

"Beyond the gate" *Sat. Eve. Post* April 22, 1930.
> Publ. in *Harper's*, CLXVII (September 1933), entitled "Beyond." In the Faulkner collection are a typescript, entitled "Beyond the Gate," and a later manuscript, entitled "Beyond."

"Big Shot" *Am. Merc.* [undated, but before Jan. 23, 1930]; *Miscellany* [undated, but before Feb. 5, 1930]; *Liberty* [undated, but before Feb. 14, 1930]; *Forum* [undated, but before March 7, 1930]; *Sat. Eve. Post* April 14, 1930.
> Unpublished, but there is a typescript, entitled "The Big Shot," in the Faulkner collection. (See entry under the unpublished short story section of the manuscripts handlist.)

"Black Music" *Sat. Eve. Post* July 27, 1931; *Woman's Home Companion* Aug. 7, 1931; *Scribner's* Sept. 1, 1931; Ben Wasson [uncancelled, undated].
> Publ. in *Doctor Martino and Other Stories*, New York, 1934.

"Brooch" *Forum* Jan. 29, 1931; *College Humor* Feb. 13, 1931.
> Faulkner's story "The Brooch" was published in *Scribner's*, XCIX (January 1936). Despite the disparity in dates, the likelihood of this

being the story published in 1936, or a version of it, is established by a manuscript note by Faulkner, dated January 1, 1931, on the verso of p. 7 of a carbon typescript of a version of this story in the Faulkner collection.

"Built a Fence" *Sat. Eve. Post* Nov. 29, 1930 [entitled "Built Fence"]; *Scribner's* Dec. 20, 1930; *Am. Merc.* Jan. 29, 1931.
Unpublished.

"Centaur" *Scribner's* Aug. 11, 1931; *Harper's* Aug. 23, 1931; *Am. Merc.\** Oct. 5, 1931.
Publ., entitled "Centaur in Brass," in *Am. Merc.* XXV (Feb. 1932).

["Centaur in Brass" *see* "Centaur"]

"A Dangerous Man" *Forum* [undated, entitled "Dangerous Man"]; *Am. Merc.* Feb. 6, 1930.
Unpublished.

"Dead Pilots" *Woman's Home Companion* April 23, 1931.
It would seem likely that this is the story "All the Dead Pilots" that was published in *These 13*, New York, 1931 (publication date was Sept. 21). It is possible that the story was submitted to *Collier's*; see footnote ten.

"Death Drag" *Scribner's* Dec. 16, 1930; *Sat. Eve. Post* Jan. 5, 1931; *Am. Merc.* Feb. 1, 1931; *Collier's* April 5, 1931; Ben Wasson June 5, 1931; *Scribner's\** [undated, but between Sept. 1 and Oct. 16, 1931]; Ben Wasson\* [undated, but after June 5, 1931].
Publ., entitled "Death-Drag," in *Scribner's*, XCI (Jan. 1932). On the sending schedule Faulkner encircled the title where it appeared in the column under the name of the agent who placed it, Wasson, and in the column under *Scribner's* he encircled it and added Wasson's name. The *Collier's* entry may instead refer to the *Woman's Home Companion*; see footnote nine.

"Divorce in Naples" *Forum* May 21, 1930 [entitled "Equinox"]; *Scribner's* June 20, 1930; *Am. Merc.* June 30, 1930; *Blues* Oct. 1, 1930; Ben Wasson April 7, 1931.
Publ. in *These 13*, New York, 1931 (publication date was Sept. 21). A manuscript version in the Faulkner collection is entitled "Divorce in Naples," with the cancelled title "Equinox."

"Dr Martino" *Sat. Eve. Post* March 5, 1931 [entitled "Martino"]; *Woman's Home Companion* March 16, 1931 [entitled "Martino"]; Ben Wasson June 5, 1931; *Sat. Eve. Post* Sept. 1, 1931 [entitled "Martino"]; Ben Wasson\* [entitled "Martino"; un-

* An asterisk indicates that Faulkner encircled the title of the story on the schedule to show that it had been accepted.

dated, but after June 5, 1931]; *Harper's*\* [entitled "Martino"; undated].

> Publ., entitled "Doctor Martino," in *Harper's*, CLXIII (Nov. 1931). On the sending schedule Faulkner encircled the title where it appeared the second time under the name of the agent who placed it, Wasson, and added the name "Harpers"; in the entry under *Harper's* he encircled it and added Wasson's name.

"Drouth"  *Am. Merc.* Feb. 8, 1930; *Forum* March 7, 1930; *Scribner's* April 21, 1930; *Scribner's*\* May 1, 1930.

> Publ., entitled "Dry September," in *Scribner's*, LXXXIX (Jan. 1931). A manuscript version in the Faulkner collection is entitled "Drouth."

["Dry September" *see* "Drouth"]

"Dull Tale"  *Sat. Eve. Post* Nov. 14, 1930.
> Unpublished.

["Elly" *see* "Selvage"]

"Equinox" *see* "Divorce in Naples"

"Evangeline"  *Sat. Eve. Post* July 17, 1931; *Woman's Home Companion* July 26, 1931.
> Unpublished.

"Fire & Clock"  *Am. Merc.* Jan. 23, 1930; *Sat. Eve. Post* Feb. 6, 1930; *College Humor* Feb. 14, 1930; *Cosmopolitan* March 1, 1930.
> Unpublished.

"Fox" *see* "Fox Hunt"

"Fox Hunt"  *Forum* [entitled "The Fox"; undated, but before March 7, 1930]; *Miscellany* [entitled "Fox"; undated, but before Feb. 5, 1930]; *Liberty* [entitled "Fox"; undated, but before Feb. 14, 1930]; *Sat. Eve. Post* Dec. 29, 1930 [entitled "Fox"]; *College Humor* January 9, 1931 [entitled "A Fox"]; *Woman's Home Companion* March 11, 1931 [entitled "Fox-Hunt"]; Ben Wasson\* April 7, 1931; *Harper's*\* [entitled "Foxhunt"; undated].

> Publ. in *Harper's*, CLXIII (Sept. 1931). On the sending schedule Faulkner encircled the title where it appeared in the column under the name of the agent who placed it, Wasson, and in the column under *Harper's* he encircled it and added Wasson's name.

"Hair"  *Am. Merc.* March 20, 1930; *Sat. Eve. Post* April 3, 1930; *Sat. Eve. Post* January 1, 1931; *Woman's Home Companion*

---

\* An asterisk indicates that Faulkner encircled the title of the story on the schedule to show that it had been accepted.

January 10, 1931; *Scribner's* January 29, 1931; *Am. Merc.** Feb. 27, 1931.

> Publ. in *Am. Merc.*, XXIII (May 1931).

"Honor" *Scribner's* March 25, 1930; *Am. Merc.** April 22, 1930.

> Publ. in *Am. Merc.*, XX (July 1930). It would seem very likely that this is the same story as "Point of Honor," submitted to the *Sat. Eve. Post* March 7, 1930.

"The Hound" *Sat. Eve. Post* Nov. 17, 1930; *Scribner's* Nov. 29, 1930 [entitled "Hound"]; *Am. Merc.* Jan. 29, 1931 [entitled "Hound"]; Ben Wasson* April 7, 1931 [entitled "Hound"]; *Harper's** [undated; entitled "Hound"].

> Publ. in *Harper's*, CLXIII (Aug. 1931). On the sending schedule Faulkner encircled the title where it appeared under the name of the agent who placed it, Wasson, and in the column under *Harper's* he encircled it and added Wasson's name.

"Idyll in Desert" *Am. Merc.* [undated, but before Jan. 23, 1930]; *Liberty* [undated, but before Feb. 14, 1930]; *Forum* [undated, but before March 7, 1930]; *Sat. Eve. Post* Feb. 4, 1931; *Scribner's* March 2, 1931; *Harper's* April 18, 1931; *Woman's Home Companion* [undated, but between April 11 and 23, 1931]; Ben Wasson* June 5, 1931.

> Publ., entitled *Idyll in the Desert*, in a limited edition by Random House, New York, 1931 (publication date was Dec. 10).

"A Justice" *Woman's Home Companion* April 11, 1931; *Harper's* May 5, 1931 [entitled "Justice"].

> Publ. in *These 13*, New York, 1931 (publication date was Sept. 21).

"The Leg" *Sat. Eve. Post* Dec. 14, 1930; *Scribner's* June 8, 1931; Ben Wasson [uncancelled; undated, but after June 5, 1931].

> Publ., entitled "Leg," in *Doctor Martino and Other Stories*, New York, 1934. The reprinting in the 1950 *Collected Stories* is entitled "The Leg."

"Lizards" *Sat. Eve. Post* May 27, 1930; *Sat. Eve. Post** Aug. 7, 1930 [entitled "Lizards in"].

> Publ., entitled "Lizards in Jamshyd's Courtyard," in *Sat. Eve. Post*, CCIV (Feb. 27, 1932). For a change in the date this story was first submitted to the *Post*, see footnote four in Table II below.

["Lizards in Jamshyd's Courtyard" see "Lizards"]

"Martino see "Dr Martino"

"Miss Z. Gant" *Am. Merc.* [undated, but before Jan. 23, 1930]; *Scribner's* [undated, but before March 25, 1930]; *Miscellany* Feb. 5, 1930; *Southwest Review** March 16, 1930.

---

* An asterisk indicates that Faulkner encircled the title of the story on the schedule to show that it had been accepted.

Publ., entitled *Miss Zilphia Gant*, by the Book Club of Texas, [Dallas,] 1932, with a Preface by Henry Nash Smith. According to Mr. Smith, Faulkner was asked to submit a story to the *Southwest Review*, then edited by Smith and John McGinnis. When the typescript of "Miss Zilphia Gant" arrived, the editors liked it, but felt that it might offend some readers, and persuaded the Book Club of Texas to bring it out instead, an arrangement that was satisfactory to Faulkner. (Letter from Henry Nash Smith to JBM, June 15, 1960.)

"Mistral"    *Sat. Eve. Post* June 19, 1930; *Scribner's* July 12, 1930.
> Publ. in *These 13*, New York, 1931. The *Scribner's* entry was cancelled with many lines, apparently to obliterate the entry rather than to indicate rejection of the story.

"Mountain Victory"    *Sat. Eve. Post**\*** September 24, 1930 [date cancelled, and above it inserted the new date October 4, 1930].
> Publ., entitled "A Mountain Victory," in *Sat. Eve. Post*, CCV (Dec. 3, 1932).

"Peasants"    *Scribner's* Aug. 25, 1930.
> No Faulkner story by this title has been published, but it possibly refers to "Spotted Horses," which was originally published in *Scribner's* in June 1931, and appeared, revised, as an episode in the section entitled "The Peasants" of the novel *The Hamlet*, New York, 1940.
>
> If this is so, there remain several unsolved problems connected with the listing here. Why is there no entry for "Spotted Horses"? Why does Faulkner mark as accepted by *Scribner's* a story, "Aria Con Amore" (*q.v.*), which was not published, at least under that title?

"Per Ardua"    *Sat Eve. Post* Feb. 5, 1930; *Liberty* Feb. 14, 1930; *Scribner's* Aug. 30, 1930; *Liberty* Dec. 30, 1930.
> Unpublished. Though the Royal Air Force motto, "Per ardua ad astra," supplied the title for another Faulkner story, "Ad Astra" (*q.v.*), that these are two stories, not one story with alternate titles, is indicated by the fact that Faulkner was still submitting "Per Ardua" after "Ad Astra" had been accepted.

"Point of Honor"    *Sat. Eve. Post* March 7, 1930.
> Unpublished. However, the similarity of this title to "Honor" (*q.v.*) and the way it fits into the dates at which that story was sent out, argue rather strongly that the two titles belong to the same story.

"Red Leaves"    *Sat. Eve. Post**\*** July 24, 1930.
> Publ. in *Sat. Eve. Post*, CCIII (Oct. 25, 1930).

"Rose for Emily"    *Scribner's* [undated, but before March 25, 1930]; *Forum**\*** [undated, but before March 7, 1930; Faulkner noted it elsewhere as sold to *Forum* on Jan. 20, 1930. See p. 85.]
> Publ., entitled "A Rose for Emily," in *Forum*, LXXXIII (April 1930).

---

**\*** An asterisk indicates that Faulkner encircled the title of the story on the schedule to show that it had been accepted.

"Rose of Lebanon"  *Sat. Eve. Post* Nov. 7, 1930; *Woman's Home Companion* Jan. 10, 1931; *Scribner's* July 23, 1931.
> Unpublished, but there is a manuscript in the Faulkner collection.

"Selvage"  *Scribner's* [entitled "Salvage"; undated, but before March 25, 1930]; *Forum* April 16, 1930; *Liberty* May 2, 1930.
> Unpublished under this title, and in this form. But in the Faulkner collection are a manuscript and a typescript, entitled "Selvage," and a manuscript, entitled "Elly," which is a substantial revision of "Selvage." The story "Elly" was published in *Story*, IV (Feb. 1934), somewhat revised from the manuscript.

"Smoke"  *Sat. Eve Post* [undated, but before Feb. 5, 1930]; *Sat. Eve. Post* Dec. 22, 1930; *Sat. Eve. Post* Oct. 5, 1931; *Scribner's* Oct. 16, 1931 [uncancelled].
> Publ. in *Harper's*, CLXIV (April 1932).

["Spotted Horses" *see* "Peasants"]

"That Evening Sun"  *Scribner's* Oct. 6, 1930; *Am. Merc.*\* Oct. 28, 1930 [entitled "That Eve. Sun"].
> Publ., entitled "That Evening Sun Go Down," in *Am. Merc.*, XXII (March 1931).

["There Was a Queen" *see* "Was a Queen"]

"Thrift"  *Sat. Eve. Post*\* Feb. 14, 1930.
> Publ. in *Sat. Eve. Post*, CCIII (Sept. 6, 1930).

"Two on Bench"  *Sat. Eve. Post* Sept. 12, 1930 [entitled "2 Bench"]; *Scribner's* Sept. 24, 1930.
> Unpublished under this title, and in this form. But in the Faulkner Collection at the University of Texas is an incomplete manuscript, entitled "Bench for Two," which became, substantially revised, the story "Pennsylvania Station," published in *Am. Merc.*, XXXI (Feb. 1934).

"Thru the Window" *see* "Was a Queen"

"Turn About"  Ben Wasson Jan. 9, 1932 [uncancelled].
> Publ. in *Sat. Eve. Post*, CCIV (March 5, 1932).

"Was a Queen"  *Scribner's* [entitled "Thru the Window"; undated, but before March 25, 1930]; *Sat. Eve. Post* Aug. 23, 1930; Hal Smith Sept. 12, 1930 [uncancelled]; Ben Wasson [uncancelled; undated, but after June 5, 1931].
> Publ., entitled "There Was a Queen," in *Scribner's* XCIII (January 1933). The manuscript of an early version of this story in the Faulkner collection bears the cancelled title "Through the Window."

---

\* An asterisk indicates that Faulkner encircled the title of the story on the schedule to show that it had been accepted.

# II. ALPHABETICAL LIST OF PLACES SENT:

A. *Agents*:

Hal Smith
    Was a Queen         9-12-30  *[uncancelled]*

Ben Wasson
    Divorce in Naples     4-7-31
    Hound*                 "
    Fox Hunt*             "
    Dr Martino         6-5-31
    Death Drag         "
    Idyll in Desert*      "
    Martino* - Harpers[1]
    Black Music     *[uncancelled]*
    Death Drag*
    Was a Queen     *[uncancelled]*
    Artist at Home   *[uncancelled]*
    The Leg        *[uncancelled]*
    Turn About      1-9-32   *[uncancelled]*

B. *Annual*:

*American Caravan*
    Ad Astra*         3-25-30

C. *Magazines*:

*American Mercury*
    Big Shot
    Miss Z. Gant
    Idyll in Desert
    Fire & Clock      1-23-30
    A Dangerous Man  2-6-30
    Drouth          2-8-30
    Ad Astra        3-5-30
    Hair            3-20-30
    Honor*          4-22-30
    Divorce in Naples   6-30-30

  * An asterisk indicates that Faulkner encircled the title of the story to show that it had been accepted.
  1 Faulkner added the name of the magazine with which Wasson placed the story in this case, encircling the title of both story and magazine.

| That Eve. Sun - * | 10-28-30 |
| Hound | 1-29-31 |
| Built a Fence | 1-29-31 |
| Death Drag | 2-1-31² |
| Hair* | 2-27-31 |
| Centaur* | 10-5-31 |

*Blues*
| Divorce in Naples | 10-1-30 |

*College Humor*
| Fire & Clock | 2-14-30 |
| A Fox | 1-9-31 |
| Brooch | 2-13-31 |

[*Collier's* see "Death Drag" and "Dead Pilots" under *Woman's Home Companion*]

*Cosmopolitan*
| Fire & Clock | 3-1-30 |

*Forum*
| Big Shot | |
| The Fox | |
| Dangerous Man | |
| Rose for Emily* | |
| Idyll in Desert | |
| Drouth | 3-7-30 |
| Selvage | 4-16-30 |
| Equinox | 5-21-30 |
| Brooch | 1-29-31 |

*Harper's*
| Idyll in Desert | 4-18-31 |
| Justice | 5-5-31 |
| Centaur | 8-23-31 |
| Foxhunt* | Wasson³ |
| Hound* | " |
| Martino* | " |

---

* An asterisk indicates that Faulkner encircled the title of the story to show that it had been accepted.

2 Faulkner appears first to have dated this entry 2-3-31, then to have cancelled the first 3 and written a 1 before it.

3 For these three titles Faulkner listed the agent who had placed them with the magazine.

*Liberty*

Big Shot
Fox
Idyll in Desert
Per Ardua          2-14-30
Selvage            5-2-30
Per Ardua          12-30-30

*Miscellany*

Big Shot
Fox
Miss Z. Gant       2-5-30

*Saturday Evening Post*

Smoke
Per Ardua          2-5-30
Fire & Clock       2-6-30
Thrift*            2-14-30
Point of Honor     3-7-30
Hair               4-3-30
Big Shot           4-14-30
Beyond the gate    4-22-30
Lizards            5-27-30[4]
Mistral            6-19-30
Red Leaves*        7-24-30
Lizards in*        8-7-30
Was a Queen        8-23-30
2 Bench            9-12-30
Mountain Victory*  10-4-30[5]
Rose of Lebanon    11-7-30
Dull Tale          11-14-30
The Hound          11-17-30
Built Fence        11-29-30
The Leg            12-14-30
Smoke              12-22-30
Fox                12-29-30
Hair               1-1-31

* An asterisk indicates that Faulkner encircled the title of the story to show that it had been accepted.

4 Faulkner first dated this story 5-16-30, then cancelled the 16 and inserted the 27 above it.

5 Faulkner first dated this entry 9-24-30, then cancelled the whole date and inserted the 10-4-30 above it.

| | |
|---|---|
| Death Drag | 1-5-31 |
| Aria Con Amore | 2-2-31 |
| Idyll in Desert | 2-4-31 |
| Martino | 3-5-31 |
| Artist at Home | 3-16-31 |
| Evangeline | 7-17-31 |
| Black Music | 7-27-31 |
| Martino | 9-1-31 |
| Smoke | 10-5-31 |

*Scribner's Magazine*

| | |
|---|---|
| Thru the Window | |
| Miss Z. Gant | |
| Rose for Emily | |
| Salvage | |
| Honor | 3-25-30 |
| Drouth | 4-21-30 |
| Drouth* | 5-1-30 |
| Divorce in Naples | 6-20-30 |
| Mistral | 7-12-30[6] |
| Peasants | 8-25-30 |
| Per Ardua | 8-30-30 |
| Two on Bench | 9-24-30 |
| That Evening Sun | 10-6-30 |
| Hound | 11-29-30 |
| Built a Fence | 12-20-30 |
| Death Drag | 12-16-30 |
| Hair | 1-29-31 |
| Aria Con Amore* | 2-13-31 |
| Idyll in Desert - | 3-2-31 |
| Artist at Home | 6-6-31 |
| The Leg | 6-8-31 |
| Rose of Lebanon | 7-23-31 |
| Centaur | 8-11-31 |
| Black Music | 9-1-31 |
| Death Drag* - Wasson[7] | |
| Smoke | 10-16-31 [*uncancelled*] |

* An asterisk indicates that Faulkner encircled the title of the story to show that it had been accepted.

6 This title and date were cancelled with many lines, apparently to obliterate the entry rather than to indicate rejection of the story

7 Faulkner here added to the title the name of the agent who had placed the story with this magazine.

*Southwest Review*

*Woman's Home Companion*

* An asterisk indicates that Faulkner encircled the title of the story to show that it had been accepted.

[8] Faulkner used a ligature to indicate that this date went with both "Hair" and "Rose of Lebanon."

[9] The addition of the name of this magazine, which belonged to the same company as did *The Woman's Home Companion*, may mean that Faulkner submitted it first to one and then the other, or that he sent it only to *Collier's*. The address was the same for both magazines.

[10] After this title and slightly above the line Faulkner added a capital C, encircled. One possibility might be that it stands for *Collier's* (see preceding footnote).

INDEX

# INDEX OF PERSONS

Not indexed are: actors, writers, and other movie personnel in Parts I and V; editors, translators, and writers of introductions for foreign editions in Parts I, III, and IV; individuals to whom acknowledgment is made for items lent to the exhibition or assistance rendered to this book.

writes for television, 155; wins Nobel Prize in 1950, 5, 49; awarded Legion of Honor, 49; commencement addresses at daughter's graduation from high school and junior college, 49, 50; other addresses 50-1; twice wins National Book Award, 50; other awards 50-2; trip to Japan for State Department in 1955, 46, 53, 60n.; trip to Greece for State Department in 1957, 51

Ford, Ruth, adapts and acts in *Requiem for a Nun*, 36n.

Garrett, George P. 59n.

Gilmore, Sam 24, 90

Green, Raymond 9, 10

Jelliffe, Robert A. 60n.

McClure, John, review of *The Marble Faun*, 10; review of *Sherwood Anderson & Other Famous Creoles*, 11

O'Neill, Eugene, Faulkner's article on, 8

Pearson, Norman Holmes 59n.

Romaine, Paul 45

Roth, Russell 59n.

Scott, Zachary 47, 159

Shenton, Edward, illustrator of works by Faulkner, 27, 31, 39

Sidney, George 156, 157, 158, 159, 160

Smith, Harrison 175

Smith, Henry Nash 59n., 61, 174

Spratling, William, 11, 12, 13; Faulkner writes introduction for his book of drawings, *Sherwood Anderson & Other Famous Creoles*, 11-12

Stone, Phil 9, 10, 29

Stone, Philip Alston 29, 35

Verlaine, Paul 8

Walser, Richard 52

Wasson, Ben 8, 17, 38, 81, 170, 171, 172, 173, 175

Wolfe, Thomas 52

184

# INDEX OF WORKS BY FAULKNER

of a Cow," "Barn Burning," "Fool about a Horse," "The Hound," "Lizards in Jamshyd's Courtyard," and "Spotted Horses"

*Idyll in the Desert* see under SHORT STORIES

*Intruder in the Dust* ex. cat. 32-3; manuscript 32, 75; typescript 32, 75-6; reproduction of typescript listed, 76n.; Engl. eds. 111; translations 32, 33, 127, 129, 130, 131, 132, 133, 136, 138, 140, 142, 144, 147, 148, 150; motion picture of, 48, 161

*Knight's Gambit* ex. cat. 33-4; setting copy 77-8; dead matter, samples, and layout 78; Engl. ed. 111-2; translations 34, 127, 129, 132, 133, 142; title story (short novel) based on unpubl. short story of same title, 33, 34, 77-8; see also the short stories included in this collection: "An Error in Chemistry," "Hand upon the Waters," "Monk," "Smoke," and "Tomorrow"

*Light in August* 6; ex. cat. 22-3; manuscript 22, 23, 60, 66-7; typescript 60, 67; Engl. eds. 22, 104-5; translations 22, 23, 125, 127-8, 129, 130, 131, 132, 133, 136, 138, 140, 143, 144, 147, 150; motion picture rights sold, 162; discarded title "Dark House," 67

*The Mansion* 44, 44n.; reproduction of typescript listed, 59n.; Engl. ed. 116; translations 125

*The Marble Faun* 5, 12, 24, 29; ex. cat. 9-10; typescript 10; typescript reproduced, Fig. 26; date written, 10

*Miss Zilphia Gant* see under SHORT STORIES

*Mosquitoes* 5, 13; ex. cat. 12; manuscript missing, 60; typescript 12, 60, 61, 64; typescript reproduced, Fig. 6; translations 128, 129, 133, 140, 146; Al Jackson legend in, 12

*Notes on a Horsethief* see *A Fable*

*Pylon* 25; ex. cat. 25-6; manuscript 26, 59n., 60, 67; reproduction of manuscript, Fig. 13; typescript 25, 67; Engl. eds. 106-7, 116; translations 25, 26, 128, 132, 134, 136, 140, 141, 142, 146; motion picture of, entitled *The Tarnished Angels*, 161

*Requiem for a Nun* (novel) ex. cat. 36-8; manuscript 36, 78; typescript 36, 78; galley proof 36, 78; reproduction of

galley proof, Fig. 22; Faulkner's note to his editor on, 36, 60n.; Engl. eds. 112; translations 37-8, 128, 129, 134, 136, 140, 144, 147, 148; motion picture rights sold, 162; a part incorporated in *Big Woods*, 79

————(play version) Ruth Ford's adaptation, 36n.; translations 37, 130, 134, 136; productions listed, 36n.-37n.; Faulkner attends Greek production, 51; program and poster of French production, 37; program, poster, and photographs of German production, 37; letter to Faulkner from Lemuel Ayres on, 78-9

*Sanctuary* 6, 20, 40, 47, 167, 168; ex. cat. 18-20; manuscript 19, 59-60, 66; manuscript reproduced, Fig. 12; reproduction of manuscript listed, 66n.; typescript 19, 60, 66; galley proof of first version, 19; Engl. eds. 102-3, 116, 117; translations 20, 125, 128, 129, 130, 131, 132, 134, 136, 138, 140, 142, 143, 144, 145, 146, 147, 148, 150; motion picture of, entitled *The Story of Temple Drake*, 48, 161; Faulkner's introduction to Modern Library issue of, 17, 18-9

*Sartoris* 5, 6, 13, 14, 16, 35, 40, 41; ex. cat. 14-6; manuscript 15, 59, 61, 64; manuscript reproduced, Fig. 9; typescript 15, 60, 64-5; typescript reproduced, Fig. 8; Engl. issue 103-4; translations 15, 128, 129, 134, 140, 145, 147; originally entitled "Flags in the Dust," 15, 64, 65; first book of Yoknapatawpha series, 5-6; Faulkner bases part of motion picture script on, 160

*Soldiers' Pay* 5, 10, 13, 14; ex. cat. 12; manuscript missing, 60; typescript 12, 60, 61, 63; reproduction of typescript, Fig. 5; Engl. eds. 101; translations 128, 129, 134, 137, 140, 142, 143, 146

*The Sound and the Fury* 6, 17, 40; ex. cat. 16-17; manuscript 17, 59, 65; manuscript reproduced, Figs. 10, 11; reproduction of manuscript listed, 65n.; typescript 17, 60, 65; Engl. eds. 102; translations 17, 123n., 128, 130, 134, 137, 140, 149, 150; Faulkner's unpubl. letter to Ben Wasson on, 17; projected 1933 Random House ed. of, 16, 17; Faulkner's unpubl. note on quoted

based on, 162-3; originally planned as first chapter of *The Hamlet* 43, 62

"The Bear" (*Sat. Eve. Post* version) 31, 39; relationship to "Lion" and the chapter of *Go Down, Moses* entitled "The Bear," 31

"The Bear" (*Go Down, Moses* version) see under *Go Down, Moses*

"The Bear" (*Big Woods* version) tearsheets used as setting copy, 79

"A Bear Hunt" 39; tearsheets used as setting copy in *Big Woods*, 79

"Bench for Two" *see* "Two on Bench"

"Beyond" (also entitled "Beyond the Gate") 170; manuscript 81; typescript 81

"The Big Shot" (unpubl.) 170; typescript, 35, 87

"Black Music" 170; manuscript 82

"The Brooch" 170-1; manuscript 82; typescript 82; television play based on, 48, 155, 162

"Built a Fence" (unpubl.) 171

"By the People" 43; typescript 44; incorporated in *The Mansion*, 43n.

"Carcassonne" typescript 82

"Centaur in Brass" 41, 45, 171; incorporated in *The Town*, 45

"A Courtship" 35; typescript 82, 85

"Crevasse" *see* "Victory"

"A Dangerous Man" (unpubl.) 171

"Dead Pilots" *see* "All the Dead Pilots"

"Death Drag" 25, 171; manuscript 25, 82; typescript 82

"Delta Autumn" typescript 31, 74; incorporated in *Go Down, Moses*, 31; a part incorporated in *Big Woods*, 39, 80

"Divorce in Naples" (also entitled "Equinox") 171; manuscript 82; typescript 82

"Doctor Martino" 171-2; manuscript 82; typescript 83

"Drouth" *see* "Dry September"

"Dry September" (also entitled "Drouth") 172; manuscript 83; typescript 83; tearsheets of French translation by Maurice E. Coindreau in Faulkner collection, 83

"Dull Tale" (unpubl.) 172

"Elly" (also entitled "Salvage" or "Selvage") 172, 175; manuscript 83; typescript 83

"An Empress Passed" *see* "There Was a Queen"

"Equinox" *see* "Divorce in Naples"

"An Error in Chemistry" 33-4; typescript 77; entered in *Ellery Queen's Mystery Magazine* detective short-story contest in 1946, 33-4; first book appearance in *The Queen's Awards*, 1946, 34; tearsheets used for setting copy in *Knight's Gambit*, 77

"Evangeline" (unpubl.) 172

"Fire and Clock" (unpubl.) 172

"The Fire on the Hearth" typescript 73, 74; relationship to "An Absolution" and *Go Down, Moses*, 74

"Fool about a Horse" 29, 42; manuscript 42, 69; reproduction of manuscript, Fig. 21; typescript 42, 69-70; reproduction of typescript, Fig. 20; incorporated in *The Hamlet* 42

"Fox Hunt" 172; manuscript 83; typescript 83

"Go Down, Moses" typescript 31, 74-5; relationship to final chapter of *Go Down, Moses*, 31; Faulkner changes name of character from Henry Coldfield Sutpen to Samuel Worsham Beauchamp in, 61

"Gold Is Not Always" typescript 73; incorporated in *Go Down, Moses*, 73

"Hair" 172-3

"Hand upon the Waters" typescript 76; tearsheets used for setting copy in *Knight's Gambit*, 77

"Honor" 173; "Point of Honor" a possible alternate title, 174

"The Hound" 29, 41, 173; incorporated in *The Hamlet*, 41

"Idyll in the Desert" 173, 176, 177, 178, 179, 180; ex. cat. 21-2; manuscript 22, 83; no translation of, 125

"A Justice" 173; manuscript 83; a part incorporated in *Big Woods*, 79

"Knight's Gambit" (unpubl. short story version) 33; typescript 34, 77; relationship to short novel in *Knight's Gambit*, with change of character's name from Charles Weddel to Charles Mallison, 34

"Landing in Luck" 8

"The Leg" 170, 173; manuscript 83; typescript 83-4

"Lion" 31; incorporated in *Go Down, Moses*, 31

"Lizards in Jamshyd's Courtyard" 29, 173; incorporated in *The Hamlet*, 41

"Love" (unpubl.) manuscript 87; typescript 87

"Miss Zilphia Gant" 173-4, 176, 178, 179,

180; ex. cat. 22; manuscript 22, 84; typescript 22, 84; translation 125, 128, 140; certificate of copyright registration, 22, 84; book club edition announcement quoted from, 22; Henry Nash Smith's letter on publication of, 174

"Mistral" 174; manuscript 84; typescript 84

"Monk" tearsheets used for setting copy in *Knight's Gambit*, 77

"Moonlight" (unpubl.) typescript 87

"Mountain Victory" 25, 174; manuscript 84; typescript 84

"Mule in the Yard" 42, 45; manuscript 42, 45, 80; manuscript reproduced, Fig. 23; typescript 80; incorporated in *The Town*, 45

"My Grandmother Millard" 43; typescript 43, 84

"An Odor of Verbena" see under *The Unvanquished*

"The Old People" typescript 74; incorporated in *Go Down, Moses* 74; tearsheets used as setting copy in *Big Woods*, 79

" 'Once Aboard the Lugger' " 35

"Pantaloon in Black" typescript 74; incorporated in *Go Down, Moses* 74

"Peasants" possible title for "Spotted Horses," 168, 174

"Pennsylvania Station" 175; manuscript 84; typescript 84-5

"Per Ardua" (unpubl.) 174

"Point of Honor" see "Honor"

"A Point of Law" typescript 73; incorporated in *Go Down, Moses* 73

"Red Leaves" 21, 174; manuscript 21, 85; typescript 21, 85; a part incorporated in *Big Woods*, 79

"Race at Morning" galley proofs used for setting copy in *Big Woods*, 80

"A Rose for Emily" 20-1, 168, 174; manuscript 21, 85; typescript 85

"Rose of Lebanon" (unpubl.) 175; manuscript 87

"Salvage," "Selvage" see "Elly"

"Shall Not Perish" typescript 34, 35, 82, 85; Faulkner's television play based on, 92, 162

"Shingles for the Lord" typescript 85

"Skirmish at Sartoris" 27; incorporated in *The Unvanquished* 27

"Smoke" 33, 168, 175; manuscript 33, 76; typescript 33, 77; typescript and tear-

sheets used for setting copy in *Knight's Gambit*, 77; television play based on, 162

"Snow" (unpubl.) typescript 87

"Spotted Horses" 29, 40-1, 69n., 170; "Peasants" a possible title for, 170, 174; relationship to "Father Abraham," "Abraham's Children," and *The Hamlet*, 41

"The Tall Men" typescript 86

"That Evening Sun" 175; reproduction of manuscript listed, 59n.; typescript 85-6

"There Was a Queen" (also entitled "An Empress Passed" and "Thru the Window") 25, 42, 175; manuscript 24, 25, 41-2, 86; typescript 25, 42, 86

"Thrift" 35, 175; manuscript 35, 86; typescript 86

"Thru the Window" see "There Was a Queen"

"Tomorrow" typescript 76; tearsheets used for setting copy in *Knight's Gambit*, 77

"Turnabout" 87, 175; manuscript 86; motion picture based on, 47, 48, 155, 156-7, 161

"Two on Bench" 175; manuscript entitled "Bench for Two," 175; revised as "Pennsylvania Station" 175

"The Unvanquished" story revised for chapter entitled "Riposte in Tertio" in *The Unvanquished*, 42

"Vendée" incorporated in *The Unvanquished*, 42

"Victory" manuscript 86; typescript 86; story "Crevasse" originally constituted part of, 86

"Was" typescript 30-1, 73, 74; reproduction of typescript, Fig. 16; incorporated in *Go Down, Moses* 31, 73

"Was a Queen" see "There Was a Queen"

"Wash" incorporated in *Absalom, Absalom!* 26

"The Wishing-Tree" (unpubl.) typescript 35, 87; Faulkner inscribes copy for Philip Alston Stone, 35

"With Caution and Dispatch" (unpubl.) typescript 35, 87-8; reproduction of typescript, Fig. 25

untitled (unpubl.) typescript 88

VERSE:

"Adolescence" (unpubl.) typescript 91

"L'Apres Midi d'un Faune" 5, 7-8

## LIST OF ERRATA

22.21   eighth ] seventh

29.13   stories "Barn Burning" and ] story

37.31*n*   November ] September

43.16–17   drastically cut and rewritten to form one episode (pp. 15–
      21) of ] omitted from

64.24   carbon typescript ] typescript

64.26   is ] is almost

64.34   107 through ] 107 through 156; there is a gap in the text
      here (pp. 109–111 of the published book) ; 157 through

73.17   1941 ] 1940

77.7   33,000 ] 33,000-word

78.37   Ayres ] Ayers

79.1   Ayres ] Ayers

88.6   2. ] 2; and to the sketch "Frankie and Johnny" in "New Or-
      leans," *Double Dealer*, VII (January–February 1925), p.
      103.

99.34   elswhere ] elsewhere

136.12   IN ] IM

136.13   *in* ] *im*

161.9   92/93 ] 92–93

162.17   *"Shall Not Perish,"* ] *Shall Not Perish,*

183.11   Ayres ] Ayers